Fishing for Light

a satire

Nathaniel Sewell

Fishing for Light

By Nathaniel Sewell

Copyright 2013 Nathaniel Sewell
All rights reserved.
ISBN: 0615856705
ISBN 13: 9780615856704

Dedication

For Glenn, For Tom
And those within the Charleston
Court friendship circle,
and of course, Joe.

Inspirations

"E=MC^2: Energy equals mass
times the speed of light squared."
~Albert Einstein

"Trust your instinct to the end, though
you can render no reason."
~Ralph Waldo Emerson

Chapter One

On December 22, 1990 inside a university hospital complex, Edward Tiberius Wilcox was born at exactly 3:07 Coordinated Universal Time. After the physician snipped the umbilical cord and untethered Edward from his mother Sophia, the obstetrics nurse inspected him. She did not document any obvious defects. His APGAR score registered as a 9, he had brown hair, blue eyes, and an average Caucasian body shape and size. She wrapped him in a soft baby blanket. Then she kindly grinned as she handed him over to his father, Adam, who immediately began to cry as he held his warm son for the first time. His mother's brown hair tangled and matted along her sweating forehead, she simply beamed up at her men. For the departing delivery team it was just another day, but it was *not* just another day for Adam and Sophia. From their combined 46 chromosomes, they had created a unique life. It was as random and common as their first meeting on an early Monday morning at the curved counter within a busy Starry Eyed Coffee Hut. That day the barista had wondered who had ordered the black coffees.

"What's up with this?" the Barista had asked.

"I like it black," Sophia had said. She shrugged.

"Me? Oh it was my father," Adam had said. He glanced over at Sophia. "Drink it black, so I wouldn't be disappointed."

"Oh?" Sophia said. She finger twirled with her straight hair. She whispered, "Mine too."

At that moment, Adam and Sophia had an instant lover's connection. In the blink of Sophia's hazel colored irises, they were married. As they frolicked during their indoor Caribbean honeymoon, Edward's conception was not the result of any selective breeding process by powerful families trying to protect vast generational wealth. For they had no kingdom for Edward to inherit, they passed on to him the only widow's mite they equally possessed; they bathed his DNA with their unconditional love.

For the next three months, Adam and Sophia sleeplessly cared for their precious child. During that time, they did the customary things, and they even sent in a birth notice to the Nashville Sun. But not long after, Professor Quan noticed the name in the Lifestyle section on page D6, about mid-way down in tiny black print, Edward Tiberius Wilcox.

"Tiberius?" Professor Quan said. He chuckled. "Must be a Star Trek fan?" After he spread the newspaper across a stainless steel laboratory table, he circled the name with a black ink pen. "No, Tiberius was a Roman emperor from the time of Jesus. Edward's a king's name." From a paper cup, he slowly sipped his green tea. "How interesting-" As he glossed his forefinger across the newspaper, the name caused his instincts to nag at him. And he always listened to his instincts because he thought that was how God talked to him. He snapped open his astronomy logbook. From his astronomical calculations, he realized Edward was born at the exact moment of the Winter Solstice. And it had been the clear night he was observing Orion's Belt when he saw a Kingfisher build its nest as a Delphian shooting star streak across the Appalachian sky. He knew that happened as rare as a cosmic super bubble. Professor Quan fidgeted with his kaleidoscope; he gazed through the eyehole at the colorful reflected symmetry, aware his particles of time would eventually dwindle down his hourglass. And his creation Ms. Prosperina was quietly becoming quite powerful. She would seek him. He knew it. She knew it. She could not hurt him. But what he did fear was the thought she might discover her ancestral organic material, material that he and Captain Lovins hid deep within the earth encased in a lead box.

So, Professor Quan asked Captain Lovins to do a background check into Edward's parents and his whereabouts. He easily located Adam and Sophia's Nashville address, and early one morning hidden behind a thick, barnacled hundred-year-old live oak, Captain Lovins crouched down near the Wilcox's backyard. He stared up into the sparkly night sky.

"Light from other worlds," Captain Lovins said. He sipped his black coffee as a wave of grainy steam particles washed across his hardened face. This morning's home invasion was not like performing a HALO jump off a C-130 flying just below heaven's gate, but he was happy with his ghostly existence. His cell phone vibrated.

"My genetic powder?" Professor Quan asked.

"Zip tight," Captain Lovins said. He glanced up and down the quiet residential street. "I'll make this happen."

"I've no doubt, but only that baby's saliva can come in contact with my powder."

"Have I ever failed?" Captain Lovins said as he shook his head monitoring the tick-tocks from his digital wristwatch; aware they had twenty-three seconds before Ms. Proserpina's nosey satellite constellation orbiting earth would capture their cellular data.

"Sorry, I know better," Professor Quan said. "Any fed eyes?"

"None, clean location," Captain Lovins said. He smirked. "We have thirteen seconds, his parents?"

"Sprinkle only the infant, Edward."

"Roger that, I'll text confirmation."

"Godspeed," Professor Quan said into static.

Captain Lovins snapped on his night-vision goggles. He marched south by southeast along the cracked concrete sidewalk. He leaped over the Wilcox's three feet high chain link fence topped with Occam's razor-sharp barbed ends. As he scampered forward, his boots squished into the fertile soil. He studied the foggy backyard, and the next-door neighbor's modest haunts. Kneeling down on the dense Kentucky bluegrass, the springtime chill caused him goosebumps. He scooted in behind Adam and Sophia's cinder block rental. He thought Edward likely slept carefree unaware Professor Quan theorized he was a perfect addition to his philanthropic human experiments. Captain Lovins paused. He knew breaking into the three bedroom, two bath ranch would be a straightforward exercise, but carried a cocksure awareness that each chosen baby unpredictable. Nothing from his military training compared to the pressure of influencing an infant to ingest Professor Quan's epigenetic mutation powder. If Edward woke up in a grumpy mood, his mission might get *sphincter tight complicated*.

He hustled underneath the kitchen window. With a pick and torque wrench, he applied just enough force to pop the rusty lock open. He crept inside the back patio room past a wicker chair and a writing desk. From his nylon backpack, Captain Lovins dabbed off with a cotton towel. He applied non-skid surgical covers over the bottom of his boots. Flicking on his night vision goggles infrared shield, it washed the humble interior in a blue hued glow as he maneuvered forward into the front living room. He crept past the right hand corner and down a skimpy hallway. The tongue in groove, quarter-saw oak floorboards moaned like a clipper ship's wooden fittings. As he gently pushed the hollow bedroom door forward, the chilly room smelled of baby powder and lavender, his stare focused on the sleeping Adam and Sophia. At the foot of the Wilcox's conjugal bed, he spotted Edward, asleep in a worn plastic crib. Captain Lovins bent down and deployed over Edward. But he sensed Sophia rustling under the thin cotton sheets. He submerged below the crib's horizon; he maneuvered around the crib, and twisted to watch as Sophia fitfully sat up. He studied her scratch the corner of her eyes. She verified her baby safe and sleeping nearby. She scanned the bedroom. She yawned. Then she collapsed back and snuggled close behind, Adam, who snored with short, distinct blasts. She elbowed him in the lower back, then tugged at the heirloom quilt, and squished it over her head. Captain Lovins controlled his breathing. He hunkered down and waited for Sophia to slip back into fairyland REM sleep. He had to be patient, precise, and not leave any trace residue, or Edward's parents might think he had an infection because they would know he had not been nibbling hot glazed donuts.

As Captain Lovins waited, he replaced his waterproof nylon gloves with latex gloves. Then he quietly unsnapped a pocket sized nylon pouch strapped to his waist, and unzipped the plastic cover. He cracked it open. With his dry, right hand fingertips, he pinched a teaspoon of metaphysical virgin white powder. He sprinkled the epigenetic dust, mixed with sugar granules and pulverized pig bladder, across Edward's plump lips that purred from his fragile lungs innocent breath puffs. As Professor Quan had predicted, Edward licked his velvety soft lips as he ingested the sweet concentrated substance into his pink tissue. His saliva the catalyst for an instant cellular tempest attacking his helical shaped DNA structure, altering his life's instruction manual.

Edward happily blinked his eyelids as if his mother had kissed his forehead, he hazily smiled, he wiggled his arms up in a feign attempt to touch Captain Lovins, he swabbed Edwards's mouth with a baby-cleansing wipe. Edward lazily closed his eyes, sighed and started to suck his thumb.

"Love, always," Captain Lovins whispered as he backed out the bedroom.

Chapter Two

Twenty-three years later just beyond Nashville's outer-loop, inside a spartan one-bedroom apartment, Eddie flicked on his father's old Mr. Coffee machine. Stark-naked fluorescent tubular ceiling lights blurred his vision as the gurgling coffee maker began to gasp steam and drip addictive brew. After a random godless lightning bolt stung a nearby laurel oak, he ducked down below the white-on-white Formica counter top. He heard a crack and then a dead thump. Eddie crawled over to his kitchen window; he stared down two stories at the soul-less tree with a black charred limb stump thrust toward heaven. He shook his head. He knew his natural reaction was no match for the one universal constant: the speed of light. He studied up at the guilty dark-grey thunderclouds and wondered if special providence hid up there and had decided to zap him. He would already be flying into a white haze, as an oven roasted, Ralph Waldo Doll toward his long since deceased father, Adam.

But his cell phone vibrated. The tracking device sounded like a trapped bumblebee within the irregular shaped ceramic bowl, a bowl his mother Sophia had made years before at her church pottery class. It had been a Father's Day gift for Adam. It had rested at the left corner of his father's glass covered office desk, full of multi-colored candy next to the formal family photo. Until the day they had to pack up all of Adam's possessions after his fatal heart attack.

Eddie yawned. He blinked his eyelids, staring down at the cell number. He coughed to clear his throat.

"You okay?" Eddie asked.

"Wake up," Jim Bob said. His twangy voice trumpeted.

"I'm up, what?" Eddie said. "You in jail?"

"Naw dummy, I'm workin'."

"Good for you, what do you want?"

"Is it rainin' over there?"

"Yep, what do ya want?"

"I was smokin' out back, barely downed my coffee, thought we're gettin' invaded by space aliens."

"Yeah, I can see why you might think that."

Eddie stared up at the starless textured ceiling. He could almost smell the bacon fat, cigarette smoke-infested diner.

"Get your skinny hind-end over here."

"No, I'll be late as it is in this mess."

"Then come by after work, just a sec," Jim Bob said. "Hey Darlin', order up."

"Why?"

"Big news," Jim Bob said. "Hold on a sec-"

Eddie opened the cupboard above the coffee maker. He pulled out his father's favorite mug. *What was so secretive about another multi-level marketing scheme?*

"Women are all the same," Jim Bob said.

"I guess-"

"Although Ardee's pretty hot, just sayin'-"

Eddie poured steaming coffee into the priceless mug.

"So what's the big news? Magical weight loss vitamins? No wait, boost your testosterone and grow a giant unit?"

"Naw, can't be sayin' on this phone, top secret like."

"Really? Like the IRS is monitoring us. Been stealing gold foil, wrapping your head channeling the pyramids again?"

"Ain't you funny. This time it's different, like, like I don't need another shift for the money," Jim Bob said. He whispered. "But I'm workin' tonight anyways, if you get what I'm sayin', amigo."

"Really? I'll be by after work?" Eddie said. He took a sip of coffee and shook his head. He chuckled.

"That'll do, I'm workin' through dinner time," Jim Bob said in whispered tone.

Eddie stepped under a warm shower. Unfiltered city water cascaded over his unblemished pasty white skin. After he rinsed off, he dressed in rumpled khakis and a vanilla long sleeve button down, as the brewed aroma enticed his tragically scarred brain.

Eddie sipped the hot, bland coffee and clicked on his television. His senses instantly accosted by a Humperdinck Used Car commercial. Bobby Humperdinck, an elementary school friend, wore denim Bib overalls and a frayed straw hat. He flicked confederate dollar bills in the air while holding a black haired chimpanzee in a red, white and blue diaper.

"Com on down to Humperdinck Used Cars, if we can't make a trade, I'll kiss Bobby Junior, the price-slashing chimp!" The camera zoomed in as Bobby intently pointed his menacing forefinger up at the lens. "On … the … lips!"

Bobby Junior shrieked, the primate pounded its chest and spontaneously waved its paws in the air as if an inflamed cult follower.

"Goofball," Eddie said, "but he can sure peddle cars." He sighed. He muted the one-way communication tube. He shut his eyes. He sat motionless for several minutes listening to the rain sizzle against his apartment building. It sounded like bacon frying in his mother's cast iron skillet. When he was a little boy, the smoky, sugar cured fragrance was his alarm clock. He would spring out of bed, wide-awake, wearing his Superman Underoos; his red gossamer cape was his spinnaker sail as he scampered downstairs toward the kitchen.

"Why it's a bird? No, no, now don't tell me," Adam said. He had black Elvis like hair, kind eyes and a velvety smooth southern accent.

"I'm not a *bud*," Eddie said in child speak. His tiny fingers gripped into his father's left thigh. He smiled up at his father's still youthful face.

"Hey love, who can this, be?" Adam asked Sophia. Adam patted Eddie on the back, as he sipped his black coffee from a tall white mug.

"Dear me, I'm not sure," Sophia said. She turned away from the double oven full of baking buttermilk biscuits. She wiped her hands off with a bright, sunflower printed apron.

"I'm super me," Eddie said. He giggled and wiggled. He stood up on his red stocking tiptoes, arms stretched wide apart as if about to take flight to protect Nashville.

"Wonderful, but I think you mean, Superman," Adam said. He chuckled. "Come sit a spell and eat your oatmeal, you need lots of energy to save the planet from the communists."

"What's a *common-est*?" Eddie asked as he crawled up onto his fathers lap.

"Never mind Superman, let me spoon you up some delicious oatmeal," Adam said.

"I don't white oat meal." Eddie crinkled his face.

"Well, you better get used to it," Adam said.

"Listen to your father," Sophia said. She pointed her forefinger over at Adam. "Someone's cholesterol was a bit high."

"Yap, yap, yap-" Adam winked at Eddie, as he held him close.

Eddie giggled. He looked at his father. It was the one time of day that they would talk, and his father was not distracted with the afternoon newspaper. His father loved bacon, just a little crisp, eggs sunny side up with plain wheat toast. And it was Adam who had taught Eddie the secret to drinking coffee. His coffee not concealed with sugar, cream, or any of that frap-a-lap-a-whatever that might silently alter your body.

"Son, it's like life, learn to drink it black, then you'll never be disappointed," Adam said. He hugged his son. "And always know, I love you-"

"Okay, pa," Eddie said.

Chapter Three

Down the interstate highway system, as Eddie sipped bland coffee, inside an innocuous steel building within Nashville's light industrial warehouse district, a secret IRS unit toiled. Reflected hellish lamp light splashed across Agent Prince's freckled face. He swiftly picked up his office phone.

"Prince?" Agent Machiavelli asked.

"I think I've got the type *perp* you've been looking for," Agent Prince said as he steamrolled his pudgy fingers through his buzz cut red hair.

"Why? Hold that thought," Agent Machiavelli said. Agent Prince watched him strut from his supervisor's desk from the center of the open floor planned cube world, acknowledging a few subordinate agents. He shifted in behind Agent Prince. "What's up?"

"I noticed him, name is, ah, Calhoun, first name, Jim Bob."

"Fake name, who names their kid *Jim Bob*?" Agent Machiavelli said. He snorted. "That's just cruel."

Agent Prince peeked up at his devilishly calculating boss.

"The guy's been selling autographed items, and believe it or not, *athletic supporters* on WePay," Agent Prince said.

"Now that's bizarre," Agent Machiavelli said. He grinned. "I guess it would make sense, organic material."

"I cross-referenced him and investigated. He has used his credit card, just last week, he purchased a home theater system, and had a lot of on-line, ah, activity."

"So?" Agent Machiavelli said. He chuckled. "You're such a rookie, calm down, I've been at this for a longtime, don't get your emotions involved, clouds your judgment."

"It's true, that's what got my attention," Agent Prince said. He shrugged. "But he's not unique, Scarletto Johnsonvillia, that Italian beauty queen. She blew her nose on the Jay Leonardo TV show. They auctioned the tissue on WePay, I think they got several grand for it."

"Yeah, we checked that out, before your time," Agent Machiavelli said. "It's creepy, it's not illegal, yet. Higher ups are lobbying to control buying and selling of all human organic material, but nobody messes with the IRS, we'll keep these or this bumpkin under control."

"Bumpkin yes, creepy for sure," Agent Prince said. He coughed to clear his throat. "The guy's a fry cook over at an SB&E."

"Man, I love bacon, I'm addicted to their whipped-cream coffee concoction," Agent Machiavelli said. He rubbed his sweaty left hand palm over his middle-age-spread. "Course then the wife would beat me once she found out I was cheating on my diet."

"Ah, me too, well, he only has a high school education," Agent Prince said. He poked at his computer screen. "Although he did get a D in English at UT-"

"Get with it," Agent Machiavelli said. He tapped his right hand fingertips along the brown laminate work surface.

"His checking account has been close to absolute zero, until just the last nine months when he started depositing five thousand dollar increments, all in cash." Agent Prince sat up straight. "Also, I think he's addicted to on-line pornography."

"Porn?" Agent Machiavelli said. He crossed his thick arms.

"Yes sir," Agent Prince said. "The credit card, he has to use it for his on-line, ah, activities."

"Bad news for him," Agent Machiavelli said. He pursed his sanguine lips. "Nasty stuff out there frying our kids' brains."

"Oh, I guess, he's not a druggie," Agent Prince said.

"No, try desensitized, alters the brain," Agent Machiavelli said. He grunted. "Not to mention it's the end of imagination, you know what's under the hood."

"Sir?" Agent Prince asked.

"Think, Prince. Think about our perp. He's lost in life, likely no girlfriend, few close friends, probably sits at home playing video games, you know, not politically savvy," Agent Machiavelli said. He leaned back against the fabric cube wall. "Goes along with the crowd come election time, you know the type, lacks any self-control, takes the easy path."

Agent Prince paused for a few seconds.

"Didn't think about him like that," Agent Prince said.

"And that's why I'm in charge," Agent Machiavelli said, "but see if our perp has filed a tax return. Perps always think they can hide from us, but money always does the talking." He slapped Agent Prince on his right shoulder. Several nearby agents glanced up from their cube stations. Agent Machiavelli started to fidget with his shiny silver belt buckle, he stared up at the ceiling tiles.

"Sir?" Agent Prince asked.

"Flipping eggs will not get you that kind of cash. Email me your report, even the innocuous stuff. I want it *this* afternoon, so I can present the evidence to Judge Plato in the morning." Agent Machiavelli tapped his black wingtip dress shoe against the plastic bottom of the cube station. "We might need to go stake out this Jim Bob character."

"Yes Sir," Agent Prince said. He grinned. "You, ah, you all right?"

"Cash, right?" Agent Machiavelli asked. He pointed down at Agent Prince who was fidgeting in his office chair.

"Sir? Yes, he made deposits in small denominations, enough to buy stuff, and you know," Agent Prince said. He sat up straight in his office chair. "Then his account goes back toward zero."

"Never mind," Agent Machiavelli said. He scanned the busy open floor office plan. He thought Dr. Yin and Mr. Screwtop would be rather intrigued. "Old buzzards aren't dead after all."

"Sir?" Agent Prince asked.

"But they're getting sloppy in their old age," Agent Machiavelli said as he backed out of Agent Prince's cube. He mumbled. "Can it be Quan?"

"Who? I don't understand?" Agent Prince asked.

"Genetic material, fresh DNA," Agent Machiavelli said. As he sauntered away, he turned around. "Wonder if they have a social media page?"

"Sir?" Agent Prince asked. "Isn't that what we do?"

"Check the social web sites, anything to do with trading *unique* human material, autographed hats, clothes, I think we've been looking at this wrong, for all these years."

"Who?" Agent Prince asked. He shrugged.

"Sorry, I'll need to check your security clearance, there is a lot more to this than might seem on the surface, and you're a rookie," Agent Machiavelli said. He scratched his flabby chin. "But this matches their modus operandi, they are brilliantly low key, disciplined."

"Who?" Agent Prince asked.

Agent Machiavelli stared at Agent Prince.

"Careful what you ask for, but they reason you're here, I'm here," Agent Machiavelli said. He marched back toward his desk. "Sometimes ignorance is bliss, but good work."

Chapter Four

Hidden within the frothy early morning haze of Nashville's downtown skyline, as Eddie drove toward work within the commuter traffic, Bertrand Screwtop closed his six-panel oak office door. He stood on the thirteenth floor of the Batman shaped building, at the high-powered commercial litigation firm of Lewis, Milton, Wormwood & Screwtop. He combed his smooth fingertips through his thinning, curly light brown hair. He slid behind his desk onto his button backed, brown leather chair. He sipped coffee from his favorite Kentucky Derby mug. Then he dialed a secret transatlantic telephone number.

"Mr. Screwtape, I presume your demonic self has good news," Ms. Prosperina said, English was not her primary language.

As he clicked through his computer screen, he opened the cyber client folder. He clicked on her picture. She was a diminutive middle-aged woman with blonde hair; she had hardly a wrinkle across her blank face digitally staring back at him.

"Well, I'm not exactly sure," Bertrand said. His southern accent was subtle, as he had refined it from years of practice so his Yankee clients did not think him daft. "But, I have good information, the people you seek have emerged."

"I trust you will not give me false expectations, like Dr. Yin," Ms. Prosperina said. Bertrand could hear her puff on a cigarette, and a drag that sounded like fizzing antacid tablets.

"Understood, my contacts believe it's them." Bertrand coughed to clear his throat. "It appears someone paid an exorbitant amount for some, ah, shall I say, rather personal sporting goods equipment, athletic supporters worn by a star running back."

"Star?" Ms. Prosperina said.

"Sorry, American football," Bertrand said. He fingered with the sharp cress of his suit pants. "All American football star, ah, similar to a famous soccer player."

"Oh, a man-bra, didn't want to lose his paradise," Ms. Prosperina said. She cryptically laughed. "So, the old man just cannot give up on his quest to protect the world from little old me, not much of a multiplier effect, one baby at a time."

"Ah, I suppose, you've retained me to provide information about internet commerce, but I'm not a private detective," Bertrand said. "And Dr. Yin seems like a typical scientist."

"Oh, now, now, I had my associate Mr. Oppenheimer thoroughly research you," Ms. Prosperina said. "Mr. Screwtape, you are a sneaky fellow, and he tells me you're quite the playboy."

Bertrand twisted to stare out the expansive office windows across western Tennessee and down at the dense interstate system cycling through the heart of Nashville, where

Eddie and Captain Lovins sat within the clogged traffic idling in their fossil-fueled machines pointed in opposite directions.

"It's, *Screwtop*, not Screwtape, never had a reason to marry."

"Irrelevant, I can be many different people all at the same time, my father was quite creative," Ms. Prosperina said. "I need to find him."

"Not sure how to respond," Bertrand said. He studied Ms. Prosperina's dossier, as he clicked his computer mouse, it was painfully thin of information, aside from the menacing photo. "Not sure I totally understand my role, but I do understand your business is agriculture?"

"I am amazed, I can be entangled with so many, in vastly differently locations with a minimal investment," Ms. Prosperina said. She purred. "Perhaps you should do more research about me, better than that client folder you've been studying, do you like my photo? On your computer screen I don't think it quite captures me."

"Well, I suppose," Bertrand said. He gulped. He sipped some more coffee from his mug. "You always wear black sunglasses?"

"No, but I don't think you'd want to see my eyes, besides, it will pay you financial dividends to be in my world," Ms. Prosperina said. She paused. "I have sensitive eyes. One of my investments is in bioengineering, to find replacements for people, like me. I'm quite the philanthropist, and I hope to feed the world, help my future generations."

"I suppose," Bertrand said. He loosened his tie.

"I need you to continue to focus Dr. Yin," Ms. Prosperina said. "I've quietly funded his research, he's not totally aware of me. He thinks his research is an off the books government program to grow synthetic diamonds, to figure out Professor Quan's secret formulas."

"To continue, this will take some more time, I'll need a substantial retainer, ah, our managing partner, Mr. Lewis," Bertrand said. "He will ask about the purpose of our relationship, he's annoyingly honest."

"Name your price, perhaps I'll send Mr. Oppenheimer to pay you a visit, he assists me," Ms. Prosperina said. "Tell him I am purchasing a utility, land, so forth. Good day, Mr. *Screwtop*, and remember, always drink your coffee black, you do know what's in it, right?"

The cell phone line clicked silent.

Bertrand quickly pushed his steaming coffee mug back across his leather inlay desktop. He stared at it as if it were leaking nuclear radiation. Then he studied her photograph, he quickly clicked the mouse to close the client file. Then he opened his internet browser and continued to research his client. Ms. Prosperina had a vast empire of privately held companies, they were all focused on utilities, agriculture and related businesses. He had not found any evidence she was involved in the bioengineering niche. However, he did note she had a relationship with a space technology company. But she held neither positions on boards of directors, or philanthropic organizations, nor could she be found in any form of social media.

It was as if she preferred to live in the shadows, building a vast fortune. Bertrand sat back and stared over at his steaming coffee mug. He decided it best to not to contact Dr. Yin again. He would get agitated and more nervous having someone outside of government asking questions. But he wondered who this Ms. Prosperina was, and where she came from. He knew he better find out because his partner Simon Lewis would pelt him with pesky ethical questions.

Chapter Five

Earlier in the morning mist, Captain Lovins had visited a three-month-old girl named Gloria. Professor Quan had whipped up musical maestro epigenetic dust from the Mozart sample Captain Lovins had outbid the world for off WePay. He mixed in some Horowitz, Copeland and Stravinsky samples they had captured along their life journey. He hoped she would fulfill her destiny. Because she was born the exact moment, Professor Quan saw a shooting star as he hummed a Dylan tune. He trusted the epigenetic adjustment would shoot her transcendental star to become a virtuoso pianist, but he would have to wait before he saw any results. It was the crucible of science he knew, testing and then having to wait to validate his instinctual theory. But he knew the future really belonged to Gloria's choices, and her passion to learn music. Her altered DNA chained to that nasty booger, *free will.*

Captain Lovins drove his vehicle northeast, away from downtown Nashville and onto Interstate 65. Then his sedan came to a dead stop. He glanced across the four-lane road of bumper-to-bumper southbound traffic and noticed Eddie blankly staring forward, driving a 1984 Cosgni.

"Worker-bee," Captain Lovins said. He waited for a dial tone and pressed *1 on his cell phone.

Eddie glanced over at Captain Lovins. He thought the hard looking bald headed man had a deathly stare, a stare that had caused the stubbly hair on the back of his neck to stand up. He averted his gaze back up at the distinct downtown skyline centered by the shape of the Batman building where Bertrand sat contemplating his existence on the thirteenth floor. But his fractured brain whispered for him to peek back over again. Now, the bald headed man seemed to be studying him.

"All righty then-" Eddie tried to whistle. In his own southern way, Eddie nodded his head forward and waved his left hand forefinger as if he were Farmer Wilcox acknowledging a neighbor he passed by on a narrow backcountry road.

"Man-at-large?" Professor Quan asked.

"I've completed the morning tasks," Captain Lovins said. His stare never moved from Eddie.

"Excellent," Professor Quan said.

"I cannot believe this," Captain Lovins said. He tapped his callused fingertips along the steering wheel. "This is so random."

"How so?" Professor Quan asked.

"Young man, it's him, Edward, from our 1990 or '91 list, he's stuck in south bound traffic across from me, good looking kid. I'd know his face. I've not paid much attention to him. I thought him a no brainer, he appears he has no fire in his eyes. And he's driving a socialist junker from the 80's."

"How did I screw that one up?" Professor Quan asked.

"I don't know. Sorry, I've not been paying close attention to him," Captain Lovins said. He put on his black skullcap. His car tires started to roll forward and Eddie's unblemished face disappeared behind a concrete median.

"I need to think about him," Professor Quan said. "I need to examine his sample. Weird, my instincts have been pecking at me about him, too. Now I know why. Double-check our Watch List."

"On it," Captain Lovins said. He drove his vehicle over a pothole full of muddy surface water. He almost dropped his cell phone as he slowed the vehicle near a busy intersection merging with Interstate 24.

"Dear friend, I think you should retrace Edward. I would like to figure out what he has been up to, work, friends, all the data of his life, something doesn't add up."

"You've not missed many, I'll tag his jalopy with a tracking device," Captain Lovins said. He shrugged. "That was just weird. He looks dead inside."

"Instincts I guess, but really, 'It is the stars, the stars above us, govern our condition,'" Professor Quan said.

"Okay, I'll bite, what's that from?" Captain Lovins asked.

"King Lear, never mind me, but I'm heading into Clayhole for supplies, you need me to pick anything up?" Professor Quan asked. "And I'll check in at the shop, we keep selling drill bits, amazing demand for something littered all over the earth."

"Yeah, but be extra careful, I get the sense Dr. Yin is sniffing about," Captain Lovins said.

"How so?" Professor Quan asked.

"I picked up on some conversations. They're after a knucklehead I did some business with, the moron spends money like a power drunk congressman," Captain Lovins said.

"I see," Professor Quan said.

"I hinted to lay low," Captain Lovins said. "Clearly, he is unaware the IRS monitors our every movement."

"Not to worry. I'll change into my itinerant-farmer skin," Professor Quan said. "Besides, until Ms. Prosperina pops up out of the underworld, until then, I'll sleep like a baby."

"Yeah, and some day she'll realize we provided the diamond drill bits for her collider, she'll get pissed when she finds out we have a complete set of blueprints," Captain Lovins said.

"Well, true, fatal flaws are best kept hidden" Professor Quan said. He chuckled. "She can play with particles all she wants. She'll not get her hands on the black nuggets she seeks."

"Yeah, hey, I'm going to stay here and monitor the situation, guy's a fry cook," Captain Lovins said. He glanced around at the weaving traffic. "I think I have a mess on my hands, but I'll clean it up, and in the meantime, I'll track down Edward."

"Good, I look forward to finding Edward," Professor Quan said. "I think he's the one that should be a physician, yeah, I think I imagined him as an ER doctor."

Chapter Six

Inside a cavernous, subterranean lair, lost within the lush emerald green Appalachian hills, Professor Quan stared into a high-powered optical microscope. His skin was reddish with orange undertones. He was far from packed urban neighborhoods, busy city streets, but most of all, Big Brothers' constant inquisitive eyeballs. Nearby on a faded leather lounger his pet dog's seal-brown eyes focused on her master. He slid off his magnifying goggles, latex gloves, mesh smock, and deposited them into a biohazard container. A satisfied expression emerged across his face as he slipped on a white lab coat. He scratched the dog behind its fluffy ears. He grinned down at his friend.

"Waldo, it's about what *happens* to you, and you have to remember you're loved," Professor Quan said. He adjusted his lab coat at the lapels. "Let's go for a walk, time for you to do some business, right?"

Waldo and Professor Quan left the lab; traveled up inside a wide reinforced elevator, and emerged inside a dilapidated shotgun style house. Together, they ambled out of the rickety front door. A lonely 1940s era powder blue metal porch glider set on the left side, flanked on the right side of the concrete slab porch by a wooden swing connected to the ceiling by metal chains. A cooper-bellied water snake, disturbed, uncoiled and slithered into the scrub grass. The obedient dog scurried just in front of Professor Quan down a narrow dirt path. She sniffed at dense foliage, pranced back forth in semi-circles before she stopped to relieve herself.

"Good Waldo," Professor Quan said. He chuckled as noticed several fox squirrels. "Come, Waldo." Ignorant that Professor Quan lurked, they scratched behind glossy red bryum moss covered limestone, and chewed fresh elder berries. They dug holes near Cumberland rosemary. Their cybernetic vibrations bounced off inconspicuous spider web like receptors strategically placed next to tree trunks, rock embankments, and draped across mountain azaleas. Carbon based threads that glistened with a blue diamond fleck coating. The vibrations reflected back to a primary cellular membrane spread over the shotgun shacks tin roof. Over the decades, they had created an almost impenetrable organic mesh security zone, because years before he had roamed the habitat, hunting the local rodents with his enhanced three-foot blowgun. He had shot a disintegrating dart, tipped with a microscopic wafer that dispersed into their pink tissue. At the molecular level, over the subsequent decades, the little-brained creature's natural breeding cycles advanced the micro-organic adjustments from squirrel to squirrel. The result, their sensations and feelings beamed back positive kinetic energy collected by the web sheets that Professor Quan could convert into three dimension visual images that signaled any unwanted visitor hiking within their environment, an environment that had only a single narrow dirt road that terminated in front of the dilapidated house.

Professor Quan and Waldo continued along a bisecting walking path up to a clearing within the forest that overlooked the sun-splashed valley. But he dared not emerge from the canopied tree line to reveal his real face. He remained within the shadow cast by a massive sycamore aware Ms. Prosperina's drones constantly roamed the heavens filming, probing and sensing earth, and communicating with her satellite constellation. Waldo sat back on her hind legs, she panted with her pink tongue as she looked up at Professor Quan.

"Waldo, this valley was formed from a huge meteorite, I used to go hiking along those trails when I was at Briar Hill, it's not far from here," Professor Quan said. He looked down at Waldo. She had happy black eyes, as her tongue waggled out.

"I wish you understood me, but that's okay, what I tell you would get you killed," Professor Quan said. He clenched his jaw. He leaned down on his left knee; he patted Waldo along her furry back and turned to stare down the jagged valley wall. "Down there, along that sandstone ridge, I found those plutonic diamonds. I had no clue, coated with organic material. I was just a kid, playing with science."

Professor Quan picked up an oak leaf. He smelled its oaky fragrance admiring the expansive veins that had fed the blade.

"I wonder about nature, a random asteroid slings past Jupiter, it blazes through the atmosphere, crashed into earth, with organic material packed in ice, organic material? And the ice melts, we have water, but from where?"

Professor Quan got up. He wondered about the random nature of nature, and if it was random at all, or if there was a grand design hidden from his view. He looked up into the sky through the colorful cluster of tree limbs and leaves.

"Waldo my fury friend, you could fish the stars for a zillion years, never find a thing but cold, dead space. But then again, organic material doesn't appear by magic." For some reason he started to think about Edward. He snapped his fingers.

"Come Waldo."

Professor Quan descended back into his laboratory hell. He leaned back against a yellow oak table. His bushy, black eyebrows furrowed as he inspected the stainless steel science table littered with Bunsen burners, magnetic stirrers and a genetic analyzer. Clasping his thin fingers together, he inhaled the lair's filtered air infused with a calming blended lavender, peach and hibiscus scent. He focused on a propped open reclaimed stainless steel bank vault door. Professor Quan clapped his hands. Escaping from the main lab with his dog wagging her ghost-white furry tail they ambled through the concrete reinforced doorway into rooms labeled, Genome Therapy.

The first room to his immediate right appeared from the outside, similar to a florist's cool room storage. Professor Quan tapped his fingers against the thick glass leaving behind a faint image of his fingerprint. But inside it was a full on arctic negative degree winter. On the west wall, it had a lanky ladder with rubber rollers. All the walls were covered floor to ceiling with a vast collection of paraffin vacuum-sealed conical flasks. Each vessel glistened on the edges as if sprinkled with white diamonds.

"Why is Edward nagging at me?"

Waldo sat back on her hind legs; she panted and pawed at for Professor Quan's leg. He picked up Waldo. He scratched her belly as he tightly hugged her. Professor Quan continued to pet Waldo as he twisted to walk across the chocolate chip specked terrazzo floor hallway. Inside a strange teak wood apparatus dominated the room. It had two haunting fibrous intersecting triangular sheets that hung within a rectangular frame. The sheets effused hot bubble gum pink from the blending of red sun and white moon. And it seemed to beckon Professor Quan closer as they waved back and forth like drying bed sheets in a springtime breeze. Waldo barked at it. Professor Quan put her down and she quickly scampered from the room. From the obvious wear, and the frames weathered silver graying, it was decades old. But Professor Quan knew it had never seen the light of a brilliant hot summer day, nor felt the sting from a harsh ice storm. Underneath the spider web like sheets was a strip of telescopic glass portholes segmented three-inches apart. With an amber carpet runner bisecting underneath the machine with a slight hump at the center across which the silent wavy sheets draped. The heart of the machine was an ancient blue diamond that was a perfect semiconductor for heat and light.

In the left corner of the massive room was an innocuous yellow oak roll top desk, but for the fact it glowed with an odd auburn hue. Professor Quan's scalp tingled. He glided his fingers across the desks curved closure.

"So many options, my mind was on fire."

In November of 1962, caught in the middle of fighting the Cold Epigenetic War, Professor Quan had learned the Government had taken his advanced cloning concepts, used his genetic starter mixture and created a life form in 1953. They had named it Prosperina. He would have used the name Kore, but even so, Ms. Prosperina existed. But they had no clue his own DNA coursed through her evil veins, and her DNA was not like any human. All because when he was a brilliant teenager, he had had, a thought experiment that his adult wisdom scars would have whispered to him to not take that road. At that moment, his pineal gland opened a window to his soul for self-reflection. He saw the evil in his own heart from the methods he created to alter societies, or wipe out generations without ever firing a shot. A sword hung above him that Damocles would have never contemplated.

Then one innocuous afternoon, during an aimless lunch break, a paranormal idea revealed itself as he strolled within the beehive of tourists inside the Smithsonian Institute. Standing before his answer, the immensity of the moment caused his eyelids to blink rapidly. And he had to sit down on a cushioned museum chair. He sprang back up, and stood close to the glass.

"Optics?" Professor Quan whispered. "Gravitational lensing, bending light, but at a subatomic level?" Professor Quan whispered. He tapped the protective glass with his fingers. "I bet that's where God hides, right in front of us." Condensation from his breath glossed a ghostly pattern on the glass.

"Sir?" a security guard asked.

Professor Quan glanced over at the well-built security guard.

"Just curious where they found that shiny rock?" Professor Quan asked. He nodded his forehead over at the diamond that shimmered as if a giant blue star discovered within the dark matter of outer space.

"It's a mystery, they don't know." The security guard shrugged. "Maybe from India they think?"

"Life's a mystery," Professor Quan said, "like looking through a child's kaleidoscope, or the mystery how a cuttlefish can disappear within its environment."

"I suppose sir," the security guard said, "hands off the glass please." The security guard strolled away.

"Oh, sorry," Professor Quan said. He backed up and sat down studying the illuminating object for several hours. He stayed well past his normal lunchtime, musing at his hearts affection within the mesmerized groups of tourists. Roaming back toward his government laboratory, he decided he would need to work in total isolation. Relocate far from the government's icy clutches. If he pulled off the heist, he would be a marked man for the rest of life. But how? He knew he could not do it alone. He was determined to steal the Hope Diamond; he was certain it was the key to his newest theory. For the next nine months, his instincts constantly nagged at him, unable to sleep, to rest.

Then one day it all came together in his mind. Within his secret laboratory analyzing a captured eastern bloc spy's blood, it all suddenly seemed so simple, and yet so transcendental.

"Our dead friend's DNA looks just like everybody else's, nothing remarkable," Professor Quan said.

"I guess," Dr. Darko Yin said. He was a beanstalk of a young man, and was Professor Quan's laboratory assistant.

"Dead." Professor Quan peered over at Dr. Yin. "If only I had a way to isolate his genes?"

"I guess, you're kind of being - out there." Dr. Yin scribbled a note on the chart.

"Too bad I can't just play with his genetic structure."

"Sorry, I don't understand?" Dr. Yin said. He stared down at the chart.

"I'm daydreaming." Professor Quan slipped off latex gloves and his examination glasses. He placed a thin glass specimen slide underneath his microscopes viewer. He tilted forward and squinted through his microscopes viewer lens. After a few moments, he jostled back from the stainless steel lab table. He stargazed up at the bland square ceiling tiles, as he rolled around on a cushioned chair.

"I wonder," Professor Quan whispered. A method to extract DNA from living creatures, synthesize them via laser blue light and modify their linked amino acid genetic necklaces. Rather retool their instruction manual, to engage their pineal gland to sense people like Ms. Prosperina. They would build peace and love generation to generation.

"You okay? You seem, well, troubled," Dr. Yin said. He stepped away from the laboratory. "Be back in pie."

Professor Quan sat quietly allowing his authentic artistic subconscious to emerge immersing him within the ghostly vapor of prophetic whispers. He prayed for courage, to protect unborn generations, he feared for their silent epigenetic slaughter.

"Clones?" Professor Quan said. He chuckled. He had not noticed Dr. Yin quietly slip back inside the laboratory.

"Did you say cloning?" Dr. Yin asked. He shifted closer to Professor Quan, who ogled down at the busy parking lot. He turned and weaved his way past a stainless steel lab table.

"Never mind me," Professor Quan said.

"We're just theorizing now, right?" Dr. Yin said.

Professor Quan glared down at his mesh-covered shoes as he strolled across the white tile floor.

"Twin DNA might be identical, but as they age they might choose to smoke, drink or eat junk food, so they become unique even to their twin," Professor Quan said.

"How do you know that?" Dr. Yin asked.

"I just do, my instincts told me," Professor Quan said. He stuffed his hands in his lab coat. "Listen to me, cloning is bad karma, humans are more than a collection of body parts. There is magic electricity inside us, a riddle we have no answers for inside our cells, light particles that make up the universe."

"Maybe, maybe not, you should teach another class to the graduate students with a high security clearance?"

"Why?"

"To build on your research, I bet our bosses would love to know more about your cloning ideas." Dr. Yin slanted in close to Professor Quan. He had a faint grin.

Professor Quan scrutinized Dr. Yin's face.

"I hate this homogenized world," Professor Quan said. He coughed. "Why do we have to all be stereotypes, why not be unique, be like Elvis, take risks."

"What's that?" Dr. Yin asked. "You cannot be serious, Elvis?"

"I dig Elvis, sorry, I, I'm just not focused I suppose." Professor Quan gulped.

"You're brilliant, you've probably killed off half of the KGB," Dr. Yin said sarcastically. He patted Professor Quan on the back. "And that skin sensor potion, brilliant. I can't figure out how it works."

Professor Quan clenched his jaw; he glared at Dr. Yin. As he thought of all the orphaned children, just like him.

"I'm not real proud of all that, you know my parents were crazy anarchists, but I'm not," Professor Quan said. He whispered. "You don't have to be like your parents."

Professor Quan strided out of the laboratory with Dr. Yin close behind. As they approached the building's locker room, Professor Quan stopped in front of the metal swinging double doors. He twisted his shoulders to face Dr. Yin.

"I'm tired of all this," Professor Quan said, "retirement?"

Dr. Yin backed away from Professor Quan, scratched his narrow chin. What Dr. Yin could not know, Professor Quan had sworn that very moment to never let him, nor any of his colleagues, highjack his inventions again. As if a filthy, dirty window, wiped clean, a crystal-clear picture emerged of an envisioned new life, a redemptive life, a sacrificial solitary life. He would start his own silent bioengineering war on humanity, and today was his Fort Sumter.

"Now?" Dr. Yin asked. He laughed. "You're not that old. How will you survive? I'll be totally out of balance." Dr. Yin stared at Professor Quan. He leaned against a locked metal door situated next to a tempered glass observation window.

"Oh please, they'll replace me," Professor Quan said.

"I don't think so," Dr. Yin said.

"I'll survive. My instinct is to make a drastic change. I need to get out of this rut I'm in." Professor Quan smacked Dr. Yin on the right shoulder. "I need some sunshine."

Dr. Yin shook his head, scratched behind his right ear.

"They're not going to be happy," Dr. Yin said.

"I don't care. They don't own me." Professor Quan felt a chill cycle up each nerve root of his spine. If he succeeded, he would be the number one villain on the FBI's most wanted list. A publicity shy list you never notice at the local post office.

Professor Quan pondered his idea for the next six months as he handed over the laboratory to Dr. Yin. They would kill him if they realized his intentions. And Ms. Prosperina would soon demand the plutonic diamonds he had hidden. He knew both sides wanted total control over humanity. But luckily he was an orphan, they could not easily trap him. He loved no one.

The next day, Professor Quan glanced over at Dr. Yin.

"If you wanted to start a business, how might one go about such a thing? I've no experience with such matters."

"Guess it might depend on what you want to do."

"Maybe a cake baking business? I just love mixing things together." Professor Quan gripped his hands on his hips; his face gleamed wonderment. Dr. Yin shook his head, as he icily ogled over at Professor Quan.

"Don't take this the wrong way, you do need some time away."

"Yes, yes, indeed. I think you're right, as always," Professor Quan said. He laughed nervously. "Perhaps a long vacation, find a partner, yeah, someone with experience." Professor Quan crossed his arms as he instinctively remembered meeting a Captain Lovins at a DOD cafeteria.

Over the next week, he researched Captain Lovins background; his instincts were prophetic because Captain Lovins was an orphan, he was a Special Forces soldier. Stuck working a desk job at the Department of Defense, demoted for speaking the truth about Vietnam. Professor Quan tracked Captain Lovins down, keenly aware what he was about to ask him could get him killed.

"So, you're one of those frogmen?" Professor Quan asked. He sat across from Captain Lovins at the busy DOD cafeteria.

"Pardon?" Captain Lovins said. His naval uniform perfectly pressed. "We've met before?"

"Yes, a few months back," Professor Quan said. He adjusted his jacket. He glanced down the cafeteria table at the other faces; he heard the buzz of humanity. He sipped his glass of water.

"Food sucks, black coffee kills the taste," Captain Lovins said. He poked his plastic fork into a pile of mashed potatoes. "This crap is full of chemicals."

"Sorry, I'm a bio-scientist, I'm not real proud of that," Professor Quan said.

"What's wrong with you?" Captain Lovins said.

"Sorry, I'm nervous," Professor Quan said. He coughed. He adjusted his black frame glasses. "We have something in common, we're both orphans."

Captain Lovins sat back in the plastic chair. He pushed his tray forward.

"Yeah, so what?" Captain Lovins said. He examined Professor Quan's face. "How do you know that?"

"I need your help," Professor Quan said. "I sense we are both of a common mind, that these folks are corrupt."

Captain Lovins carefully studied the diminutive man. He glanced around the cafeteria.

"Go on," Captain said. He crossed his arms. "Be careful."

"I have caused many bad things, I was young, naïve, stupid," Professor Quan. He clenched his fists. "I created inventions that allow our spies to do bad things. I created the most dangerous life form on earth."

"Wait, I've heard of you, you make new skin, all sorts of biochemical potions, or something like that," Captain Lovins said. He chuckled. "I thought you were a myth."

Professor Quan sat up straight and stared directly at Captain Lovins. He placed his hands flat on the cafeteria table.

"I am Professor Pi Dong Quan, I am brilliant, but so to speak, I accidentally opened Pandora's Box," Professor Quan said. He glanced side to side at the lunch crowd. "I see things I wish I did not see, I need to steal something, then, I have to start a war."

"Hmm, well I am a trained warrior," Captain Lovins said. He shrugged. "War? That's serious business little man."

"Genetic war, war you cannot see," Professor Quan said. He interlocked his fingers. "I need to steal the Hope Diamond."

"What the-"Captain Lovins said. He pushed his tray to the side. He menaced forward. "I'm not a thief."

"It, it has unique optical properties, it is the perfect conductor of light," Professor Quan said. He clenched his jaw.

Captain Lovins glided his hardened hands across the tabletop.

"Why are you talking to me?" Captain Lovins asked.

"I am brilliant, but, I'm not strong, I need someone smart, tough, to help me, you're not happy, I know it," Professor Quan said. He leaned forward. "I created a genetic starter, you know, like making bread, the government used it, there is a life form that appears human, but she's not really a she, it has alien organic material in it."

"Back up, what's this Hope Diamond stuff, I know nothing about genetics, I'm confused," Captain Lovins said. He crinkled his face. "But I'll give you credit, best way to tell me this is in a busy cafeteria, they'd never suspect that, smart."

"If I shoot laser light, blue light through it, I perceive I can alter DNA, create a special genetic bond, but the light, it has to be real, from the earth, just the right shape, color," Professor Quan said. He shifted in the plastic chair. "That shiny rock is perfect. If it works, I think I can create a genetic mutation."

"I don't understand," Captain Lovins said. He tapped his forefinger on the table. "My instincts, ah, what do you want?"

Professor Quan leaned forward.

"Help me steal the Hope Diamond," Professor Quan whispered. "Then help me protect humanity from her, from these people."

Captain Lovins blinked his eyes rapidly.

"Wow, slow down," Captain Lovins said. He brushed off whole-wheat breadcrumbs from his uniform pants. "If we do that, you know we've crossed the Rubicon." He shook his head. "But for some reason, I know, you're not messing with me."

"You live by a code, I've read it, I deal in code, DNA is just a biological code," Professor Quan said. He pushed his glasses back up the bridge of his nose. "You are an honest man, you would rather die than to lie. You must understand, she, it really, will grow to be more powerful than any Caesar. She will find me, I am no match for her, but I have the diamonds hidden, she must never find them, not matter what."

Captain Lovins paused for several minutes. He shook his head and crinkled his face.

"In three weeks' time, be back here," Captain Lovins said.

Professor Quan reached across to shake Captain Lovins hand.

"I welcome your background check," Professor Quan said.

"I hope so," Captain Lovins said, "for your sake."

Chapter Seven

Eddie was unaware he was again floating within Professor Quan's mental orbit as if by the randomness of a shooting star. And that his life was about to navigate in another dimension as he casually entered the third floor office suite through the smoked glass double doors.

"Why're you here?" Ardee asked with a breezy, southern accent. Her brown eyes convicted Eddie.

"Come on, this isn't such a bad job."

"True." Ardee crossed her thin arms. Her fingers nails perfectly manicured with a lovely candle apple red shade.

"Besides, I barely got through community college," Eddie said. He looked down at her.

"We'll have to discuss your future prospects sometime," Ardee said, "Somethin' better than barbeque hell?"

"You just like toying with me." Eddie sniffed her lily fragrance.

"I don't think so-" Ardee said. She leaned back in her chair. She crossed her willowy legs. "Anyways, our big-boy just came back in a great mood from one of his Civil War reenactment boon-dongles. Unfortunately, for you, his cousin Forest called to complain about you, you ruined his breakfast. He could not drink his, red eyed, black eyed, frappe mocha latte frothy cream with sprinkles. I had to go get him another one."

"Thanks," Eddie said. He shrugged. "Just drink it black."

"I'll spray your cube down with air-freshener later," Ardee said. She playfully winked at him.

"Good idea." Eddie loped a few steps from Ardee's desk, he sighed as he forged into the office suite. He turned the corner into his windowless cubed, pale vanilla oblivion.

"There you are my good man, say, how long you been with Insurance Professionals?" Clevenger said. He was five-foot-seven inch, portly middle-aged man with a mangled Civil War lieutenant goatee.

"Almost two years, Mr. Rollins." Eddie said. He stepped back from his office cube doorway. He twisted his head trying to minimize Clevenger's cockroach killing halitosis.

"Now, call me Clevenger, anyways, one of our Blue Ribbon Agents, now that's a - BRA." Clevenger held his fat hands outward in a pastoral position as if to pontificate. "Now BRA's are why Insurance Professionals has been so successful, a magical distinction that supports and separates our clientele."

Eddie tried not to burst into laughter.

"Forest Bedford, a BRA for the last ten years, called me this mornin' concerned you're out to get him. He said you declined an Azeem Ibraahamm Joseph Abdul Skyhook Smith, M.D., or something or other."

Eddie crinkled his pug nose. He looked up at the starless square ceiling tiles. "You mean, Azim Ibrahim Yoshef Abdul Skywalking Smith, M.D.? His application was incomplete, part of it's written in Farsi." He did not need to review the three-inch thick underwriting file Clevenger held open. Eddie pictured each page in his mind like a vivid slide show. "Dr. Smith has been sued nine times, he's a known drug addict, a registered sex offender." Eddie folded his arms across his chest. He leaned back against the fabric wall. "I declined the submission, it was not even close to the underwriting guide."

Clevenger yawned. He wiped off creamy foam from the hair above his lips.

"Well, I can understand you might be hesitant to provide Dr. what's-his-face with a quote. But, I think you really should reconsider," Clevenger said.

Eddie gave Clevenger a puzzled expression. Clevenger sheepishly stared down at his well-worn wingtips.

"Besides, Forest's my cousin three-times twice removed, he drives me crazy with his nasally voice." Clevenger waddled up from Eddie's office chair. He burped. He rubbed his belly.

Eddie twisted, as he covered his nose with his fingers.

"I'll call him back to explain I'm not out to get him. A physician, who might be a *terrorist*, is an automatic decline. Nothing you or I can do about that," Eddie said as his eyes watered.

Clevenger grinned through his mangy goatee.

"You're so clever, old Forest's a serious redneck, you know, he's still in the KKK, he looks like a fat gnome," Clevenger said.

He waddled away from Eddie's cube. "I think the old – terrorist - word will guarantee no more nasally sounding telephone calls."

Eddie sat back in his office chair. He spent the rest of the day aimlessly underwriting insurance submissions. Later that same day Ardee happened by his office cube.

"I feel like a prisoner living out a life sentence," Eddie said. He grinned up at Ardee. He slinked back in his office chair and crossed his legs.

"Find some meaning for your life, let's get a drink?" Ardee asked. Her left hand was on her hip. "This ain't purgatory."

"Sorry, I promised Jim Bob I'd stop by," Eddie said. He nervously chuckled. He sat up. He attempted to avoid eye contact with her.

"Feel free to give me a ring after you dine on that artery-cloggin' stuff," Ardee said. Her curvaceous body stood pigeon toed in Eddie's office cube opening.

"Jim Bob this better be good," Eddie whispered.

"Edward," Ardee said. "Come here."

Eddie bounced up from his office chair.

"What's wrong?" Eddie asked.

"That thang-" Ardee pointed down at a spider dancing along a silky web behind the edge of Eddie's cube and interior wall along the marshmallow vanilla hard plastic baseboard.

"It's just a spider. Too bad for the fly though." Eddie bent down to study the fly death scene.

"Make it go away," Ardee said. "Spiders, they're evil."

"I think it's a, Spruce-fir Moss Spider or something like that," Eddie said.

"So?" Ardee said.

"My dad pointed one out like this years ago, we were hiking in the Smoky Mountains. I *think* they're endangered. Let's just take it outside."

"Why don't you just kill it? It's evil," Ardee said.

"I don't know, I don't like killing anything," Eddie said. He shrugged. He collected his plastic trashcan and swept the spider inside. As they walked outside, Eddie was curious why Ardee was fascinated with the spider. Her intoxicating brown eyes tracked the insect's movements around the container bottom.

"Never knew you were the out-a-doors type?" Ardee asked.

"Just like to breathe in fresh air," Eddie said.

Eddie found a grassy spot next to their office building. He gently encouraged the spider from the container near several green velvet boxwoods and a Fraser fir.

"Sit with me for a moment," Ardee said as she patted her hand on a concrete bench shaded by several oak trees. Eddie slid in next to Ardee. They watched the spider scurry away to freedom. "I need a cigarette."

"You're a smoker?" Eddie asked.

Ardee dug in her purse. She pulled out a pack of cigarettes.

"There's a lot you don't know 'bout me. I did not know you liked to go campin'. We could go and only need one sleepin' bag," Ardee said. She nudged Eddie with her elbow.

"Behave. I haven't been in a long time, used to go with my dad," Eddie said. He acknowledged a few co-workers leaving for the day, and the once full parking lot quickly emptied.

"What's he like?" Ardee flicked her lighter. She ignited the cancer stick. He twisted his butt on the hard seat.

"Passed away years ago, never mind," Eddie said.

"I'm sorry," Ardee whispered. She patted Eddie's forearm. She crossed her legs. She studied Eddie's face. She released plumes of smoke from her full lips.

"Just the way things are-" Eddie said.

"I don't know what happened to my father, he left us when I was a baby, never met him," Ardee said. "Is your mom alive?"

"Yeah, she still lives over in Brentwood," Eddie said, "How 'bout you?"

Ardee frowned. She took another drag of her cigarette. She paused for a few moments and glanced at a row of dogwood trees. "That's a little complicated, we don't talk anymore."

"Sorry," Eddie said.

"No need to be sorry." Ardee looked away from Eddie. She dabbed her eyes with the back of her right hand.

"Spider didn't mess around, crawling to freedom," Eddie said.

Ardee ogled back at Eddie.

"It's been almost three years now, she's not happy with me, I broke-off my wedding engagement, so she cut me off," Ardee said.

Eddie stared down at Ardee's fashionable dress pumps.

"I'm sorry," Eddie said.

"Stop sayin' sorry all the time, nothin' to be sorry about, she didn't seem to care he hit me. It was only once, he was drunk, but that's all it took," Ardee said. She sat up straight. "Life's too short to put up with that."

"Yeah, no good reason from that," Eddie said.

"What reason? Stupid is more like it. My mother and her ways, she was fixated on his family money," Ardee said.

"Not sure what to say, all I can remember is my father always told my mother he loved her, loved me," Eddie said.

Ardee patted Eddie on top of his left hand. She paused for several minutes staring past the evening sky into deep space.

"If I wanted that," Ardee said with a laugh. "I'd rather marry Clevenger and put-up with his Civil War re-enactment crap that my dead ancestors would find disgustin'." She glided her forefinger across his forearm. "I think a lit candle and a simple prayer for the fallen is better, those were real people that died, it ain't real brave, just acting brave."

"I think Clevenger would have out-kicked his coverage," Eddie said. He coughed. "He won the sperm Olympics."

"Sperm Olympics?" Ardee asked.

"Haven't ever heard that? Some people get lucky just being born," Eddie said. He shrugged.

Ardee puckered her lips. She grinned at Eddie.

"You're silly, ever been in love?" Ardee asked. Smoke plumes escaped from her lips like water over a steam baths lava coals.

Eddie gripped the bench with his fingertips.

"Not really-" Eddie said.

"Why are you so afraid?" Ardee asked.

"Sorry," Eddie stopped mid-word. "What I mean is, I don't understand."

"You're afraid, that's no way to live," Ardee said. She held her breath. She rhythmically released smoke between her perfect lips as she intently stared into Eddie's eyes. "Boys don't play hard-to-get."

Eddie averted her stare. He glanced across the parking lot and the busy Hubble Parkway over toward the fake log cabin Uncle Dante and Aunt Virgil's Hellish Barbeque Pit. A blending of Apple wood, Ash and White Oak smoke plumed above the center-point red brick chimney.

"Who were you engaged to?" Eddie asked.

"Bobby Humperdinck, son of the late, great Darryl Humperdinck, trust me, a real jerk," Ardee said. He huffed.

Eddie sniggered.

"What? What's so funny?" Ardee asked.

"Small world, I went to grade school with him, known him most of my life, Bobby's always been a total jerk. Girls used to just hang all over him," Eddie said. He leaned forward. "I guess they thought he'd change, but he's a sperm Olympic champion for sure, used car lots aren't sexy, but they sell a bunch of cars."

"Depends on where you're sitting," Ardee said. "Money and good looks don't make you special, it's what's behind your eyeballs, and you have extraordinarily kind eyes."

"Behave. I laugh every time I watch his weird commercials. He got lucky in life, born to the right family," Eddie said.

"And that demonic *chimp*, I think he has somethin' goin' on with that rodent. He's a creep." Ardee said. She glared past Eddie. She crinkled her mouth. "Some people think they can get away with anything, he's just a lucky jerk, whatever-" Ardee put her thumbs and forefingers into a 'W' symbol.

"Yeah, he's definitely been lucky," Eddie said.

"Don't take this the wrong way, but I've been workin' here for awhile, and I've noticed you can do this job with your eyes shut. Clevenger thinks you have a photographic memory. And I think you're ten-times smarter than Bobby."

"I don't have three cents to my name," Eddie said. He sheepishly crinkled his face.

"Never mind that," Ardee said. She waved the thought away. "Why don't you go back to school? I'm a hard worker."

"I don't know, really wish I had a better answer," Eddie said. He shrugged his shoulders. He stared up into the azure sky blending blue to gray toward a dark, forbidding night.

Ardee flicked the ash off her cigarette. The shards floated away, as if weightless lost memory snowflakes.

"Aren't we the pair? I'm getting' too old to be shy, if you want to get dinner some night," Ardee said.

"I hear ya," Eddie said as he decided to inspect his shoes.

"Not sure you do." Ardee extinguished her cigarette. She patted Eddie on his left shoulder.

"Okay, not sure what to say." Eddie grimaced.

"I best be goin'-" Ardee said. She collected her purse.

Eddie sensed the smoky evening air. He let the Co2 release gradually from his lungs as he watched Ardee stroll toward her car. He returned to his cube to collect his collectivist stamped keys and left his workday world behind. He turned the key and ignited his forest green fossil-fueled modern chariot. He drove unmolested through rush hour traffic, and navigated down Hubble Parkway toward his favorite heart unhealthy restaurant, The Sausage Bacon and Eggs Diner. The single story building had a red painted wooden-plank exterior, trimmed with flat white paint, and crowned with a happy animal protein, pink-neon signage. Eddie loped through the high gloss off-white double doors. His nostrils sensed the inescapable bacon grease fragrance.

"Here you go, dear. You know where to sit?" The host was shaped like two lemony balloons, pasted together trying to separate to freedom. She handed him a laminated menu featuring fowl, cow, and swine entrées paired with three optional narcoleptic inducing starches.

"Yeah-" Eddie coasted past her, into the smoking or second-hand smoking dining areas separated by a latticed wall adorned with fake folk art memorabilia. Eddie sat on a thick, lacquered, yellow oak swivel seat at the end of the red, white and blue-checkered Formica topped customer counter.

"Come on now, it's almost Christmas Jim Bob. I need that there special now," a server said. She had a beehive hairdo with a red and blue polyester uniform and white leatherette shoes.

"Order in, Jim Bob make it a rush," another weight challenged server said. She menacingly pointed at Jim Bob.

"At least I do not work here," Eddie whispered.

"Need something honey?" a server asked.

"Coffee, full test," Eddie said.

The staff congregated like expectant mothers for Jim Bob to birth-out short orders back across a slick commercial grade stainless steel counter top.

"Simmer down, old Jim Bob only got three hands," Jim Bob said. He had an unconscious, giggly, twang.

"Don't care," an older server said. Eddie thought her facial features resembled a Red-tailed Hawk.

"Now, now, ain't any way to treat a man-wolf," Jim Bob said. A white smock tied around his bulging waist, underneath a short-sleeve, white cotton collared shirt. He noticed Eddie and skirted his pear shape around the cook station.

"How's it goin'?" Jim Bob said. He smacked hands with Eddie. He picked his nose with his thumb and fore finger. He wiped it on his grease-stained smock.

"Dude, stop *tickling* your brain," Eddie said. He glanced around the restaurant.

# # #

Outside the restaurant, Captain Lovins had parked his sedan on the SB&E's eastside parking lot. The dark tinted windows eliminated any prying eyes from peering back at him. In his right gloved hand, he held a device that resembled a tiny satellite dish antenna.

"Tickle what brain?" Captain Lovins said. His jut-jaw clenched, he sipped black coffee from a Styrofoam cup.

# # #

On the western side of the restaurants parking lot, two federal agents were in the back of a black cargo van. The interior stripped bare to reveal its metal skin. Bundles of AV cords, telephone wires cinched together to resemble veins, and arteries. Last week, after Agent Machiavelli got Judge Plato's consent, they had installed surveillance equipment in the diner at strategic locations underneath the server counter, above the back prep area, and inside the stainless steel cook station.

"How's this guy kept a job?" Agent Nietzsche asked.

"No idea," Agent Frederica said. She examined a flat screen video monitor. She dialed in better audio reception. "This place smells like a barnyard."

Back inside the restaurant, Eddie took in a deep breath as he tried to settle his stomach.

"Jim Bob, come on back here," the servers said in unison.

"Sorry, hanger-dangers, you just got to go in," Jim Bob said. "Simmer down girls." Jim Bob poured some coffee into a white cup.

"You'll wash your hands?" Eddie asked. He shrugged. "Man, we drink a lot of coffee."

"Yeah, I like it black, too, sort of comforts me. Hey, you want to try one of my special items?" Jim Bob asked.

"Why not, at least I'll die a slow painful death preceded by uncontrollable vomiting and diarrhea," Eddie said. He grinned.

"Come on, have I ever let you down?" Jim Bob said. He chuckled.

"Dude, are you kidding?" Eddie said.

"Forget that. Let me whip somethin' up for my best buddy. Tell you what - I'll even pick up the tab, my treat."

"What? You're so cheap you re-use toilet paper," Eddie said.

"Hey, my paper got two sides," Jim Bob said. He wiggled. He scratched his substantial belly. He then slid in close to Eddie.

"Been workin' a new angle," Jim Bob whispered. He leaned on his thick forearm. "Sort of the sperm Olympic idea you have."

"What?" Eddie said. He sat back.

# # #

Captain Lovins heard something peculiar about Eddie's voice. He smashed on a baseball cap, and strolled inside the restaurant. He stopped to ask the host directions to the bathroom, even though the sign marked just to her left. He marched inside, waited three minutes. He came back out and glanced over at Eddie. Edward? Captain Lovins thought. He twisted his shoulders to examine some post cards for a country music wax museum, highlighting a wax Elvis with big collars and a cape. Then he ambled back toward his sedan.

# # #

"Jim Bob, did you leave for vacation?" a server asked.

"Gentlemen, what's for dinner?" Earl asked. He was a regular with thin blond hair. His bow tie twisted cockeyed.

"Hey Earl," Jim Bob said. Eddie acknowledged him.

"Don't be talking about my sperm Olympics stuff, someone might have me committed," Eddie said.

"Hey, speakin' of that, had that hot little actress in her this mornin', what's her face?" Jim Bob asked.

Earl snapped down his newspaper.

"Let me guess, Regan Fryingpan?" Earl asked.

Jim Bob scratched his hairy chin. He snapped his fingers.

"Yeah, that was her," Jim Bob said.

"Who?" Eddie asked.

"She's from here I think," Earl said. He cackled. "I think Jim Bob's in heat."

"Shut up dummy," Jim Bob said.

"Yep, that's right, bet she's got some magic DNA," Earl said. He elbowed Eddie.

"Thanks, dude," Eddie said at Jim Bob. Jim Bob wobbled back and forth.

"Hey, never mind him, there're too many folks roamin' round here tonight. Why don't you come by Friday night?" Jim Bob asked.

A skinny server leaned in to interrupt their conversation. She had horrible coffee and cigarette breath.

"You workin'? I got bills to pay," the server said.

Eddie pushed back from the counter. He coughed.

"Man sakes they're all over you tonight," Earl said.

"Alright now, I'm comin'," Jim Bob said. He waved her away. He mumbled. "If you keep it all on the low down, I'll show you some magic. It'll change your life, come by Friday night?"

# # #

Captain Lovins flipped off the baseball cap and dropped it on the backseat. He immediately dialed Professor Quan.

"Yes?" Professor Quan said.

"You will not believe this, but Edward is friends with that idiot cook," Captain Lovins said.

"The fry cook?" Professor Quan said. "You were going to pay him visit."

"Yeah, I screwed up, thought he was harmless," Captain Lovins said. He mashed the gas pedal as he sped back toward their lair hidden within the cradle of Appalachia.

"Screwball and Edward friends? I'd never put them together," Captain Lovins said. "Weird, I got side tracked, had not had the time to paste a transponder onto Edward's car, he just shows up out of nowhere."

"This is not random," Professor Quan said.

"No kidding, we have a big problem, the FBI was on the other side of the restaurant," Captain Lovins said. "They are onto this bozo, but we lucked out, the goofball was about to tell Edward his little business secret, but he got spooked, he invited Edward to his house, this Friday."

"Not good," Professor Quan said.

"Not good," Captain Lovins said. "I'm headed your way, I need to get prepared, Friday night, I need to stake out the house."

"This is a problem," Professor Quan said. He paused. "But it's also an opportunity."

"How so?" Captain Lovins said.

"It's as if some force is bringing Edward to us," Professor Quan said.

# # #

Back over at the FBI surveillance position.

"Call Agent Machiavelli, I guess this will go down Friday at Calhoun's house," Agent Frederica said.

"Yeah, I'm on it," Agent Nietzsche said.

# # #

Back inside at the restaurant counter.

"What're ya peddling this week Jim Bob?" Earl asked. He folded the newspaper as he shook his head.

"Never mind," Jim Bob said. He glanced at Eddie. "Friday?

"All right," Eddie said. He shrugged. "I'll be there."

Chapter Eight

Back in 1962, exactly three weeks later, decades before the time of Edward, at precisely noon within the busy Department of Defense cafeteria, Professor Quan sat directly across from Captain Lovins. Within his rectangular lunch tray set a paper cup full of water and a wrapped whole-wheat club sandwich on a hard plastic plate.

"So, tell me what you learned," Professor Quan said. He appeared a bit heavier. He wore a baby blue bowtie. He slid his black framed glasses back up his nose. In front of him, set a six inch square box topped with a golden bow.

"Pardon?" Captain Lovins said. He studied the ruddy, pock marketed face. "Weird, your voice is the same, but-"

"It's me, I'll show you how, but later," Professor Quan said. He put his hands up. "But first, I want you to carefully examine my face. Do I look real? And I want to know what you learned about me. A man like you would always do a complete background check, you would not miss any detail."

Captain Lovins closely scrutinized Professor Quan's face.

"I've only heard rumors," Captain said. He pointed at the box. "What's up with this?"

"I'll explain, but first tell me," Professor Quan said.

Captain Lovins shrugged.

"Assuming this is you, well, you were born in Miami, January 30, 1932, a leap year, your father was named, Pi Dong, your mother was Maria Lopez Delores. Your father was a Japanese spy, your mother, a Luddite, a South American separatist movement."

"Anarchists at heart," Professor Quan said. He grinned.

"Well, the Hoover boys detected your mother after she tried to get free healthcare for some illegal orange pickers. They caught you all in the Florida Straits trying to escape to Cuba on a raft shaped like a swastika," Captain Lovins said.

"That was not a pleasant day, it was a left handed swastika," Professor Quan said. He sighed. "Helicopters, speedboats, my father was a Hindu. He thought the shape would give us luck. My mother was a Catholic, but didn't practice since the Jesuits wouldn't welcome her into their order, not the nun type."

Captain Lovins scratched his clean-shaven, square chin.

"He was shot dead in 1942 trying to escape from the Jerome War Relocation Center," Captain Lovins said. He tapped the table with his forefinger. "They deported your mother to Cuba. We sure like to wear a white hat, but I wonder."

Professor Quan adjusted his black framed glasses.

"She was a rather passionate woman," Professor Quan said. He sighed. "I never saw them again, just figured they were dead."

"Yeah, but the government decided to keep you, as a prized brain washable pet," Captain Lovins said. He shook his head. "190 IQ, not bad for a little kid, they justified keeping you using US v. Wong Kim Ark and the Fourteenth Amendment, but they always have excuses for what they want, now don't they?"

"Then, you learned about Briar Hill?" Professor Quan asked.

"Orphanage for smart kids?" Captain Lovins said. He chuckled.

"I suppose," Professor Quan said. He drank some water. "It was a secret science school, trained me to be a scientist. I guess I'm used to being alone, it can be an advantage."

Captain Lovins pulled out a folded piece of notebook paper.

"Yeah, I wrote this down, make sure I got it right, by the time you were thirteen, a Ph.D. in Molecular Genetics and a Ph.D. in Theoretical and Applied Linguistics by time you were fifteen, 190 IQ?"

"Good, glad you to know those facts," Professor Quan said.

"Helps to have SCI clearance, I've got a lot more," Captain Lovins said. He smirked. "But you knew that, right?"

"Correct," Professor Quan said.

"A random name was associated with you, Prosperina," Captain Lovins said. He twisted his shoulders. "Which is funny if you know anything about Roman myths, not my bag, this the girl?"

Professor Quan adjusted his collar and loosened his bow tie.

"Yes, but she is not a female, enough chit chat," Professor Quan said. He waved away the conversation. "I'm going to tell you something and then do something, and then I'll give you this box." Professor Quan slowly breathed out. He glanced at the nearby souls munching down their tasteless processed food. "Knowing, just knowing, could get you killed." Professor Quan looked over at Captain Lovins. "They won't waste the time to arrest you. Do you want me to continue? If not, I will leave."

Captain Lovins leaned back in the chair. He sensed it was a moment he could never take back; but his instincts prodded at him to listen, to keep an open mind.

"You really want that diamond?" Captain asked.

"It's a bit deeper," Professor Quan said, "you'll see."

"Go ahead then, I'm not afraid," Captain Lovins said.

"That, I am certain," Professor Quan said. He sat up straight in the plastic chair. "Excuse me for being a bit long winded."

Captain Lovins blankly stared back at Professor Quan.

"With all the resources of the government at my fingertips, incubators, a sterile hood, tools to remove and implant cells. One morning I scraped off organic material I noticed coated the surface of a plutonic diamond meteorite. I discovered them near the Middlesboro Crater, not far from the Cumberland Gap, where Daniel Boone guided settlers. It's not far from Briar Hill."

"Thanks for the history lesson," Captain Lovins said.

Professor Quan frowned. He fiddled with the box.

"They were not lumps of coal. I knew they were different, you could hike past them, and not even notice because they blended in with the lumps of coal. But in fact, they had traveled from deep space, formed from within the atmosphere of a dying star, a black star. I think a massive explosion destroyed the host planet, I don't know why, but I think it was within the goldilocks zone, it could support life. After a gravitational slingshot past Jupiter, part of its host, some of its life force glazed across the asteroid pieces hurdling toward earth."

"Life force?" Captain Lovins asked.

"Remember I was kid, organic material, bacteria, I had not a clue what it really was," Professor Quan said. He shrugged.

"That took some stones," Captain Lovins said. He grinned.

"Youthful indiscretion," Professor Quan said. He huffed and twisted the box back and forth. "I mixed pure human cells with the liquefied organic material, I added all sorts of animal cells, like cuttlefish cells, but then I really screwed up."

Captain Lovins tapped the table with his forefinger. He coughed to clear his throat.

"You talked," Captain Lovins said. "They hooked you in."

"Correct, I was naïve," Professor Quan said. He stared down at this brown leather shoes. "I told them I had made a genetic starter, sort of like a bread starter, I love to bake, mix things together, well, I told them all they needed to make a clone was an unfertilized human egg cell and of course, a fertile woman. I showed them in my notes, if they allowed it to multiply, like they added sugar to yeast, remove the nucleus from the unfertilized egg, then implant new cells inside the coat of the egg, hit it with electricity, like a lightning bolt from God, the cells should fuse together, reorienting the DNA. Then implant it into the female, and bang, nine months later a clone baby. But in this case, not a purely human life form, or a clone of a single person, I made a dangerous mess of things."

Captain Lovins leaned his elbows on the laminate-topped cafeteria table. He covered his face with his hands. He closed his eyes for several minutes. He shook his head.

"This is not a brave new world," Captain Lovins whispered.

"She is the most powerful weapon ever created, she lacks emotions, she can change her appearance, from her own familial DNA. I sense she has talents that I do not understand. She could be sitting next to us, we'd not know, unless I sensed her. I can sense where she is, I know what she is thinking, a rather odd feeling," Professor Quan said. He stared across the cafeteria. "I think it has something to do with the pineal gland."

"This is serious," Captain Lovins said.

"She's brilliant, only a teenager for now. She thinks like the Nazi's, the best way to manage a population is through food, water and air. I sense she has already figured that out."

"Damn, you make my skin crawl," Captain Lovins said.

"Now, I know she exists, I have a responsibility, these government people will protect her. But they don't understand she is more than a petite female form," Professor Quan said. He fondled with the golden bow affixed to the top of the box. "For now, a child, but she knows I exist as well, but she cannot read my mind, I don't know why."

"Why a Nazi?" Captain Lovins asked.

"She has some rather special DNA," Professor Quan said.

"A Nazi?" Captain Lovins said. "You didn't?"

"Plural, Nazis, sort of an evil primordial soup, I did not understand I was playing a dangerous game. I had access to all sorts of tissue samples, she is not a simple XX chromosome pair," Professor Quan said. He paused to inspect the square ceiling tiles. "In part, the reason I have a responsibility, to act, to get ahead of her. We can't just kill her, that would leave us blind to what she has already done or what she intends to do. I can't just destroy the meteorites, I'd lose the samples, to study, and if I pulverize them, I'd release the material into the environment, it's complicated."

Captain Lovins tapped the tabletop with his forefinger.

"I'll say, but no, you mean *we* have responsibility," Captain Lovins said. He icily stared at Professor Quan. "I'm in, but we'll need resources, can't just live off the land."

"Oh, good point, open this box," Professor Quan said. He slid the box across the table, over to Captain Lovins. "Look inside."

Captain Lovins slowly loosened the golden bow to release the top of the six inch cubed box. As he slid off the top, he noticed inside it was heavily cushioned. But what he saw from the reflected cafeteria light dazzled him and puzzled him at the same time. He held his breath. Then he stared back over at Professor Quan who morphed into his true self. His skin returned to its smooth, reddish tone, his weight seemed to evaporate into the air. And his shirt collar appeared a few sizes too big for his neck. Captain Lovins exhaled; he cautiously glanced side to side at the nearby lunchtime crowd. He realized they had not paid them any attention, and no one seemed to notice his startled expression.

"How did you do that?" Captain Lovins whispered. He felt frozen in space.

Professor Quan leaned forward. He chuckled.

"Which - that?" Professor Quan asked. He smiled. "I knew no one would notice, they are all quite typical, most people ignore their surroundings, they'd walk over a dying man on the street."

Captain Lovins stared inside the box. He quickly closed it, and tightly retied the golden bow. He clutched it within his strong hands as if it were an injured sparrow.

"Ah, I, ah, figured you could alter your appearance," Captain Lovins said. He looked over at Professor Quan. "I've heard of that, I think, not sure how you just did that, reappearing, but I thought you needed me to steal this, you just handed it to me like it was a stinking birthday gift. I can't think."

Professor Quan adjusted his black framed glasses.

"That is not what we seek," Professor Quan said. He casually pointed over at the cubed box. "I made those shiny rocks, it took me a bit of time, but I figured out all the angles and facets to the real thing. I think it's an exact duplicate, but it's not real. In fact, nothing inside that box is a real diamond. I created them all from me."

Captain Lovins shook his head. He leaned back; staring down at the box, he continued to clutch it with his fingertips. He slowly breathed out through his lips.

"And the, ah, skin?" Captain Lovins asked. He waved around Professor Quan's face with his forefinger in the air like an orchestra conductor.

"I imagined how she can alter her appearance, organically, the whole cuttlefish thing, she does it for fun," Professor Quan said. He unbuttoned his shirt collar. "What you've heard of is a biochemical reaction I created, add a few skin cells to the type profile you want to appear as, put it into one of my base mixtures and it replicates into a skin like sheet. Our spies use it, they wrap it over their faces. They use another invention to alter their vocal chords, it thickens, modifies how they sound. If they are fluent in a language, they seem authentic."

Captain Lovins blinked his eyelids rapidly.

"Seriously?" Captain Lovins asked.

"The trick that I've never told them about, the heat source has to be shot through a real diamond, from this earth, synthetics work, but rarely, and after one use, they crack easily. I think the Hope Diamond can be used over and over, it has to do with the conductor properties."

Captain Lovins pulled the box off the table.

"Okay, but, it's not possible to just make diamonds," Captain Lovins said.

"Oh now, just because you never heard of it, does not make it impossible," Professor Quan said. He kindly grinned. "I figured that out years ago, how do you think we finance wars?"

"What? Smashed coal?" Captain Lovins asked. He scratched behind his ear.

"No, my hair is a better source for carbon, highly compressed pure carbon, it is blue from with just enough boron," Professor Quan said. He smiled. He acted as if he was sprinkling salt on Captain Lovins sandwich. "I bet someday, they'll be as common as a grain of sand. I'll show you how I did it, it's really not that big of a miracle once you realize it's just fundamental science and so forth, I think we can create our own mining bit company, one way to fund our work."

"So you say," Captain Lovins said.

"You know, it's really about light, there is something about light, electricity, how it affects our cells, the real mystery," Professor Quan said. He drank some water from a paper cup. "So, do you think you know how we'll get that shiny rock hiding in plain sight over at the Smithsonian?"

"I think so, Occam's razor," Captain Lovins said, "right?"

"Ha, you are beginning to see me," Professor Quan said.

"Let me guess, we'll just walk in there, Captain Lovins said.

"They'll never realize it's gone," Professor Quan said. He folded his bow tie and stuffed it into his pants pocket. "I know you can set this experiment up relatively quietly."

"Yeah, I know what to do," Captain Lovins said.

Chapter Nine

Forward back into the time of Edward, he locked his metal desk drawer. His cube was cluttered with thick underwriting files stuffed with long forgotten insurance applications.

"Hey, want to get a drink," Ardee said. She sheepishly vacillated near Eddie's cube opening.

"Friday sure took it's time," Eddie said. He glanced over at Ardee. He glided his fingers along the edge of his car keys. "Not sure you can alter time, I, promised Jim Bob, you know."

"Sure, I understand," Ardee said. She stared down at the brown commercial carpet as she continued along between the cube world and toward the office's front smoked glass doors.

"Jim Bob, this better be good." Eddie whispered as he watched Ardee leave.

Eddie drove his gas-powered rust-bucket past the Brentwood Interstate 65 exit, where he typically turned off to visit his mother. He gazed down the black topped two-lane road, and thought only a few miles further down Three Jewels of the Tao Road across an arched wooden bridge over the Acheron River was the lush forest green, resplendent cemetery where his father eternally slept without dreams. He gripped the steering wheel as he aimlessly weaved through traffic. It had happened on a Wednesday, December 28, without any warning, Edward's oceans powerful cellular currents pushing him to become special became dead breathless.

#

It was after nine o'clock, the emergency room waiting area was crowded with colorful tattooed Gun & Knife Club members. A few illegal human aliens were being monitored nearby by bored radio squawking law enforcement. No one watched the mindless television spew unreality reruns, a few flicked through well-worn magazines. Every four minutes, Bobby Humperdinck and his crazed chimp tempted fate with another used car commercial. A few honest souls cried, or prayed for mercy as they changed their social networking status from married to single. Eddie and his mother hurriedly scooted past them and up to the ER night desk. A night nurse immediately ushered them past the swinging double doors and behind a pale blue curtained off area. She sat them down, and offered them water.

The nurse immediately guided Dr. Noah over to them. He was a long-limbed man with an angular face, he wore surgical greens and a staff coat with his name stenciled in powder blue above the hospital emblem. He sat down and pulled the curtain behind him as he fumbled with the patient chart.

"Mrs. Wilcox, I suspect," Dr. Noah said. He glanced up at Eddie who stood behind his mother gripping her shoulders. Eddie thought he had a face that was no longer curious about life.

"He's our son," Sophia said.

"I think your husband had a significant athermanous plaque build-up, my instinct tells me a genetic defect, it occluded his coronary arteries," Dr. Noah said. He paused as he continued to fumble with the patient chart. Eddie noticed his father's name written in the panel in black block letters.

Next door, Eddie saw his father's pure white cotton dress shirt, red club tie and wing tip dress shoes stuffed inside a plastic storage container. Atop a metal gurney, he thought he saw one of his father's motionless naked feet peeking out from underneath a stark white hospital sheet. He must be tired or heavily drugged, Eddie thought.

"Sorry to say, we know he bit into an apple, then he likely felt like a thunderbolt smacked him from inside his chest. It was likely an extremely quick, flood like sensation," Dr. Noah said. He closed the metal patient chart. He leaned his elbows on his knees. He talked slow and methodical as he stared directly into Sophia's eyes.

"No," Sophia whispered. She shook her head. She stared down at the cold tile floor. "This can't be-"

Dr. Noah reached over to grasp Sophia's shaking hands.

"We worked on him for several hours, I did everything I could, I did everything my training has taught me. I'm sorry, he's past away." He shifted on the hard plastic seat. He clenched his jaw. "I wish I had better news."

"No, no, he's not even forty," Sophia said. She whispered as her lower lip trembled. "We were supposed to grow old together."

Sophia took in a deep, exaggerated breath. For Eddie, his mother's wisdom disappeared that night into another world, a world of her own. The spark in her eyes dimmed, as she retreated into a fantasyland of cotton candy and bunny rabbits where no one ever faced reality.

As Edward's face flushed scarlet he stumbled away from his mother, sensing he floated alone in a silent blurred surreal space. He pushed past the curtain, he stumbled forward, but an angelic nurse gently gripped his waste; she hugged him and guided him to a cushioned chair. As he blankly stared down at the floor tiles, his mind was traumatized that exact moment, as if a nuclear weapon detonated within his brain causing thermal radiation to incinerate all the positive particles within Eddie's soul. All the magical epigenetic dust Professor Quan had lovingly formulated that Captain Lovins had sprinkled across Eddie's newborn lips tragically altered. His DNA had biochemically switched on the wrong protein instructions.

# # #

Eddie's jalopy coasted in front of a gas pump at a dingy mini mart. He was not like most people; he was quite aware his internal engine lacked a spark as if a brand new high-performance engine hidden away inside a silent burley tobacco barn. He thought it a curse that he was self-aware that he was a loser.

The humid night air lathered his face, he dabbed dry his faint tears. The terse odor of gasoline tingled inside his nose. After a redneck teenager driving a chrome-infested four-wheeler, gunned his souped-up engine. Eddie danced back into reality to dodge drips of gas falling toward the bottom of his khaki pants leg.

"Come on," Eddie said, "get your shit together." He slipped his debit card into the payment slot. He got back into his car.

And he foraged another four miles south toward Jim Bob's ancestral habitat. Traveling just over the speed limit heading west, the placid environment transformed past Eddie from the stale, vanilla, multi-use commercial office and shopping complexes into rolling acreage of homogenous residential developments. Eddie steered his car onto the right hand lane canopied overhead by soaring oak and ash trees. The two-lane road bordered mile after mile of tar covered four plank fences. Not too far past the last gated community, Eddie pressed the brake; he turned his jalopy onto a dirt and gravel path, marked by a dented metal mailbox. As he drove along the gravel driveway, Jim Bob's hovel emerged; it was a rosy red brick, ranch style, with a black shingled roof streaked with white water stains. The exteriors custard cream trim paint dotted with decay marks revealing the underlying wooden structure. Eddie parked near the rickety single truck garage. He strolled across the irregular gravel driveway, blotted with wispy grass clumps, perpendicular to a concrete walkway up to the front door. Eddie rubbed his forearms because of the late evening chill. And a nervous sensation caused the hair on the back of his neck to spring to life, like a cluster of sea anemone bolted to a barrier reef, waiting to squeeze the life light out of an unsuspecting fish.

# # #

"Edward? You of all people should not be here," Captain Lovins whispered. Concealed a quarter mile away behind a row of random volunteer pine trees lying flat like a sniper, he squinted into his high-powered binoculars. His baldhead topped with a black skullcap. His face smoothed with zigzagged Roy G. Biv military paint. He shifted his binocular angle, to over a thicket of dead azaleas. He observed the federal agents scramble into their attack positions like a pack of crazed hyenas.

# # #

"Can I get a read on this new guy?" Agent Machiavelli said into the wireless headset microphone. He sat on a black mesh chair inside a van, camouflaged by a military tarp, parked near an abandoned tobacco barn.

"In position sir, I can confirm it's the guy from the restaurant," Agent Prince said. His voice crackled with static.

"Roger that, it's him," Agent Tacitus said. He had crotched under the back kitchen window. His 9mm weapon pointed down.

"Once we have our evidence, I will say 'collection time' for go," Agent Machiavelli said. "What's our confidence from the surveillance placement protocol?"

"High confidence sir, all systems functioning, good visuals," Agent Cromwell said. He monitored three hidden camera feeds. One positioned inside the living room, another above the front door, and another screwed into the kitchen window.

"Homer? Homer?" Agent Machiavelli said into his walkie-talkie. He only heard static. "Typical, in limbo-"

# # #

Eddie dodged beer cans, discarded pizza boxes, and found remnants from last night's barbecue feast scattered across Jim Bob's front porch. Eddie pounded with his left hand on the cracked pine wood door, aware the doorbells been broken since Slick Willie skillfully dodged wars, and economic meltdown before his Cuban cigar snagged him at the wrong clambake.

"Hey man, you in there?" Eddie asked. The loose knob turned. The door swung inward after a brief, extra tug by Jim Bob.

"Sorry 'bout that, need to get that fixed," Jim Bob said.

"Need help?" Eddie asked.

"Naw, come on in here, my man," Jim Bob said. After Eddie loped past him, Jim Bob took a suspicious inspection back across his scruffy front yard.

As Eddie neared the family room, he blinked his eyes, adjusting to the blazing one-hundred-watt incandescent light. A hardwood floor hallway was to his immediate right that led to three modest bedrooms. His shoes sunk into the spongy carpet padding under the family rooms new chocolate brown carpet. The room had a pungent fresh paint odor.

"Jim Bob?" Eddie asked.

"Times've changed, my man," Jim Bob said.

Eddie stuffed his hands within his khaki pants pockets. The living room had an overstuffed brown leather couch, lounger, and cherry hexagon shaped side tables. A sixty-inch helium and hydrogen plasma television hung within the vacuum of the front load-bearing wall.

"You making meth?" Eddie crossed his arms.

"Heck no, I ain't on drugs, want some coffee? Hey, like my furniture?" Jim Bob said. He cackled. He shook his hairy body side to side like a two-legged manatee. "I got a question for you, asked out that hot girl at your office?" He collapsed on to a leather lounge chair.

"Who?" Eddie turned his shoulders to study the movie theatre sized television. "Naw, it's late for coffee."

"Ardee, you know who," Jim Bob said as he pointed his pudgy finger at Eddie. "That girl needs a fireman."

"Ah, she's looking for a gold medalist," Eddie said.

"Whatever, you and your crazy sperm ideas," Jim Bob said. He chuckled. He yawned and scratched his groin. "Listen here now, got big news, I've connected to the worldly-wide-web." Jim Bob pointed his forefinger at his thick block of a head.

"So what," Eddie said. "That's not news."

"I was thinkin' at the SB&E one night, lookin' down at some biscuits and gravy, oh, I'd made them so pretty." Jim Bob said as he hound dog sniffed his thick nose. "The smell brought me back to my days as an athlete."

"You were simply born before your time," Eddie said. He shook his head. He leaned his elbows on the chair back. "You shouldn't think, it will only hurt your head."

"Can you just smell it? Remember after football practices that sweaty smell, cup smelled like rotten cottage cheese?"

"Not really, my mom had a washer and dryer, dude."

Eddie felt stomach acid creep up his esophagus.

"Anyways, while I was a freshman at UT, I got to know Leonardo Starfire," Jim Bob said.

"How'd you get to know him?" Eddie asked.

"Leonardo and me both flunked old English, but seems he had some special assistance." Jim Bob gave Eddie a weird, green-eyed, wink. "I just flunked, but old Leonardo felt bad for me, he convinced his secret friends." Jim Bob made a quotation mark sign with his thick fore and middle fingers. "They influenced Professor Tom More to let me slide with a D." Jim Bob stared expressionless into space. "Gave the old boy an autographed football, but he gave it back, got so mad almost lost his head."

"That's one way, I guess," Eddie said. He gazed up at the textured starless ceiling. "I'm such a loser."

"Proud of that D, after supper a while back, I got a little buzzed one night, and called old Leonardo." Jim Bob slinked up. He strutted to the center of the living room. "I asked him for the favor of a signed Volunteer jersey." He pounded his chest, crouched down into football linebacker fundamental position.

"You're amazing." Eddie said. He chuckled.

"Well, I set me up an account on that there WePay, sold old Leonardo's master work of a game jersey for fifteen hundred dollars," Jim Bob said. He happily shook his head. "Leonardo called some of his teammates for me, I started workin' on them, I had made quite a bit of dinero."

"Congratulations, I think," Eddie said. His left hand filtered his eyesight as if he is trying to block out a disgusting vision. "Do me a favor, first cross your legs or something. You're silk jammies, things are peeking out."

Jim Bob peeked down at his tubular personage.

"Sorry, that thing has a mind of its own," Jim Bob said. He waved his right hand in the air. "Speakin' ah your sperm Olympics, and such, I sold some funny stuff to this weirdo, said he'd buy stuff that famous athletes and popular people wore or what not, paid me a bunch of cash."

Eddie twisted his back to Jim Bob.

"That's weird man, don't be tellin' people I said anything," Eddie said. He covered his face with his hands. He strolled near the television, glided his finger along the warm, glowing screen. "So, I see you spent the money."

"My prized possession, I named her, Jolene," Jim Bob said.

"Jolene?" Eddie glanced back at Jim Bob. "You name boats, not TVs."

"Cause of this hot waitress, Jolene, she don't even notice me, unless I get behind on her orders," Jim Bob said.

"Jolene?" Eddie said. He furrowed his eyebrows.

"Yep," Jim Bob sipped his drink. He slinked back in the chair.

Eddie blinked his eyes. He took in a deep breath through his mouth.

#

Back at the surveillance van, Agent Machiavelli and Agent Cromwell puzzlingly stared at each other.

"Is he serious?" Agent Cromwell asked.

"Can't be, no one's that stupid," Agent Machiavelli said.

#

Eddie rubbed his eye sockets. He strolled toward the front door. "Well, Jolene is cool," Eddie said.

"I like her crazy eyes, like she might stab me," Jim Bob said. He chuckled. "Believe me, I get her orders done first."

"I had no idea signed stuff got so much money?" Eddie said.

Jim Bob squirmed in his new leather chair.

"Well, it's just this one particular dude," Jim Bob said. He set his drink on the side table. "Secretive, never met him."

"You reported the money on your tax return?" Eddie asked.

Jim Bob tumbled out of the chair.

"Naw, but I've been real careful like, it just the internet," Jim Bob said. He adjusted his pajama top. "Not like they can see me, or what not."

"Better let them know, or they might come and take Jolene."

"Jolene, Jolene, Joe Clean," Jim Bob sang. He wiggled. "I like that Dolly."

"You're in rare form," Eddie said.

Jim Bob grunted. He disappeared into his kitchen. He returned with a refreshed drink and a crumpled bag of potato chips.

"Want some? Can I get you a drink?" Jim Bob asked.

"Not yet-" Eddie said. For some odd reason he could not seem to calm down and relax, he thought of Ardee. He wondered what she was doing, and if he should call her.

"I love my Jolene, I'd never let nothin' happen to her," Jim Bob said. He chuckled. He flopped back onto the lounger. He rubbed his belly.

"Don't you remember the IRS took down Eliot Swizzle, President of Waterbed World? He was stashing money in plastic bags inside the water beds," Eddie said. He leaned his left elbow against the back of Jim Bob's leather couch. "Needed to hide some cash for, well, professional babes, be careful."

"Hey, want to play video games?" Jim Bob asked.

"Saw the whole thing on FOXY," Eddie said.

"Mr. Fun-Hater, like I'm stupid or somethin', all the stuff's sold real confidential like over the internet, so it'll be real tough to find old Jim Bob, I got some cash here and there."

"No thanks," Eddie said, "but they don't mess around."

# # #

"I've heard enough," Agent Machiavelli said through his walky-talky. "Collection time, collection time-" Two groups of federal agents, wearing black ninja spandex outfits with night vision goggles strapped to their heads descend into the house like evil vampire bats. They shattered the front door with a battering ram. Jim Bob's eyeballs darted back and forth at the legal invaders. He squeezed into the fetal position. Eddie shut his eyes. He thrust his hands up in a classic pre-arrest position.

"Freeze-"

Jim Bob acted as if encased in a block of ice.

"You heard the man." Agent Tacitus pointed a high caliber pistol at Eddie's feet.

"Not sure if I can breathe," Eddie wheezed. His sphincter muscle blocked all outgoing deliveries.

After three tense minutes, the federal agents secured the perimeter. They were satisfied no other co-conspirators hid within the house.

# # #

Captain Lovins patiently monitored the situation from his nearby position curious what the federal agents would do next and if they were monitoring the area with their thermal sensors.

# # #

The federal agents yanked Jim Bob up on to his now protein stained leather couch.

"Are you James Robert Calhoun, III"?" Agent Machiavelli asked. He holstered his weapon.

"Yep-" Jim Bob said. He gulped.

"Mr. Calhoun, we've been monitoring your activities for the last six-months under the direct supervision of the United States Internet Trafficking Surveillance Court." Agent Machiavelli handed Jim Bob a warrant for his arrest. His goggles bounced up and down on his head, like black unicorn roaming dark fairy woodlands. "We've reason to believe you're involved in illegal sale and distribution of sports memorabilia, said collection by you of certain funds that haven't been reported to the IRS, and remitted to the Treasury."

"Aw, come on now, I can provide receipts and-" Jim Bob said.

"Mr. Calhoun you're under arrest. Agent Homer come out of limbo and cuff and stuff Mr. Calhoun," Agent Machiavelli said.

"Hey, that hurts," Jim Bob said. The agent clicked the handcuffs tight over his wrists.

"Agent Cromwell, continue the evidence collection protocol," Agent Machiavelli said. He paused for a moment. He shoved his goggles up and off his forehead. He stared at Eddie. "Mr. Wilcox?"

Eddie kept his hands and arms up.

"Ah, Eddie is fine," Eddie said. He puffed out his mouth.

"We've taped your conversation with Mr. Calhoun, I guess he got the idea for his activities from you?" Agent Machiavelli said. He waved at Eddie. "Put your arms down."

"I have no idea," Eddie said. He gulped. "Honestly."

Agent Machiavelli stared at Eddie for several seconds. Eddie felt a sweat drop glide down his back. He adjusted his shirt collar.

"You know how many times I've had a bad guy tell me that?" Agent Machiavelli said. He shook his head.

"Honestly, he called me, I, I," Eddie said.

"Yeah, I heard your conversation," Agent Machiavelli said.

He waved Eddie toward the front door. "I have no reason to keep you or arrest you, for now, but we might be back in touch, I have a hard time believing Mr. Calhoun was this successful without help. You seem intelligent enough."

"I didn't have any idea, sir," Eddie said. He was curious what the federal agent meant. He exhaled. He turned to scamper out of the house. But he waved over at Jim Bob. "Jim Bob, I'll do what I can."

Jim Bob glanced back over his shoulder as they dragged and loaded him into a black SUV.

"I think my waders are full up, here Eddie," Jim Bob said.

Eddie stared back and forth at the agents who busily flashed pictures, cataloged, and packaged Jim Bob's possessions. They had their nylon-gloved hands all over Jolene. He sprinted back to his car. He quickly got inside and locked the door. "Unbelievable," Eddie said. He laid his head in the center of the steering wheel.

# # #

Captain Lovins watched Edward get back in his car. Then he escaped from the nearby pasture. He revved his sedans engine, deciding that soon he would need to visit Edward. He had easily located Eddie's address. It was dangerous for him to reach out to Edward; Edward might not appreciate the deadly nature of their work, and then he might tip off the authorities. But maybe this was their opportunity to bait Edward's curiosity with their Wish List and then lure him back toward Professor Quan. He tapped the steering wheel with his gloved fingers. He sucked in a deep breath, and shifted the car into drive.

Chapter Ten

On the first day of spring in 1963, Professor Quan and Captain Lovins stood at the bustling city street corner of Constitution Avenue and 12th Street NW, near the back entrance to the Smithsonian National Museum of Natural History. Winter had given up its icy death march, replaced by a gentle southern breeze wisping through the yet to bloom cherry and oak trees. To their left the United States Capital dome glowed in the night sky, and not far from their relative position, staring down the National Mall past the reflecting pool loomed the silent pale marble statue of Abraham Lincoln.

"Captain, you can still turn back," Professor Quan said. He tightly clutched a black leather brief case as the constant city traffic coursed past them.

"Nope, can't turn back now," Captain Lovins said. He grunted, dressed in a pressed service uniform. "Besides, it took us some time to set this up, they will always know it's us, even if we leave, some things you cannot hide from."

"I wish I could," Professor Quan said. He sighed.

"Can I give you a piece of advice?" Captain Lovins asked.

"Sure," Professor Quan said. He turned to look up at Captain Lovins. A group of tourists lingered near them inspecting an attractions map.

"Train continuously," Captain Lovins said. "But after a mistake, what do you do?"

"Hmm, fundamental science is all about mistakes," Professor Quan said. He gripped the brief case handle with both hands. He glanced at the mixture of lobbyists, tourists, and government lifers lost in their own worlds. "All my work is a series of mistakes, but then, magic happens."

"Exactly," Captain Lovins said.

"Not sure I follow," Professor Quan said. A passing yellow taxi driven by an immigrant squeaked its brakes. He puffed smoke plumes out the driver side window.

"Always move forward, no matter what, focus on the mission at hand," Captain Lovins said. "Don't linger, gets you killed."

"Difference?" Professor Quan asked. "What?"

"You can never go back in time," Captain Lovins said.

"Well, maybe," Professor Quan said. He shrugged.

"Listen, you made a serious mistake," Captain Lovins said.

"Cataclysmic," Professor Quan said.

"Let's solve the problem, but nothing good happens from festering about something you cannot control, focus on the task, what keeps the team alive is communication and focus," Captain Lovins said. "Don't live in the past."

"Thank you," Professor Quan said. He stared over at the massive museum. "I understand, I don't want to turn into salt."

The traffic light changed from green to red, and they strolled between the white lines across the busy city street. They stopped in front a long bank of glass double doors opening and closing as tourists and workers left for the day. The odd couple stared back at their reflections. They walked forward, they flashed their high security badges, and they climbed the massive marble staircase. They turned left toward the exhibit gallery area concealed with a tall black curtain. They showed their badges to a security guard standing near the opening, the palm of his hand rested on his weapon. As they moved closer toward their goal, they could see a museum curator wearing white gloves remove the prized object. They showed their badges again to another security guard. The aged, chubby curator held the diamond in the palms of his hands.

"Please be careful," the Curator said.

Professor Quan opened his briefcase to reveal a cushioned interior covered with soft red velvet. He put on white nylon gloves and carefully clutched the shiny rocks.

"Most assuredly so," Professor Quan said. He kindly grinned at the agitated curator.

"You have six hours, then get it back here," the Curator said. He angrily glanced at Captain Lovins. "One man security detail? Are you crazy?"

Professor Quan ignored the curator and deftly snuggled the Hope Diamond within the custom-made cushion. Captain Lovins icily stared down at the nervous curator.

"Told everyone we were sending it out to be cleaned," the Curator said.

"Be calm, you should learn to be calm," Professor Quan said. He locked the briefcase.

"Easy for you, you're not responsible," the Curator said.

"I have a very simple experiment to conduct," Professor Quan said. He stared over at the curator. "Have you any idea who is behind all this? Would you like me to pass along your concerns?"

Captain Lovins stared at the Curator. He shook his head.

"Well, still," the Curator said. He mumbled. "Six hours-"

"My guard is a SEAL, he lives by a code," Professor Quan said. He adjusted his black framed glasses with his forefinger. "I and these shiny rocks are perfectly safe, we want to be low key, not draw a lot of attention, I will it back in three hours."

"Fine, I'll be waiting," the Curator said.

Professor Quan lead by Captain Lovins simply marched out of the museum and disappeared into the night. They drove their four-door sedan back toward Professor Quan's government laboratory. As they drove along, Captain Lovins made certain they were not followed by a security detail. He drove inside the parking garage. Captain Lovins had ensured all the security cameras turned off for a repair that would never take place. They switched out the real diamonds with Professor Quan's creations.

"Perfect," Professor Quan said. He opened a metalworkers' lunch box lined with lead and placed the Hope Diamond within a cushioned form. They sat back and they waited for the three hours to pass as they reviewed their plan.

"I will leave immediately," Captain Lovins said.

"Be patient, but yes, I need to give them a report that I didn't find anything useful from the experiment," Professor Quan said. He adjusted his eyeglasses. "I'll walk out of here in a few days, let the trail go cold, and meet up with you."

"Agreed," Captain Lovins said.

"Just take good care of our treasure," Professor Quan said.

"That will not be a problem," Captain Lovins said. He shoved the lunch box under the driver's seat.

"We'll need to find a better secure hiding place for this, and those meteorites," Professor Quan said.

"I'll do some scouting down there," Captain Lovins said.

After time gobbled up the required three hours, Professor Quan and Captain Lovins returned to the museum. As they emerged from the city darkness, the fidgeting curator quickly opened the museums security door.

"Hurry," the Curator said as he waved them inside and past the night security guards.

"Wait," Captain Lovins said. He motioned for a guard to approach them. "Examine this, don't break protocol."

The night guard smirked over at the curator; he noted the high security clearance badges for Professor Quan and Captain Lovins as the curator tapped his wing tipped dress shoe.

"Thank you," the Security guard said as he noted the time sheet.

They quickly climbed the stairs, and breezed past the black curtain and opened the thick security glass encased diamond display. Professor Quan unlocked the briefcase, put on his white nylon gloves and then handed the fake diamonds back over to the curator.

"Can you do me a favor?" Professor Quan said.

"What?" the Curator asked. He had on white gloves.

"I appreciate you trusting us," Professor Quan said.

"Hardly, it was not my decision," the Curator said.

"I understand, you're instincts nagging at you?" Professor Quan asked. He grinned at the curator and up at Captain Lovins.

"In a word, yes," the Curator said. He slowly breathed through his lips.

"Good," Captain Lovins said.

"Will you do us the favor, closely examine it?" Professor Quan said. "I don't want to ever be accused of damaging a government treasure, you know, from one of my experiments."

The curator shrugged. He expertly clutched the diamonds and inspected the work of art. He placed a jeweler's loop in his left eye and seemed to check each angle, each facet for any imperfection. He nodded at Professor Quan and dropped the loop into his museum jacket pocket. He replaced the diamond back onto its display setting. He adjusted the lighting, locked the display and switched on the security settings.

"Thank you for your time," Professor Quan said. And he and Captain Lovins left the museum through a side security door and disappeared into the early morning haze.

Chapter Eleven

Dr. Yin sat alone within his dimly lit lab office. Outside his office, a horde of scientists wore puke green hospital space alien scrubs. They cycled about a vast laboratory filled with conical flasks, Bunsen burners, genetic analyzers and sterile glass encased test stations. His office phone rang.

"Dr. Yin?" Agent Machiavelli asked.

"What?" Dr. Yin said. He huffed.

"We think he was nearby when we arrested the Calhoun."

"Why?" Dr. Yin asked. He tapped his fingers on his desk.

"Our thermal sensors picked-up an unaccounted for human in a nearby farm pasture, I was almost ready to investigate, and then he disappeared," Agent Machiavelli said. "Sorry, I couldn't get away from the crime scene. I kept losing Homer."

"I've heard this *crap* for years now," Dr. Yin said. He pounded his fist on his yellow oak desk.

"I'm certain it was Lovins."

"Why is it so difficult to catch a seventy-something year old man? As for Lovins, he has to be in his late sixties. How's it possible highly trained federal agents can't catch them?"

"They don't leave many clues, we'll get them."

"Let's hope for your sake you do. If we are not successful, someone will figure out the government let them go undetected for decades. With oh, about two hundred fifty million worth of government property, that is when the party stops. Do we understand each other?" Dr. Yin asked. He paused, he breathed hard into the telephone receiver. "It would be unfortunate for our names to show-up in a newspaper."

"Crystal-clear, sir-"

"Exactly, but it's not *crystal* we seek, and now I'll have to report back to Mr. Screwtop, and trust me, neither of us want to deal with his client, Ms. Prosperina," Dr. Yin said. He slammed the telephone back into its cradle. He menacingly stared through his office window at the busy laboratory on the other side of his offices rectangular smoked glass one-way window. After a deep breath, he glided his fingers across his glass covered desktop. He swiveled his chair around, tapped in his pass codes on his computer keyboard, and checked his email. He turned back around and glanced over at his half-full bookshelf. He sighed and then grabbed his cell phone.

"Yes?" Bertrand asked.

"Mr. Screwtop," Dr. Yin said.

"Well, well, I must admit I'm curious why you're bothering me this late at night?" Bertrand asked.

"I *think* we've almost got him, we'll get that diamond back."

"Almost? You know as well as I, we're running out of time." Bertrand said. "I'm not sure how much longer we can play this game."

"I understand, we're close, but it's just not the same as the *real* Hope Diamond, synthetic diamonds are close," Dr. Yin said. "but they lack something, hidden structures, at the quantum level, we'll figure it out."

"Let's *hope*, you find the SOB because Ms. Prosperina called this morning, again, now I'm beginning and ending my weeks with her gravelly voice." Bertrand said. He slowly let his lungs carbon dioxide release back into the dens atmosphere. "Thinks she's getting Mad-off'd, she's paid us, more to you, a bunch money to find these people, and some formulas, and she claims they have that diamond, I think."

"I understand," Dr. Yin said. He sucked in a deep breath.

"No, I really don't think you do." Bertrand said. Dr. Yin heard him drop ice cubes into a crystal tumbler, and the distinct pop as Bertrand opened a bourbon bottle. He could hear the hint of Brat Pack music. "Hold on a sec, not now honey, sorry, having a private dinner party."

"You there?" Dr. Yin said.

"Doctor, let's not draw a lot of needless attention," Bertrand said. "That would be bad, would get me audited."

"Science takes time," Dr. Yin said. He stared out his office window into the empty parking lot. "That special unit, they seem clueless to catch them."

"Listen to me, Ms. Prosperina appears like a kindly old lady, I bet she's barely five feet tall. But she's got these weird eyes," Bertrand said.

"Pardon?" Dr. Yin asked.

"They are abnormally large in the center, the size of quarters, one black and one red," Bertrand said. He breathed hard into the telephone microphone. "I saw them one time, I think she did it accidentally on purpose. We were having our only online conference, she only agreed to do it once. I think she was sending me a message, and man, it worked."

"Oh?" Dr. Yin said. He snapped his left hand fingers. "Heterochromatic, different colored eyes, a genetic mutation I suppose, nothing to get concerned about, really."

"Really? Easy for you to say," Bertrand whispered. "I bet she's got a third eye in the back of her head."

"Maybe she's a chimera? Let me guess, she's a shape shifter, she can disappear like a Cuttlefish," Dr. Yin said. He chuckled.

"What?"

"Mixing of cells from multiple species, never mind, it's a joke," Dr. Yin said. He coughed. "Not a good one."

"I'm not laughing. It's as if you're staring into a dead void and being absorbed," Bertrand said. "She's a total mystery, her tentacles are primarily into agriculture but she's been investing quietly into particle colliders, her businesses are everywhere, but hidden. And I get the hint she's into selling body parts, or such things, anyway to make a buck. And I guess making fake diamonds, well, a girl's best friend, right?"

"I'm doing my best." Dr. Yin said. He shook his head.

"You better," Bertrand said. "I'd hate to have her man-servant Mr. Oppenheimer show up." The cell went dead.

Chapter Twelve

Sunday afternoon, Eddie navigated his gas-guzzler across the unguarded Tennessee and Kentucky boarder foraging along Interstate 65 northeast from Nashville. He maneuvered off the pushy interstate and drove down a lonely two-lane blacktopped country road. He chuckled as the GPS announced in an odd, female voice with an English accent, "Destination on left", as he neared the Dorian-Hyde correctional campus where the Feds locked arch criminal Jim Bob Calhoun away from normal society. It had a colorful kaleidoscope of manicured overgrowth as if a safe urban park setting within a canopied tree big top, but surrounded by a ten-foot high barbed wire fence.

"This is crazy," Eddie mumbled. He veered his car to the right of a cinder block guard station. Two visible surveillance cameras were bolted underneath the shingled roof fascia. Black signage with white letters *welcomed* him to Dorian-Hyde Federal Penitentiary. A husky guard guided a sniffing German shepherd around his totalitarian metal death trap. It barked. It snarled up at Eddie. A guard with a sawed-off Napoleonic bone structure, strided up to the left quarter panel of Eddie's jalopy, as Eddie rolled his window down.

"Sir, can we help you?" the guard asked.

"Visiting a prisoner," Eddie said. He coughed.

"Got a name?"

"Jim Bob, ah, Jim Bob Calhoun-"

The guard snickered over at his compatriots.

"Sorry, Calhoun's our hero," the guard said. "I.D.?"

"Sorry?" Eddie asked. He handed over his driver's license.

"Calhoun's a legend, first guy we've ever locked up for swindling and money laundering with used jock straps," the guard said. He turned his narrow shoulders. "Ain't that right boy's? He ain't any Mad-off mind you, but the boy has got skills." Two of the guards with their M-16 pointed down, sinisterly grinned over at Eddie.

The guard retreated to the shacks eastern-side, shaded from the suns two o'clock position. A lone male Cardinal chirped a prayer, as the northern breeze caused the long leaf trees to rattle together, sounding like rutting elk. Eddie sniffed the faint hints of sulfur smoke from nearby burning fossil fuel.

"Mr. Wilcox, follow the marked signs, to building D."

"Yes sir," Eddie said. He weaved his car to building D after he survived a security maze that probed his every thought, hidden desire and any unspoken hope to copulate with Ardee.

"Mr. Wilcox, sign in here, remove all contents in your pockets. Take off your shoes and belt, and then place the items in front of the window," the guard said. He pointed down at the sheet. "Sign here, please."

"Yes sir," Eddie said. He printed his name in capital block letters, he signed in chicken-scratch cursive underneath.

"Sit on the left side, use the center chair," the guard said. "Do not move around. We will bring the inmate to you. You will have exactly fifteen minutes." An electronic switch buzzed. The steel door popped open with a thudded clunk.

The visitor's room was centered with a simple particleboard table, separated by a foot high plastic barrier down the middle. Surrounded by facing military gray metal chairs, Eddie settled on the middle seat. His sweating palms rested on the dank tabletop. At least nine minutes elapsed before the catty-corner steel door clinked open. Two overly muscled guards guided a clean-shaven Jim Bob by his arms. Jim Bob scooted his chained feet forward. He wore an orange prison jump suit. His last name was in black block numbers.

"Man, I'm up a creek without them fancy waders," Jim Bob said. The bland room smelled of personal odor and tension.

"Jim Bob?" Eddie said.

"I know, I know, I'm stupid, again." Jim Bob said. He nervously cackled. "I was just wantin' to do somethin' with my life, be like one of your sperm Olympics people, livin' on top."

Eddie rubbed his forehead.

"Get it together," Eddie said.

"I'm tryin', they took all my stuff, like you said, they took Jolene. They been tellin' me I am goin' to owe the government back taxes, interest or somethin' or other - like that. I ain't got seventy-five-thousand dollars." Jim Bob said. He slouched on the hard, ice-cold metal chair.

Eddie glanced at the guards and slinked forward.

"Cash buried in the yard?" Eddie whispered.

"Nope, spent every nickel," Jim Bob said.

"Seriously? Seventy five thousand," Eddie asked.

"Seriously, I don't know what happened, it's like I had a hole in me. I just couldn't fill it up or nothin," Jim Bob said. He slouched back and crossed his meaty arms.

"Sorry," Eddie said. Carousel twittered his thumbs. He glanced over at the security guards. He studied an obvious camera hidden by a smoked glass bubble, bolted near the ceiling above the visitor's door.

"Money is nothin," Jim Bob said. "They're sayin' I'll spend a long time in here, goin' put me on trial, man I'm scared."

"Selling some signed football jerseys and jock straps can't get you this deep into trouble," Eddie said.

Jim Bob stared away from Eddie. He scratched his belly.

"Well you see, I, I was lookin' round that internet. I found some real dirty places," Jim Bob goofily said. He glandered back over at Eddie, his eyes now wide-open, his head cocked back.

"Porn? Don't tell me you started buying stuff from those on-line sites? That's sick dude," Eddie said.

"Afraid so," Jim Bob said. He giggled as he glanced over at the two security guards. "I couldn't help myself, I 'bout nearly pulled king-of-the-jungle clean off."

The baby-faced of the two colossal security guards frowned. He shook his head glaring over at Jim Bob.

"What?" Jim Bob asked. He wiggled forward.

"Dude, that's just bad karma," the baby-faced security guard said, as the dower-faced security guard nodded in agreement.

"Yeah, bad stuff Jim Bob, those *are* real people, but many of them are on drugs, abused children," Eddie said. He frowned. "It'll fry your brain."

"Hmm, I guess," Jim Bob said. He crinkled his lips.

Eddie rubbed his neck as he studied his brown shoes.

"But I don't think that'll get you in trouble with the Feds, unless you messed around with kids?" Eddie asked haltingly.

Jim Bob smacked his beefy palms on the table. He hurriedly waved his fingers back and forth in front of his chest staring over at the security guards.

"Aw, no dummy, I ain't any creep," Jim Bob said.

"Calm down," Eddie said.

"Ain't that right?" Jim Bob asked the security guards.

"Yep," the security guards said in baritone stereo.

Jim Bob leaned forward on his left elbow. He crinkled his face as he turned toward Eddie.

"We got one here, those *pre-verbs* inside, I hear he ain't long for this world," Jim Bob whispered. He gulped. "I think even the inmates have a *code* against them types." Jim Bob blew air out of his mouth, his puffy cheeks puffer-fished as he scanned the windowless environment. "Even the white-collared types willin' to send that rascal to H-E-double-tooth-picks, if you know what I'm sayin.'"

"Calhoun, back it up," the baby-faced security guard said.

"Yes, sir," Jim Bob said. He clutched his hands over his face. He rubbed his eye sockets and shook his head as if trying to release a brain wave. "These times I miss my dad, he'd know what to do."

"Unbelievable," Eddie said.

"I know," Jim Bob said, "like I'm livin' a bad dream."

Eddie stared up at the twelve-inch square beige and black specked starless ceiling tiles.

"You sold this junk on WePay? I still cannot understand how the Feds targeted you. Or, why you owe them seventy-five thousand dollars?" Eddie said. He crossed his arms and leaned back on the creaky metal chair. "How much did you make?"

"Oh, 'bout two hundred thousand dollars," Jim Bob said. He cocked his head left. He winked at Eddie.

"Not bad, Captain Jock Strap," the baby-faced security guard said. The security guards laughed and elbowed each other.

"But now you pay," the dower-faced security guard said.

"Seriously?" Eddie asked.

Jim Bob had a half-wit expression.

"Afraid so, think they're goin' to throw me in a dark-hole and forget about me like a Kentucky coal miner," Jim Bob said.

"You must've been selling a lot of man bras," Eddie said. He blinked his eyes rapidly. The armpits of his shirt revealed irregular curved perspiration marks. "I must admit, I'm not familiar with WePay, or what not, I peddle insurance."

Jim Bob quizzically stared at Eddie.

"See here, to be honest, I don't think it's just the money, they seem to be hintin' around about some other people, a

Professor or what-not. I think they think I know somethin," Jim Bob said.

"Just tell them everything," Eddie said.

"Don't worry, I did, but they sure are mad at whoever else is out there," Jim Bob said. He scratched behind his ear. "They threatened to call a Dr. Yin on me, whoever that be, inject me with truther serum, or put me in solitary."

Eddie aimlessly stared down as he glided his fingertips across the particleboard tabletop.

"I ain't always stupid," Jim Bob said.

"I know," Eddie said. "I don't know what to say."

"You've always been real smart," Jim Bob said.

"Never mind me," Eddie said. He shrugged. "We need to come up with ideas. I don't have any money, my mom is not rich, we're on our own Jim Bob."

"Why have you always been my friend?" Jim Bob asked. "We're as different as black coffee and an ice cream soda."

Eddie kindly grinned at Jim Bob.

"I know you," Eddie said. "Known you my whole life, you're as predictable as the sun coming up."

"Well now," Jim Bob said.

"I trust you," Eddie said. He faintly grinned. "I know if I called you in the middle of the night, no matter what, you'd help me, right?"

"Yeah, I figure so," Jim Bob said.

"That's something not for sale," Eddie said. He smiled at Jim Bob. "I remember my father telling me, keep life simple, uncomplicated, don't judge people, take them as they are."

"Ah, shut up," Jim Bob said. "I got get outta here, the coffee sucks, I had the shakes for two days."

The old friends paused silently for a few moments.

"I'm not sure what to do," Eddie said. "Lawyer?"

"Well, come to think of it, I might've an idea," Jim Bob whispered. He squinted with his eyelids as if oblong alligator slits emerging from beneath a fresh water stream.

"Yeah?" Eddie said. An odd tingling sensation cycled up and down Eddie's spine. Jim Bob put his hairy elbows on the table.

"Well, I'd Leonardo's athletic supporter," Jim Bob said.

"Stop," Eddie said. He put his moist palms up.

"Now hold the phone. I know, but darn it, old Leo was known for his big unit." Jim Bob said. He spread his plump hands apart, like retelling a fishing story about the time he caught a twelve-inch Big Mouth Bass. "Just as a joke, but heck, I must've sold four or five of them at five-thousand dollars a whack."

"No flipping way?" Eddie said. He shut his eyelids.

"Here me now, I sold all the jock straps, same weirdo I think, using different names, accounts and such, but then came back askin' me," Jim Bob said. He put his paws up in the air. He wiggled his chubby fingers to indicate quotation marks. "Other stuff, told me he would pay me in cash with untraceable crisp tens and ones."

"I'll bite, what's other stuff?" Eddie said. He spread his fingers jail cell style across his face.

"Dude sent me a big old list, creepy stuff. Like one thing was, if I could get a strand of that actress Regan Fryingpan's hair, or anything from that playboy golfer Lionel Forest."

"Seriously?" Eddie asked.

Jim Bob tilted his head downward. His eyebrows crinkled forming a deep reflective wrinkle up the middle of his forehead.

"Told me if I got a toe nail, or anything with verifiable DNA, he'd pay me twenty five thousand big ones," Jim Bob said. He whispered under his breath. "I think they think I know these people, but I've never met'em, money would magically appear, never the same place, they were real careful like."

"You're serious?" Eddie asked. He rubbed his forehead with his left hand. He thought he might have an instant spiked fever from Jim Bob's hallucinations. "The front of my head hurts."

"Calhoun, time," the dower-faced security guard said. The baby-faced guard stomped behind Jim Bob.

"Alright, now that's just between us?" Jim Bob said to Eddie.

"Sure, whatever you say," Eddie said.

"Well, if you want, the creepy list is inside my truck, above the driver side visor. Anyways, I guess they are callin' me back to my cage. Thanks for comin', guess you're my only friendly amigo," Jim Bob said. He nervously laughed.

"Sorry," Eddie said.

As Jim Bob scooted away, he glanced back at Eddie as he wiped back tears from his puffy cheeks.

"Thanks, don't' forget what I said, maybe you might be able to rustle up some fast cash, spring me outta here."

Chapter Thirteen

Forged to their life long mission, after completing an exhaustive search, Professor Quan and Captain Lovins determined the ideal location for their lair was within the southeastern corridor of the United States, known as Appalachia. After they secretly acquired a vast track of land from a mining company that bought some of their unique diamond tipped drill bits, land that they had removed most of the mountaintop, Captain Lovins skillfully built the laboratory complex within a dead coalmine. The region's forgotten inhabitants were made up of mob informants under witness protection, clannish hillbillies and their unlucky spawn. They ignored the mysterious alchemy going on up in the deep, dark, woods full of imagined magic fairies, giant Cyclops, and sinister leprechauns bouncing in and out of our dimension. And the new kids in the hills, a tough, bald headed soldier, and a ticked-off mad scientist. They happened to make drill bits for mining and excavation companies.

One fateful afternoon Professor Quan, with total commitment to his science, he extracted several pints of his own blood.

"Hate, stinking, needles," Professor Quan said. He squirmed and held his breath. Using a rubber tourniquet, he penetrated his left arm near the elbow with a number three gauge needle attached to an evacuated collection tube. With a tiny sample, through his use of the Golden Ratio, he calculated the exact cross-linked polymer gel composition. He blasted the mesh network of polyacrylamide with a lightning bolt-like electrical current he had focused through the Hope Diamond. The intense beam of pure energy made the substance appear as if a massive earthquake shook the gel residue with hydrodynamic friction as if the earth's surface had turned to grains of sand. He then stained a brilliant blue dye along the particle strip, which caused his individual molecules magically to appear. He then flooded the specimen with intense UV light and snapped a photo. Under a powerful optical microscope, he had customized to view below 200 nanometers; Professor Quan peered into the view lens. His vision blurred as he inspected his own genome. All of his genetic information stripped bare.

"I knew it!" Professor Quan said.

Nearby repairing Professor Quan's autoclave, Captain Lovins rushed into the lab.

"What's up?" Captain Lovins asked.

"I can map my DNA. I know where the genes hide," Professor Quan said. His hands shook. "They can't hide from me, I know how to find them. I don't know exactly what they do, yet, but-"

"Amazing," Captain Lovins said. He smacked Professor Quan on the left shoulder. Professor Quan webbled, but he did not wobble off his feet. Captain Lovins snapped his fingers.

"What do those hippies say?" Captain Lovins asked.

"Far-out man," Professor Quan said. He and Captain Lovins cackled. "I did it, man."

Captain Lovins glanced around the laboratory at the collection of scientific equipment.

"When do we attack?" Captain asked.

"First, we need an efficient delivery method?" Professor Quan said. He puckered his lips. "That's my next trick, might take me some time, I can isolate genes, deliver them in an easy, simple way that will minimize detection. I know for certain I can alter IQ's, I can use my profile to boost their IQ's."

"Good point," Captain Lovins said. "Not just going to walk up, hey take this pill, it'll help you get smart, sense evil."

"Exactly," Professor Quan said.

"Teach a child to fish," Captain Lovins said.

"To fish for the light inside them," Professor Quan said. "Boost their ability to absorb information, think critically."

Sparked by his discovery, Professor Quan realized the main obstacle was to devise an efficient method of implanting maturing adolescents with his amazing DNA structure. Once inside a maturing human body, Professor Quan's DNA would act like Epi genes. The new genes would simply swim through the blood stream and submerge into the human tissue, and find defective gene instructions, and simply overlay the targets helical structure like rungs along a twisted ladder.

For several weeks, he contemplated and searched his psyche for a simple answer to his dilemma. Late one night, unable to sleep, as he sprayed for bugs, an idea exploded within his supernatural brain as he carefully examined the spray canister.

"That's it," Professor Quan said. Sequence my genetic code using the Golden Ratio, blast it with the Hope Diamond. Infiltrate the specimen with unique blue light, like the uniqueness of a Blue Moon, he thought. It is all so simple now; create a biochemical reaction causing a unique peptide chain.

"Non-sexual, re-reproduction," Professor Quan whispered.

"What's wrong with you?" Captain Lovins said as he walked into the lab.

"Nothing, nothing to worry about-"

Professor Quan paced and circled his subterranean lair. He thought about all the infinite possibilities. However, he needed to set up an experiment to test his hypothesis. He watched Captain Lovins disappear into the elevator.

"A fireman, I know," Professor Quan said. He snapped his fingers. "Every male's dream, solve erectile dysfunction, forever." He cryptically chuckled. He scampered over to his microscope. He scanned along his DNA helical strands. He located the exact gene he perceived affected his libido. He knew Captain Lovins had more testosterone than a sixteen-year-old Spanish bullfighter did.

After he made the exact calculations with the Golden Radio, he picked apart the genetic material like a Swiss Watch maker. He removed his gene and replaced a synthetic specimen gene from Captain Lovins' DNA sample. He injected the liquid, mixed with a mild narcotic inside the spray cartridge, similar to an asthma inhaler with hydrofluoroalkanes to propel the liquefied material into a gaseous particle concoction.

Aware his brand of science would either alter his life or kill him, he reviewed each step from his experiments notes. He closed his eyes. He triggered the inhaler device into his mouth and allowed the spray to coat his pinkish tissue. He collapsed on his strata lounger. He waited.

Within a few moments, the potion caused Professor Quan to hibernate for several hours. When he awoke, he stalled. He played with his kaleidoscope. He whistled the Battle Hymn of the Republic. He knew he felt invigorated and a bit, weird. He stared up at the ceiling painted powder blue, dotted with wispy white clouds. He thought about a hot babe he knew from Briar Hill. He could clearly see her beautiful face. Then he took in a deep exaggerated breath, and peeked under his pants.

"Oh gracious, it works," Professor Quan said. He pushed his horizontal flagpole to half-mast and scurried down a narrow dimly lit corridor. He scrambled into his genome therapy rooms.

The square shaped room had a lanky library ladder with rubber wheels attached to a golden slide. Four flat walls, taking account for the doorway, covered floor-to-ceiling with conical flasks. Each vessel sealed with a thin rubber membrane and identified in blue, red or black ink, with corresponding names, dates and numbers. Professor Quan glanced around the room. He tapped his lips with his forefinger.

"A cowboy with a slow Texas drawl," Professor Quan whispered. "I always wanted to have a reason to wear my white Stetson Hat and lizard skin boots, let me think."

He left the cold room and went to inspect his Skin Sensor machine; it had a teak wood frame with twelve tiny vermillion lotus hooks. The triangular shaped mirrors pointed inward. Each mirror spaced a half inch apart. Across the frames interior, the hooks held micro-thin carbon based pink spider web like sheets. Two 220-volt electrical cords connected to the bottom left vertical panel, just below an oval shaped rubber knob. Above the knob, there was a panel that appeared to be a keyless garage door opener. It had backlit green buttons with a digital timer. It did not appear to have any load bearing member to support the heavy frame. It was steadied by a guide wire screwed into the top center of the nine foot cross beam. It was pulled taught into the steal ceiling joists with the angled beams resting on two square mouse pad couplings bolted into the spongy rubberized floor.

Professor Quan stepped in front of the roll top desk. He studied a laminated world map hung behind the desk. He memorized several number sequences taped to regions within Texas.

Professor Quan decided the red state ink should mix with red state ink sub-region to create the typical voice inflections and accent. He pressed a black button on the right side of the desk; it disengaged the green leather desktop cover. It popped up, and revealed rows and trays of self-inking stamps. Each numbered with a red, blue and black sequence. As he pulled up on a red lever, rows and trays rotated until he located the correct section, and glided his fingers across to select the stamps. He snapped them together like puzzle pieces. He locked them into a square tray, and then flicked a switch and the device began to vibrate. After he flicked the switch, the Skin Sensor machine started to hum as the strong electrical current coursed through the machines circuits. The device swayed, the teak wood frame began to move as if a light breeze was blowing drying bed sheets in the backyard behind a mid-western farmhouse.

"Almost forgot," Professor Quan said. He scampered back into his laboratory. He unhooked the Hope Diamond from its magnetic coupling. He slipped on white nylon gloves and gently grabbed the diamond with his fingertips. He went back to his Skin Sensor machine, unscrewed the center porthole beneath the frame, and locked the big blue diamond inside a cushioned chamber that resembled a grocery store bar code box scanner. It was nestled between the two black diamonds that would offset each other with positive and negative energy. His system was now in total balance.

Brilliant reflected laser blue light emerged from the box top like a communist party disco lounge. It bounced off the frames mirrors. It caused the machines mesh sheets to liquefy, but not one drop hit the floor. Each node levitated, as if balanced in a zero gravity vacuum.

"Excellent," Professor Quan said. He smacked his hands.

Back inside the adjacent room, he snapped his fingers as he remembered a spy from Texas who had died in a Russian gulag. He had been a nice fellow, with a smooth Houstonian drawl with each word understandable and soft.

"Now where is he?" Professor Quan said. He studied his vast collection of conical flasks.

Captain Lovins opened the cold room door.

"What's up?" Captain Lovins asked.

"Road trip," Professor Quan said. "Let's get the Roadmaster warmed up."

"I'm confused?" Captain Lovins said. "Road trip?"

"Yeah, I figured it out, this spray canister, let's find some candidates to start this experiment," Profess Quan said.

"Far out," Captain Lovins said. "Let me call the business office, let them know I'll be out for a few days."

"I'm going as a Texas business man," Professor Quan.

"I don't hide," Captain Lovins said. "But, this will be interesting, you're never boring, I'll give you that."

"Well, let's start by boosting some IQ's," Professor Quan said, "And maybe, some other things."

Chapter Fourteen

After the long trek back from visiting Jim Bob, Eddie parked his junker near the rear of his apartment complex next to the garbage bin. It had an aroma of moldy socks, rotten eggs and wasted melted butter. Sunday's clear, azure sky had surrendered to a forsaken starless amethyst black night. A crisp haunting breeze warned a low-pressure system coursed toward him another sinister carnival ride of lightning, thunder and rain. He yawned as he loped toward his apartment stairs sensing the parking lots toasty warm blacktopped surface. Past several older cars, Eddie noticed a four-door sedan parked near his usual spot. It seemed out of sequence, it was spotlessly clean, and it was backed into a space. It shimmered under the parking lot halogen lights like a threatening black dragon. Eddie stopped to examine the mysterious car with dark tinted windows. Unaware that he was staring directly at Captain Lovins.

"Dang it," Captain Lovins whispered, he sat as still as a dead man.

Eddie shrugged. He moved along. He meekly climbed the back concrete stairs, gripping the rusting iron railing as he trudged up toward his second floor apartment. He reached the concrete landing, but he decided to peek back down at the shiny automobile.

"That's spooky," Eddie said.

# # #

From his scouting regimen, Captain Lovins had quickly driven the vehicle to a new spot, but a location that still gave him an easy building access point.

"That was stupid," Captain Lovins said. He clicked open the glove box. He removed a common white business envelope. He got out and crept toward Eddie's one bedroom apartment. He scaled the forward stares, spied as Eddie unlocked his metal door, and disappeared into the apartment.

# # #

"Home sweet, home," Eddie mumbled. He abandoned his keys and his wallet into the decorative ceramic bowl with his mother smiling face pasted at the bottom. He slipped off his brown shoes, and slung them into his bedroom. He foraged inside the refrigerator for a carbonated cola, considered sacking down, but opted to mellow out, scarf down day-old pizza and investigate WePay.com. Eddie flipped open his wireless work laptop.

# # #

After fifteen-minutes, Captain Lovins returned to his sedan, perked up from the crisp evening air. He switched on his computer pad, checked his encryption software and drafted an instant message for Edward. He easily navigated into Edward's computer, disabled the security settings and began to mirror his screen. "Time to reacquaint-"

# # #

Eddie thought the WePay site was mostly full of junk for sale. But he easily located Jim Bob's infamous jockstrap items. He stared at the creepy picture, read the description, and unconsciously laughed.

'For Sale: UT running back legand, Leonardo Starfire, done wore this here athletick supporter in a bowl. Add to your G-nome Collection.'

Eddie closed his eyes. He chuckled. He thought Jim Bob had wandered into the land of moonstruck crazy people.

But an rectangular instant message box blipped open center screen. The subject line: Jim Bob Calhoun.

"What?" Eddie said. He munched down more pizza. He clicked it closed.

Another IM popped open. The subject line: Leonardo Spitfire.

"What the-" Eddie said. His checks flushed pale red. He quickly closed the message. Then he checked his spam filter to verify it was supposedly working to block out the Russian mob.

Outside, intermittent raindrops started to pelt the apartment building. A distant thunder rumbled the shear curtains.

Another IM popped open. The subject line: Do not close this, Edward.

Exasperated, Eddie crossed his arms. Another IM popped open. The subject line: We should talk.

Eddie stared up at the starless textured ceiling.

"Have we met?" Eddie typed. A few moments passed.

# # #

"Not formally." Captain Lovins typed. His encryption software shielded his true location with a backdoor matrix protocol. Within moments, all their correspondence would automatically delete, and be swiped from Edwards computer. "Mr. Calhoun thought you might be interested in earning some part-time cash."

"How did you get my email?" Eddie typed.

Captain Lovins was pleased with the addition of stormy weather because it would minimize his detection.

"This is not an email, I have your unique IP address, it's your cyber fingerprint." Captain Lovins typed.

# # #

Good point, Eddie thought.

"Why are you bothering me?" Eddie typed.

"Mr. Calhoun." Captain Lovins typed.

Eddie felt a slight stabbing wound from his stomach acid climbing inside throat.

"Who are you?" Eddie typed.

"An old friend." Captain Lovins typed.

"Go away." Eddie typed.

"You need money." Captain Lovins typed.

"So?" Eddie typed. "Who doesn't."

"You can assist me?" Captain Lovins typed.

"Why?" Eddie typed.

"You need money, Mr. Calhoun." Captain Lovins typed.

"How'd you know that?" Eddie screamed. Adrenaline poured into his blood stream. He squeaked his ear with his forefinger; he remembered the sinister looking automobile. "Why'd you leave?" Eddie typed.

# # #

"Well his brain is not completely fried," Captain Lovins said. He took off his skullcap. He sipped some coffee from a thermos bottle. Several minutes passed as Captain Lovins pondered his next move.

"Are you familiar with our Wish List?" Captain Lovins typed.

# # #

Eddie crinkled his face, bewildered, hesitant but curious about the people behind Jim Bob's cabal. Sheets of rain began to cascade like a wispy forest waterfall. Lightning flashed in the dark sky. Eddie flinched at his own shadow cast across the mediocre vanilla painted far wall.

"He mentioned something-" Eddie typed. He intently stared at the computer screen.

"Provide me with verifiable items. We pay in cash." Captain Lovins typed. "That simple-"

"I have never seen your list." Eddie typed. Instinctively acting like a harmless moth unable to stay away from bright light before zapped by electrical current.

"Under your door." Captain Lovins typed.

Eddie pensively twisted around to focus down slowly to discover an envelope corner shoved under his front door.

"Crap!" Eddie yelled like a prepubescent eight-year-old girl. He plummeted to his knees. He crawled toward the door and yanked the envelope through the threshold with his fingertips. He crawled back across the carpet. Then he slinked back up to face his computer. His shaking fingers paused. He had to retype the words three times. "I have the envelope."

"Feel free to pursue the items." Captain Lovins typed.

"*Okay*?" Eddie typed. He gawked at the envelope in his fingertips. "But then what?"

"If you get lucky, go back to WePay, find the souvenir section, and offer the item in question with the words: Genome Collection. Use the words anywhere in the description. I will respond. And I'll assume you can spell."

"What?" Eddie said. He wiped his moist forehead. He stared at the envelope for a few moments. Then he ripped it open.

"Bizarre?" Eddie whispered. Enclosed, within the basic white business envelope, a simple single piece of notebook paper with what appeared to be just a random list of recognizable names:
Wish List
Stephano Martine Aykroyd
Ophelia Bin Frey
Biff Soxworthy Miller
Henry James O'Rahilly, Jr.
Regan Jeanne Fryingpan
Cando Hillary Grain
Peggy Bay Smitten
Lionel Bobby Forest
Deanna Elvis Crawled
Gates Warren Jobs
Sasha Night O'Canada
G. Willis Krauthammer
Farley Dresser Peters, PH.D.
Items of personal nature delivered, and verified. Exchanged items are non-returnable. Any deviation from communication protocol will end relationship.

"This is insane." Eddie typed. He flicked the paper and envelope across his kitchen counter top. He paced back and forth.

"We have a network, but our work needs to remain secret." Captain Lovins typed. "We need living samples."

"Why?" Eddie typed.

"You'll figure it out, go get an autograph." Captain Lovins typed. "Good luck - Goodbye."

The computer screen instantly went dark. Eddie hopped back as if he had touched a raging campfire. It was three in the morning, relieved no one attacked him, but he was not sure what to think of the Wish List. As quickly as the bad weather came, it had now cleared to a dark stillness, as a genteel mist hugged the apartment building. Eddie crumpled the paper into his left-hand; he slid down to the kitchen floor. He rested his back against the cold linoleum. He stared up at the starless textured ceiling. His twisted, knotted muscles released along his spine and stomach, as he drifted off into sleep.

Chapter Fifteen

On a sizzling midsummer afternoon on July 25, 1965, Professor Quan cruised along with Captain Lovins in his hulking 1957 Buick Roadmaster with white walled tires. It was the day Bob had gone electric, a decision to be true to his artistic sensibilities, but the folk community thought he had betrayed the purity of his sound. The sun's golden cascades reflected off Professor Quan's temporary skin mashing down on the gas pedal. They whizzed past the lush forest green foliage. Professor Quan pulled off his Stetson. He slung it on the bench backseat. With the convertibles top down, unfiltered oxygen flowed over the car's panoramic windshield, and rustled through his now thick dishwater blond hair.

A transitional year for America, a few short years after the assassination of JFK, the government wobbled, lost its mainsail with delusions of hope for a great central planning society. Simultaneously, it focused on a fateful policy to stop the domino theory spread of communism in Vietnam. And with the ominous backdrop of the cat and mouse game played with the Soviet Union, everyone struggled under the ever-present specter from nuclear oblivion as the secretive conflict tore at America's societal building blocks. And Professor Quan sensed within his DNA, Ms. Prosperina's life force was growing stronger each day.

"We must not waste time," Professor Quan said.

"How will we find candidates?" Captain Lovins asked.

Professor Quan pondered Captain Lovins' question. He changed the radio station with his left foot admiring the cars over-engineered gadgets. A car invented from a time when America seemed to have an unlimited future. He clutched the innocuous spray bottle he had tucked in his left breast pocket.

"I think our best approach, listen to our instincts," Professor Quan said. He gripped the huge steering wheel. "We must listen to our inner voice."

"Yeah, but the key problem will be how we're going to deliver that spray," Captain Lovins said. "We could get beat up."

Professor Quan smiled over at Captain Lovins.

"It'll not be easy. We need to go undetected, yet make certain enough spray is inhaled by the targets, and immersed within their tissue, I hope the tracking particle works."

Captain Lovins started to sweat from the intense heat.

"You're certain, this will?" Captain Lovins asked.

"Epigenetic adjustment," Professor Quan said. He sighed. "Change a destiny, and they don't even know it."

"Well, I guess we've declared war," Captain Lovins said.

"Perhaps I'll slow down, you appear uncomfortable."

"Don't worry about me," Captain Lovins said. He crossed his arms. "I'll keep you out of trouble."

Professor Quan glanced at Captain Lovins and shook his head in agreement. He wondered as they drove along the two-lane freeway toward Nashville who they would find.

"Never thought I'd bounce out of the military and be running around the south with a mad scientist," Captain Lovins said. He leaned back and crossed his legs. He fiddled with his boot treads. "My code requires me to step up and defend those that cannot defend themselves. And now that I know Ms. Prosperina exists, she or it will be hell in a pair of Pravdas."

"Yes she will. I was not aware you were into fashion?"

"Never mind, a gift for a hot Russian babe, Natasha," Captain Lovins said. He shrugged. "Dropped me for a shrimp, Boris."

"Did you ever love someone, get married, think about creating a bunch of children?" Professor Quan asked. He slightly grinned.

"Not really, I grew up alone, you know orphan child, like you," Captain Lovins said. "I kind of like my space."

"Oh, I get that, same here," Professor Quan said.

Captain Lovins stared forward. His clenched his jaw.

"Being alone, solitary, given my line of work," Captain Lovins said. He deeply breathed in. "I didn't think it fair, you?"

"I'm clueless," Professor Quan said, "nutty scientist and all, you know."

"So?" Captain Lovins said. He clapped his hands.

"I don't know, I was always hidden from the world," Professor Quan said. He shook his head. "I don't do well, in bars, dates."

"I'll let you be my wingman," Captain Lovins said. The spark of a golden sunray flashed as he blinked his eyes. "Opposites attract."

"Not really," Professor Quan said.

"Sorry?" Captain Lovins said.

"I think sometimes we think so," Professor Quan said. He rocked his shoulders back and forth. "Twins have the same DNA, but one twin drinks, smokes, lives with a lot of stress, the other lives like a nun, but the nun dies first, they are the same, but different, why?"

"But you'd be attracted to a hot babe, skinny model type?" Captain Lovins asked.

"Oh, yes, yes, I'm not dead, I think the correct word we search for is," Professor Quan said. He stared up into the blue sky. "Ethereal."

"Why?" Captain Lovins asked.

"We are the way we are," Professor Quan said.

"True, I still don't understand me," Captain Lovins said.

"I guess I married my science, it is the one thing in my life, that I am completely, totally devoted," Professor Quan said. "I think marriage, or at least the image of marriage is a farce, it's a legal reason to control, tax people."

"Yeah, marriage would suck," Captain Lovins said.

"But now, I sense like a twin might sense," Professor Quan said. "I know what she is thinking, where she is, I suspect she has the thoughts about me, I cannot totally hide from her."

Captain Lovins pensively stared over at Professor Quan.

They continued along the freeway, a metal sign just over the Tennessee border warned that Nashville loomed in the distance.

"Funny, to share your body, your true essence with another, to create a human being, a life, now, I think that takes courage," Professor Quan said. He gently turned the steering wheel to the right as they continued to blaze their own trail.

"Carnal exchange, mistakes happen," Captain Lovins said.

"I wonder, is life a mistake?" Professor Quan asked.

"I don't know, that is unanswerable," Captain Lovins said. "But you can still be my wingman."

"Okay, but you'll look past my genetic seed that has been scattered by our former employer?" Professor Quan asked.

"Ah, we are an odd couple," Captain Lovins said.

"Government people, creating death and destruction, they just stole my work, regardless of what happens to me, this is such a better life," Professor Quan said. He scratched his partially unshaven beard.

"You know, it took me a bit, I think you resemble Montgomery Clift's character in 'The Misfits'?" Captain Lovins asked. He shifted forward, he grinned. "You're hair is longer, but you have his face."

"I envisioned him, I guess my mixture worked to perfection," Professor Quan said. "Do you think my accent is close to ideal?"

"If it weren't for the fact I know it's you, I wouldn't even recognize you," Captain Lovins said.

"Good, good," Professor Quan said. He mashed the gas pedal.

The pair investigated Nashville, but they did not find anyone who met their instinctive criteria. They roamed past dusty farmers working in corn and tobacco fields. It was a time in America when people wore bright multi-colored clothes and let their hair, grow goldilocks long.

"I cannot seem to either get close enough for an evaluation, or talk to anybody long enough without coming off as, odd," Professor Quan said. He tapped his hands along the steering wheel. He stared forward through the windshield.

"Be patient, to pull the trigger," Captain Lovins said. "Like a sniper, you wait."

"I agree," Professor Quan said.

"But be ready to fire," Captain Lovins said, "focus."

Clear cobalt skies and the pleasant warm weather relaxed their nerves. Encouraged to continue their search, their instincts sojourned them toward the land of Elvis, Memphis. Hungry, they found a local barbecue joint near a bend in the serendipity of the Mississippi River, Uncle Waldo's' Boathouse & Rib Joint. The strolled inside, the restaurant smelled of free will, cigarettes and hazy smoke clouds floating under the timbered log ceiling. They enjoyed plates of Memphis style barbecued ribs. Their gaped open mouths covered in red dipping sauce. And a barmaid was relentlessly hitting on Captain Lovins.

"You ain't from round here muscle man?" the barmaid said. She wore a t-shirt that covered her chigger bites. Her bleach blonde hair pulled back in a girlish ponytail.

"Sorry Madam, no I'm not," Captain Lovins said.

She leaned over the wooden counter top, rapidly chewing gum.

"I like bald headed men. Well, you're not quite there yet, is ya? I like that smooth round surface, kind of makes me think about something else," the barmaid said. She winked. She squished the number two pencil into the corner of her mouth.

Professor Quan ignored the conversation. But he noticed two young men in separate parties, both about nineteen years old, had entered the restaurant. He intently watched them and started to wonder. The first young man had blond hair, a spindly thin body; he sat down in a wooden lacquered booth directly behind Professor Quan. With him, he had a stocky built, red headed friend.

The second young man, was taller, solidly built, and just happened to sit in a booth next to the first young man. He had a younger boy with him.

Professor Quan, was not exactly sure why, he was intrigued with them. Captain Lovins wiped the sauce from his face. He ignored the barmaid. He elbowed Professor Quan. He angled his head in the young men's direction.

"I'll monitor, over near the bathrooms, she'll likely follow me over there, so focus," Captain Lovins said. He smacked Professor Quan on his left shoulder.

Electromagnetic energy cycled up and down Professor Quan's spine. He twisted his shoulders to better eavesdrop on the first subject's conversation. Blond-haired, the young man had a natural wide toothed smile coupled with innocent fun loving eyes. He had a playful inviting appearance, similar to a giggling, three-year old boy playing tag with his mother in the backyard under a summer sun.

"Man, I'm not sure where I'm headed. Not sure what major to pick at Auburn," the blond headed boy said. He had a happy southern accent. He wore bellbottom jeans and a t-shirt with a peace symbol on it.

"Got to pick something," his friend said. He intently studied the paper menu.

"I want to do something fun, do something fun to make money," the blond headed boy said. "Too bad there ain't any pirate ships out in the gulf anymore."

"I recommend accounting or maybe engineering, both are good options," his friend said without looking up from the menu.

"You might think I'm crazy, but I feel deep down inside, life has more to offer," the blond headed boy said.

Professor Quan adjusted his cowboy hat. He leaned back in the bar stool with his thumbs hooked on his pants pockets.

"Life's about building-up your bank account, and retiring a rich man. Keep your grades up, or you'll end up getting drafted," his friend said.

Professor Quan thought the friend just parroted what his parents had told him. His life would be plain vanilla, no mint chocolate chip, sprinkles or swirls of strawberry.

"Man, agree with the money part, you might think I'm crazy, but I kind of like writing poetry. And I have been messing around with trying to learn to play the guitar. Maybe I can get some music lessons at school. Hey man, you never know?" the blond headed boy said. He nervously laughed.

"Listen, writing music, poetry or what not, that is stuff hippie losers do," his friend said. "You know, and I know, the world doesn't need another Elvis."

"Elvis is cool," the blond headed boy said.

"Besides, how are you going to earn a living? Let me guess, you'll write these songs about pirates and girls, and dance around bare foot on stage?" His friend cackled. He clapped his pudgy hands. The blond haired boy decided to study the menu.

Professor Quan twisted his shoulders. He wanted to smack the boy's friend up side his flat-topped, parrott head.

"Not real practical, am I? Maybe a change in my attitude, far from Mobiles latitude," the blond headed boy said.

Professor Quan's brown eyes turned pitch black, back lit by a blue hot flame. His rage turned to a molten fire, sick in the pit of his stomach. He realized the teenager did not have the internal support to chase after his dreams.

"Jim, don't be a loser," his friend said. "You'll end up living in your car in Key West, with all those homos."

"Yeah, I guess, got to stop day dreaming about floating around the gulf, maybe be Jimmy?" the blond headed boy said. "Jimmy sounds happy."

"Stay in school, chicks dig the rich guys," his friend said.

Professor Quan started to fidget in his wooden lacquered chair. He prayed the friend might disappear to the bathroom.

From across the bar, Captain Lovins gave Professor Quan an encouraging gaze. The look only good friends understand.

"He should learn to stay away from that human vampire," Professor Quan mumbled. He sipped his fizzing RC Cola.

"Did you say something to me, cowboy?" a busy body server asked.

"No, just talking to myself I guess. Will you please get me another RC?" Professor Quan asked.

"Why sure, sweetie, where's your friend?"

"Next to the bathroom," Professor Quan said. He nodded over toward the bathroom opening.

"Oh, see I'm late to the party," the busy body server said. "That girl Paris, she ain't got no pride-"

Professor Quan shrugged. He swung the yellow oak chair in the opposite direction. He decided to listen in on the other young boy's conversation.

The second young man had sandy brown hair. He wore a short sleeve cotton blue checked button-down and blue jeans. Another boy sat in front of him, he appeared several years younger and more diminutive in size, but had similar facial features.

"I believe in you, work hard. Good things will happen," the husky young man said. His voice sandpaper raspy, with the hint of a southern accent, Professor Quan thought perhaps from central Arkansas. Maybe some place near Hope. He loved his work mapping out accents, and matching them up for his Voice Box Protocol machine back at his lair that glowed inside out.

"Thanks Bill, it doesn't come easy like it does for you," the younger boy said.

"It doesn't come easy to me either. I spend a lot of time alone studying, just keep at it," the husky young man said.

Professor Quan twisted his torso. He brushed barbecue off his Stetson. He quickly glanced at the husky young man. He had a warm presence. He had an expression as if he never met a stranger.

"I hope to get someplace in life, you know. We didn't grow up with a lot, never stop believing," the husky young man said.

"I know you're right, I hope can I visit you up there at Georgetown," the young boy said.

Professor Quan's brain began to squirm. He needed some amazingly good luck if he were to spray them with his Epigenetic compressed particles. He wondered if the sisters of fate weaved him a friendship quilt for today.

Near the restroom doors, Captain Lovins was under full assault from the barmaid. Hidden inside his temporary skin, with his face in his hands, but then Professor Quan sensed a commotion near the restaurant's front doors.

Through a dense pack of handlers, Elvis emerged inside Uncle Waldo's' Boathouse and Rib Joint. The young men and restaurant customers where entranced by the super-star who had a striking young woman on his arm. She had Bambi brown eyes that hypnotized Professor Quan. Her soft, delicate, youthful face caused Professor Quan's initial serpentine experiment to pour buckets of testosterone into his bloodstream.

"Darn it, I need to make a Moonpie," Professor Quan said. He shrugged; he loved Elvis, but just not right now. He thought the disturbance had ruined his experiment. He swigged his RC Cola. He decided the nearby bathroom a perfect place to escape to collect his thoughts. He strolled up to Captain Lovins. The dingbat waitress disengaged her attack and gawked at Elvis.

"I'm not sure how to make this happen?" Professor Quan said. He stared down at his lizard skin boots.

"Be patient. They seem like real good candidates. But if it's not to be, we have to keep searching," Captain Lovins said.

"It's up to the sisters of fate I suppose," Professor Quan said. He turned toward the bathroom. "I'll be back."

Professor Quan stuffed his hands in his pockets and found his way through the entranced crowd and inside a bathroom stall. He sat on the toilet seat. His breathing slowed. Twirling his hat by its brim, he tried to stay in his Texas cowboy character. Finally, he relaxed, and released a non-poisonous gaseous cloud that burped like a bullfrog belching compressed air at the bottom of a pond covered with Lillie pads.

"You're killing me."

"Hey man-"

Professor Quan shot up off the plastic seat. His pants fell around his ankles. Hidden behind the stall, he instantly realized whom the voices belonged too. His heart began to thump up to his brain. He yanked his pants up. He emerged from the bathroom stall.

"Now, I'm so, so, so sorry about that," Professor Quan said. As random as life, his two young targets just so happened to be relieving themselves before two white Porcelain goddesses.

Outside, Captain Lovins noticed the boys go inside the restroom. After, he blocked the doorway acting as if he had lost his wallet. A few patrons backed away from the door after he gave them a sinister glare.

"Sorry boys, that smells worse than a buzzard's breath after a road kill convention," Professor Quan said.

Then it happened, an invisible electromagnetic door opened that allowed Professor Quan to walk through.

"Tell you what, I've a newfangled spray that's supposed to knock out the smell. Being in the oil business and all, I'm used to stink and wildcatters farting all day," Professor Quan said.

The husky young boy and the blond headed boy simultaneously turned and stared at the odd diminutive Texan wearing an oversized cowboy hat.

"My wife gave me this here, to keep for such occasions. Here let me spray it in front of your nose to dissipate that rancid odor, so, take a big, ole, deep breath, okay?" Professor Quan said. He pressed the cartridge. He triggered a full release of his brillian genome to coat the teenager's sinus cavities, until he was certain it had dispersed into their blood streams and would cycle into their DNA.

Caught by oxygenated red blood cells, that ferried the epigenetic particles into protein synthesis cycling through their maturing brains. Then a wild fire of polypeptide chains scorched across their chromosomal structures. Once the particles immersed within their human tissue, oxidative phosphorylation occurred and produced massive amounts of ATP to energize across their inner mitochondrial membranes' independent helical structures, reformed with Professor Quan's intelligence quotient and the new erectical dysfunction gene.

"Wow, that doesn't smell great, but it does stop the stink," the husky young man said.

"Yeah, I think you're right, thanks, I guess," the blond headed man said.

Professor Quan simply smiled and dropped the sprayer into his shirt pocket.

"Well boys, I think that little boost will do a lot more than kill the stink." Professor Quan said. He chuckled. He pointed at them with a pistol grip. "You boys have great lives."

Both looked at him with perplexed expressions.

Professor Quan shifted on his lizard skin boots. He sensed it was time to leave the now packed restaurant. He started to push the door open to saunter out of the bathroom. As he pushed, the bathroom door seemed jammed; someone else yanked from the other side. It caused him to slip off his over-sized boots. He struggled not to fall. But he was grabbed at the man who had just wiggled inside the bathroom.

"Ah, sorry 'bout that man, real, sorry 'bout that, Tex," Elvis said.

Professor Quan stared up into Elvis' eyes. He was still a young, handsome man in the prime of his life.

Elvis leaned over to help Professor Quan up, basking in the glory with the success of Viva Las Vegas. He seemed to have a halo over his head as he patted down Professor Quan.

"Oh, not a problem, I'm just fine, yes sir, just fine," Professor Quan said.

"Well, thank you, thank you very much. Now take care, Tex," Elvis said. Elvis patted Professor Quan on the left shoulder.

Professor Quan took a quick gulp. He exited the bathroom and located a stunned Captain Lovins.

"How did it go?" Captain Lovins asked.

"It was perfect," Professor Quan said.

Captain Lovins pointed down at Professor Quan's hands. "What's that?" Captain Lovins asked.

Professor Quan inspected his left hand palm.

"Black hair? I must've accidentally yanked on Elvis' hair, I even got a few follicles," Professor Quan said. He appeared dumbfounded "I've a thought."

"Great, I love your – thoughts," Captain Lovins said.

"No, as in revolutionary," Professor Quan said. "We need to get back to our new Kentucky home, I wonder what's in Elvis' hair?"

"Don't tell me," Captain Lovins said.

"I've a wonderful idea," Professor Quan said. "We'll be way ahead of her, within this hair, a secret hides, I sense it."

"You've that crazy stare," Captain Lovins said.

"I was looking at this all wrong," Professor Quan said.

Chapter Sixteen

Eddie clutched the Wish List within his moist hand; he suspiciously glanced around the busy office-building parking lot. He stuffed it into his khaki pants pocket, and swiftly strolled inside the office. Being late for work for the first time was an odd sensation. So he vectored for Clevenger's whereabouts.

"You're in luck, he's not around," Ardee said. Her desk was ten-feet from Clevenger's invisible halitosis stench doorway. "I trust you had an exciting weekend."

Eddie blinked his eyelids. He fiddled with his keys.

"Jim Bob got arrested," Eddie said.

"Really?" Ardee asked.

"Selling stuff on WePay, didn't pay taxes, or what-not, federal agents stormed his house," Eddie said. He paused. He scratched the top of his head. "I, I was there-"

Ardee crinkled open her mouth.

"You're lucky," Ardee said as she dagger pointed her perfectly manicured forefinger at Eddie.

"Yeah, I almost had a heart attack," Eddie said.

"See, if you'd had dinner with me, none of this would've happened," Ardee said. She seductively stared at Eddie.

"I know, I got to go," Eddie said. He shrugged. He strided inside his workstation, he collapsed onto his office chair. He snagged a manila underwriting folder, spread the correspondence across the work surface to give any passerby the impression he had work to do. Then with stealth like motion, he retrieved the crumpled list.

"What is this?" Eddie whispered.

Eddie closely studied the document. He did a quick internet search for each famous name. There were no obvious patterns or connections, Eddie thought. He pondered Jim Bob's predicament for the next three hours, staring off into space as his inbox grew a virtual email traffic jam.

"That's where the money comes into this," Eddie mumbled. He folded the Wish List into a square and slipped it into his front pants pocket. Eddie's adrenaline-rushed morning had drained his body of all its electrolytes, bewildered, he decided to leave the office mid-afternoon and risk his life, dining across the freeway at Uncle Dante & Aunt Virgil's Hellish Pit Barbecue Station.

"I'll be back in a half-hour or so," Eddie said. He marched past Ardee's desk.

"Take your time Jeannie Bean," Ardee said. She winked at him. "I'd come along, sorry, have to cover the phones."

"Want something?" Eddie asked.

"I do love that barbeque hell," Ardee said, "nothing this time, but you have to take me soon."

"All right," Eddie said.

Uncle Dante & Aunt Virgil's Hellish Pit Barbecue Station or as Ardee called it, barbeque hell, had been located at Hubble Parkway and Plymouth Rock Avenue since late 1965. The founding couple Dante and Virgil were now dry rubbed and basted by their barbecue-maker near the mouth of the river Styx. They had willed the restaurant to their son; Virgil, Jr. Eddie loped past the restaurant's wooden front door. He grabbed a free newspaper and sauntered up to the clear lacquered, yellow oak front counter.

"Pulled pork platter," Eddie said. "Please."

"Why sure, young man," Virgil, Jr. said. A brown bear of a man with a baritone voice, he strolled to the back counter and slid a menu ticket across the stainless steel counter top toward the sweating, kitchen staff hidden by greyish smoke plumes. "Where's that sweet child, Ardee?"

"Back at the office," Eddie said. He shrugged. "Sorry, can I get extra hushpuppies."

"Of course, best in the south," Virgil, Jr. said. After a couple of minutes, Virgil, Jr. double-checked the order. He slid the barbeque lunch, wrapped in shiny space station tinfoil over to Eddie. "I think that girl's sweet on you."

Eddie glided his tray down toward the petite, prepubescent cherry bubble gum chewing, check out girl Charon.

"Guess so," Eddie mumbled. "Love your hushpuppies."

Virgil, Jr. heartily chuckled. He half-smiled over at Eddie.

"It's my daddy Dante's secret recipe, sort of like how to find happiness, get away from evil," Virgil, Jr. said. He grinned with his thick husky chest out. "It's all right there, you just have to shine a bright light on it to seek heaven."

"Yeah?" Eddies said.

"I think you tell that story ten thousand times a day," the check out girl said. She pushed in the cash register change pan. "Here's your change - sweet thing."

"Hush, child", Virgil, Jr. said. He smiled at her. "That's God talking to you, cooking's 'bout love, it tells people who you really are, pure, simple food barely touched by man, it's how you satisfy the soul." He gleamed over at Eddie. "My momma Virgil always said that."

"You crazy," the check out girl said.

Eddie nibbled at a crusty golden brown and delicious hush-puppy. He glanced back over at Virgil, Jr.

"You might be crazy, too?" the check out girl Charon said to Eddie. "But I guess you can keep comin' back, so I have a job."

"You enjoy now, young man," Virgil, Jr. said. He scowled at the girl. "Hush child, or I'll take away your ferryman permit."

Eddie pinpointed his usual corner high-top table within a setting of nine other round high top tables. He opened his newspaper and slipped out the sports section. After another sliver of pork disappeared, Eddie almost choked. Quickly, he swigged his drink, causing fizzed carbonated cola particles to float past his face.

In the upper right corner, the newspaper headline:

'A Lionel Tracks to St. Judith'

"That's weird," Eddies said. He coughed to clear his throat. The article, written by sports columnist Ricardo O'Reilly,

148

detailed Lionel's last minute addition to the St. Judith Classic, in Memphis. Lionel thought it would be a good tournament to help the children.

What a coincidence, Eddie thought. He was rather close to Nashville. He gazed out the restaurant's panoramic double pain windows, segmented by fake plastic muttons, as the dense midafternoon Hubble Parkway traffic cruised past.

"Sperm Olympic gold medalist for sure," Eddie said. "Wow, talk about lucky!" He bongo drummed his barbeque stained hands on the table. A nearby older woman gawked at Eddie.

"Young man?" the older woman asked. "You okay?" She scanned across the restaurant section to find Virgil, Jr.

"Oh, sorry," Eddie said. He blushed.

"Young fella, you okay?" Virgil, Jr. asked.

"Sorry, no, no," Eddie said. He bit into a hushpuppy. "I'm good, I'm good."

Virgil, Jr. shook his square head. He meandered back to the front counter. A weird sensation cycled through Eddie's body, transfixed, as if the sisters of fate beckoned him to cross a river Dante never contemplated. His scalp and neck tingled with electromagnetic intrigue as if his instincts were guiding him toward a bright constant light.

Eddie shook his fists. He crumbled his lunch into a tin foil ball. He streaked back across the active highway toward the office building; he skated atop the woolen thatched commercial carpet, and swerved in front of Clevenger's office. His chest pulsed. He aimlessly stared forward.

"Where's Clevenger?" Eddie asked. He wiped his eyebrows with his thumb. He stared into the stinky empty office.

"I told you, he's not in," Ardee said. She sat up high in her office chair. "I'm worried 'bout you."

Eddie twisted and shuffled over in front of her desk, with his hands on his hips. He pointed down at her office phone.

"Call him-" Eddie said.

"You're serious?" Ardee asked.

"Yeah, call him-" Eddie said.

"Who are you?" Ardee asked.

"I'm me, just get him," Eddie said.

"Okay, but I kind of dig this," Ardee said. Ardee shrugged, she pressed the auto dial button and handed the phone receiver up to Eddie. "Don't get yourself fired."

"Mr. Rollins," Eddie said.

"Ah, hello?" Clevenger said.

"It's Eddie," Eddie said.

"Eddie? Am I day dreaming," Clevenger said.

"No, I'm sorry for the last minute request, ah, I read in the newspaper Lionel decided to play in the St. Judith Classic in Memphis. I'm hoping to take Friday off to go see him play."

"Really? You never take time off?" Clevenger said. "Give me ten minutes."

Clevenger waddled with his manatee like frame into the office suite. He perplexingly stared at Eddie. He glanced down at Ardee. Ardee shrugged her shoulders.

"I'm not taking the day off," Ardee said. She frowned.

"Come on in," Clevenger said. He waved Eddie to follow him into his office. He flicked on the lights.

"Thanks," Eddie said. He sat across from Clevenger.

"I'll allow it, be straight with me, you looking for another job? Never knew you are such a big golf fan. Come on now, be straight," Clevenger said. He pointed over at Eddie.

"Ah, thought it might be cool to see the real Lionel," Eddie said, "you know, up close, I've never seen someone famous, you know, in person."

"I guess I can understand that," Clevenger said. He combed his mangy goatee with his fat fingers. After a few uncomfortable moments, he smacked his right hand on the desktop. "Tell ya what - I've an old buddy down there."

"Clevenger do you need anything?" Ardee asked. She stood near the office door studying Eddie and Clevenger.

"No dear," Clevenger said.

"Then it's okay?" Eddie asked. He glanced over at Ardee, and then looked back at Clevenger.

"Sure, but my buddy has these special tickets he offers me every year, you can be inside the ropes and get real close to them players, walking along with them and their caddies."

"Really?" Eddie asked.

"Interested?" Clevenger asked. He scratched behind his neck. "Coolest thing I've ever done. But they never had Lionel play down there, it'll be circus."

"Yeah," Eddie said.

"Give me a few minutes to track my buddy down," Clevenger said. He waved Eddie toward the door. Eddie loped out of his office. "If I get him, I'll call ya back."

Clevenger closely watched Eddie leave. He pulled out his old-fashioned Rolodex. He flipped through the cards until he found Charles 'Chuck' Rollins. Clevenger twisted his shoulders, his spine popped. Charles' name was crossed through with black ink, replaced with, 'Charlene'. A new address in Germantown, scribbled above the old address. With his office phone, he pressed in the number.

"Hello?" Charlene asked. Clevenger paused as he held his breath. "Clevenger? I have the number saved."

"Ah, hi there, ah, Charles, darn it, I mean Charlene. I'm sorry," Clevenger said. He cleared his throat. He fidgeted with his Robert E. Lee civil war chess set figurine.

"Not shocked you might be calling, now that Lionel's decided to play in the St. Jude?"

"Ah, I can't make it, but I've got one of my best employees, I do like this young man." He twisted the figurine in his thick fingers. "I was wondering if you could do a favor for me and momma, and help him out."

"Terrific, if he doesn't mind putting up with me," Charlene said. She huffed.

"He's real easy going," Clevenger said. He leaned his elbow on the desktop. "I have to tell you something, he's my best employee, and I'm not sure he's a big golf fan."

"Got ya, think he has an interview?" Charlene asked.

"Yeah-" Clevenger said.

"Tell him he can stay at our new house," Charlene said.

"That'd be great," Clevenger said.

Charlene paused. Clevenger could hear her breathing.

"You *DID* tell him about me?" Charlene asked.

"Ah, well, not yet, I wanted to see if you even had the tickets first, but I promise he'll know what he's in for," Clevenger said. He glided his pudgy fingers across the glass-topped desk.

"I see - in for," Charlene said.

"Sorry, cousin, that didn't come out right," Clevenger said.

"Forget about it," Charlene said.

"Thanks," Clevenger said. "Thanks, Charles."

"You know we still care about you and your momma. You're always welcome to visit," Charlene said. "Give the young man my cell number, and by the way, it's Charlene."

"Sorry, sorry, thanks, thanks cousin," Clevenger said. The cell line clicked silent. Clevenger reclined back on his black leather chair. He turned to inspect the ten-year old picture of his cousin's family; it was tucked into a corner on his credenza. Cousin Charles had always been lucky. He had boyish good looks, a bright perfect smile and a keen business mind. He had built an investment brokerage company, Turnbull, Ltd. But all his ambition changed when they picked a winning sequence for the Tennessee Lotto. Clevenger shook his head to chase away the new image of Charles. He wondered what happened to Charles after he won three hundred million dollars. Clevenger pressed his speakerphone, he pressed in Eddie's extension.

"Hello," Eddie said.

"I've some good news," Clevenger said. "Come back."

"Cool," Eddie said. He dashed back to Clevenger's office.

"Man, sakes, you're faster than a one eyed goat in Ethiopia, during Meskel, have a seat," Clevenger said.

"Can I get you boys anythin'?" Ardee asked.

"No I'm good, Eddie?" Clevenger asked.

"No thanks," Eddie said. He shrugged at Ardee.

"Well all right then," Ardee said. Befuddled, she glanced at Eddie, just before she disappeared from view.

"I convinced my old buddy, well," Clevenger said. He paused for a moment and glided his fingertips along the edge of his partners' desk. "It's my first cousin, Charlene." He coughed. "He'll, I mean, she'll guide you into the tournament. The great news is one of those special inside the ropes tickets has your name on it, no kiddin' around."

"Unbelievable," Eddie said. He could sense his heart beat pounding through his chest. He thought how random it was that Lionel would be within driving distance, and this weird wish list had mysteriously been shoved under his front door all because Jim Bob got caught peddling signed jock straps.

Clevenger crinkled his bushy eyebrows. He puckered his lips as if he had bitten into a tart lemon.

"I best let you know the whole story," Charlene said. He tapped his fingers along the desk top.

"Sorry?" Eddie said. He sat back in the leather chair.

"See now, ah," Clevenger said. He fumbled with the figurine of General Robert E. Lee. He carefully, lovingly set it back on his prized Civil War chess set, next to the Stonewall Jackson and General Beauregard figurines.

"Yeah?" Eddie asked.

"Charlene's my first cousin on my mother's side, grew-up down there in Memphis, so everybody knows him, darn it, I mean her," Clevenger said. He squirmed on the black leather chair. "See, Charlene used to be, ah, well, Charles." Clevenger blurted. His face contorted into a slaphappy contortion.

"Ah, you mean, a she?" Eddie asked. He stared past Clevenger at a plaque with a list of all the past BRA winners.

"Yep, and he's still married to his wife, Raquel, and to put a cherry on top, son-of-a-gun won the three hundred million dollar lotto. Wife's hot as a neutron bomb, luckiest SOB I've ever known," Clevenger said. He stared out he office window past Eddie. "I think, sort of-"

"I'm not sure what to say." Eddie said. He wobbled.

"Still want to go?" Clevenger said. "Charlene invited you to stay with them, so you can leave early, drive down Thursday."

"I'll go," Eddie said matter-of-fact. He wondered what storm he was headed into, and why he even decided to go.

"They're mostly nice folks though. They have two teenagers. Other than them winning the lotto and Charles, they're just like anybody else," Clevenger said. His eyes squinted as if a bomb exploded near his desk. "Did I just say that?"

"I don't know what to think-" Eddie said.

"Me neither, but it'll be all right," Clevenger said.

"I'm going," Eddie said. He intently shook his head.

"Here's Charlene's address and cell number, go have a good time, I don't know what to tell you," Clevenger said. He shifted his tubby body forward. "We think the world of you here, so, be careful and find your way back."

"Yeah, be back our way," Ardee whispered. She was partially concealed by the office doorjamb.

Eddie glanced back over at Ardee. Her penetrating stare caused him to blush, as if she was willing him toward her.

"You must been Mata Hari in a former life," Clevenger said.

"Mata Hari?" Ardee asked. "Was he a fashion designer?"

Chapter Seventeen

Bertrand's cell phone glowed within his ornate study's darkness, like an interstellar beacon from a dead planet. Bertrand snapped into reality. He grabbed the remote control to turn off the wide screen television he had fallen asleep watching. His mind was in a foggy haze from the effects of top shelf bourbon and mindless reality television shows.

"Mr. Screwtape?" Ms. Prosperina asked. She cackled.

Bertrand held the cell phone away from his ear. He gulped and wiped his tangled hair back over his head.

"This is a surprise," Bertrand said.

"I was having such a delightful morning, had the whole family here yesterday, then I had a call from Mr. Oppenheimer," Ms. Prosperina said.

"Oh?" Bertrand said. He pushed forward on the couch.

"Your people are so inept, rather sad wouldn't you say?" Mr. Prosperina said.

"Not sure I understand?" Bertrand said.

"Alas, Mr. Screwtape, the internet can be rather useful from time-to-time, with satellites, all the mindless social media chatter and of course, tracking devices in cell phones," Ms. Prosperina said. She paused. "You let Professor Quan's protector get away, again, alas, you and Dr. Yin, a poor decision on my part, why is this so difficult?"

"Yes, we're working a plan," Bertrand said. He paused and puckered his thin lips. "He's elusive, they're both elusive."

"You disappoint me, I had such high hopes for us," Ms. Prosperina said. "Perhaps Mr. Oppenheimer should handle this."

Bertrand scooted further forward on his leather couch. He wiped sleep from his eyes. He coughed with his fist at his lips.

"No, no, I can get this done," Bertrand said.

"Sloppy, I think that is what you might say in English, in my native tongue, I call it *schlampig*," Ms. Prosperina said, with a special emphasis on *pig*.

"We've made progress, per our agreement," Bertrand said. "This is all new to me."

"Mr. Screwtape, I do not intend to become famous, fame, a fool's bargain for reality stars, to be gawked at by the Roman mob. I'm just a quiet old woman living in Europe," Ms. Prosperina said. She hissed. "I have a future generation to care for, I don't have time to waste."

"I don't understand," Bertrand said. His forehead crinkled a long wrinkle between his plucked eyebrows.

"You've left me to make decisions," Ms. Prosperina said.

"Not sure I follow," Bertrand said. His heartbeat banged in his ears. With Ms. Proserpina's reputation throughout the underworld community, she did not accept failure or medaling.

"May I introduce you to Mr. Oppenheimer?" Ms. Prosperina said. "He's my friend."

Bertrand stopped breathing. He sensed in the far corner of his expansive private study, paneled in cherry, a sinewy Tarantula of a man unwind from the shadowy corner. He had a buzzed blond haircut, his face, expressionless.

"Please, this-" Bertrand said. He guffawed. He instantly slinked back against his couch; he sucked in rapid, shallow breaths.

"Now, now, Mr. Oppenheimer is not there to kill you," Ms. Prosperina said. "That would be quite untidy. To kill just ends your usefulness, he brought you a gift from me."

Mr. Oppenheimer bent down near Bertrand. He pulled out an innocuous white business envelope. He placed it on the antique coffee table in front of Bertrand.

"What do you want from me?" Bertrand asked.

"Oh, I'm so excited for you to open it, that is what I want right now," Ms. Prosperina said. She sinisterly purred. "I'm sure you'll forgive me from the bottom of your demonic soul."

"I'm sure," Bertrand said. He haltingly picked up the envelope.

"Tell me Mr. Screwtape, tell me what you think of my gift," Ms. Prosperina said. She cryptically hissed.

Bertrand opened the back flap of the envelope, within, a quarter inch thick collection of scanned photos of his favorite niece. He had never married. Instead, he had chosen a different path, a path of self-indulgence, a career, money and a vast menu of women and wine. But his niece Sarah, a freshman at Vanderbilt, the embodiment of innocence.

"Dear God," Bertrand said. He rapidly flipped through the scanned pages of photos. "Just kill me, please, leave her be-"

"Oh, too late for that," Ms. Prosperina said. "Look closely, it's okay, God's not watching. In the background, I think Mr. Oppenheimer quite photogenic, don't you think?"

"I am quite proud," Mr. Oppenheimer said. His cell phone patched into the conversation, he flicked on his cellphone earpiece and clipped the PDA to his belt. He squatted down in front of Bertrand. "She is quite the spunky vixen, quite a character, pretty."

"Just kill me," Bertrand said. "I'm begging, leave her be."

"So, I think we will all agree, it's about temptation," Ms. Prosperina said. She grunted. "Most in life get to be the bunny rabbit, but I get to be the falcon. I am curious. Do you think she might like to drink coffee? Maybe tempted by sugar and cream, maybe chocolate sprinkles, we have numerous addictive options, but that would be too easy. My preference, an older, handsome young man, with a black heart, lust can be quite powerful for a pretty, naive girl. Hmm, to then be dead inside, numb, like you, Mr. Screwtape?"

"Ya, she seems quite eager to me," Mr. Oppenheimer said. "Hmm, a tight, fit young girl, but we only teased her, this time, ah, if I were a younger man, but I drink coffee - black."

Bertrand flipped through the photos of an innocent teenager partying at school. He saw clearly in the background, in the shadows at each location, the college bar she snuck into with a fake ID, smiling into the camera with new friends, behind her, Mr. Oppenheimer. At the afterhours burger joint with Mr. Oppenheimer at a nearby table, a handsome young man, with thick Elvis like hair, but with dead eyes. Sarah could not take her eyes from the young man. From within the photos, she stared at him. The eyes of a girl yearning to be a woman, but her life choices dangled above her.

"Pain, it can come in so many sweet forms, to much sugar, cream, chocolate," Ms. Prosperina said. She hissed. "Why, Mr. Screwtop, even you had your innocence stolen, what it must feel like to have lived a life of secrets, now, her protector?"

"Ya, you have been the good shepherd," Mr. Oppenheimer said.

"Her favorite uncle, yes you are. The one who would do anything to protect her, so, will you be there for her?"

Bertrand shut his eyes. They had meticulously picked into his childhood. Exposed, stripped of his dignity, he was prepared to die, to protect her.

"Ya, Madam, Mr. Screwtop appears to be swayed by your argument," Mr. Oppenheimer said. He tightened his gloves over his long, angular hands. "But he seems weak to me-"

Bertrand blankly stared over at Mr. Oppenheimer. Aware he had danced with the wrong girl.

"What do you really want? You've quietly slithered into sugar cane crops, dairy farms, utilities, not sure of what else, I think you're even into body parts."

Ms. Prosperina lightly chuckled. From a light crackling, it sounded as though puffed on a cigarette.

"Ah, good boy, you are a smart one, Mr. Screwtop," Ms. Prosperina said. She purred. "I'm not hard to find, you just have to seek me. I'm everywhere, my structure is almost in place, I just need two black diamonds. Then the particles pulverized within a collider, collect the particles, ah, it will make the coffee taste so, so much better. So much more rich, full bodied coffee swimming in sugar and cream, so quietly addictive, so decadently life altering, then my subjects are fat and obese within the blink of an eye."

"Why?" Bertrand asked. He stared down at the wooden floor.

"You will see," Ms. Prosperina said. "My people hunger for souls, they hunger for light, my creator, Professor Quan, he senses me. I sense him. We are entangled for eternity. But I need to find him, before he knows I'm nearby, otherwise, he might do something rash, and that would disappoint me. You don't want to disappoint me, again, for innocent, Sarah?"

"No, no, what am I to do?" Bertrand said. He realized her tentacles wrapped and sucked at the building blocks of life.

"Good, acceptance," Ms. Prosperina said. "First lesson, never love, ever, love exposes needless problems, innocent light. Why do you think Professor Quan chose an orphan for his protector?"

Mr. Oppenheimer snagged the photos back from Bertrand. He slipped them back into his hip pocket.

"He looks like an endangered white tailed baby deer in the woods," Mr. Oppenheimer said. He snickered. "Like the time we took Juan's sacks of coffee beans and his burro."

"Stop, you have such the humor," Ms. Prosperina said. She

sighed. "Mr. Screwtop, I own you. There is nothing you can hide from me, I sense your inner most thoughts. You will not fail me again, your pretty niece, the only person you love, pity, pure love is so sweet, but genetically defective."

Bertrand stared over at Mr. Oppenheimer.

"Yes," Bertrand said. He gulped. "I understand."

"You will continue to feed information, anyone coming and going inside your firm. I can sense him, he is making plans, he has been at this for decades, find him."

"Yes," Bertrand said. "You'll leave her alone? I'm begging."

"I don't negotiate, but for now, she is safe from me," Ms. Prosperina said. She puffed and breathed against the cell phone receiver. "But in a moment, you'll forget most of this conversation, good bye."

Mr. Oppenheimer whipped out a dagger needle and plunged it into Bertrand's neck. He did not resist. He collapsed sideways onto the leather couch. His eyes blank, almost comatose.

"He is out," Mr. Oppenheimer said. He pulled out the needle, and replaced it inside a hard plastic container.

"Stay there," Ms. Prosperina said. "Shadow the agents, they'll clumsily lead us to Professor Quan."

"Yes, Madam," Mr. Oppenheimer said.

"Use your best judgment," Ms. Prosperina said. She quietly paused. "This exercise with Dr. Yin has become bothersome and tedious. Mr. Screwtop is not much of a lawyer, but you have injected him, we own him, we can track him."

"Yes, Madam," Mr. Oppenheimer said.

"But Dr. Yin has overpromised, I think you should pay him a visit, he seems to be wasting our resources," Ms. Prosperina said.

"Yes, Madam," Mr. Oppenheimer said.

"There is a water treatment facility I plan to purchase near Nashville, and some farm land, corn, soybean," Ms. Prosperina said. "Let me think."

Mr. Oppenheimer reached down, he squeezed Bertrand's wrist to check his pulse. He shoved a pillow under his neck.

"Mr. Screwtop sleeps," Mr. Oppenheimer said. He unclipped his cell phone; he pointed it down at Bertrand, who was splayed across the leather couch. His cell phone camera flashed, and then he emailed the photo to Ms. Prosperina's cell phone. He quickly left the house, and casually walked toward his four-door sedan. He kept the cell phone on allowing Ms. Prosperina time to think. He knew better than to ask her for instructions, or prematurely end the call.

"Thank you for the photo," Ms. Prosperina said. "Pity, he is so unfit, just begging to die."

Mr. Oppenheimer got back inside his car.

"Yes, Madam," Mr. Oppenheimer said. He started the engine.

"I sense my father frequents Nashville," Ms. Prosperina said.

"Yes, Madam," Mr. Oppenheimer said.

"I have to be cautious, he can read my thoughts, it is a one way door … I cannot read his," Ms. Prosperina said. She paused. "Go ahead and collect Dr. Yin, I think I should come visit my attorney Mr. Screwtop, we'll have a conversation with Dr. Yin. I think he should see how I view the world, and send my father a message."

"Yes, Madam," Mr. Oppenheimer said.

"Don't do anything drastic," Ms. Prosperina said. "I will be flying in soon, make the preparations." Then the cellular line clicked dead.

Chapter Eighteen

As Earth constantly orbited the Sun, 1965 kindly passed forward all its love, insight and tragedy into 1966, and then 1967 then thoughtlessly barged forward only to be absorbed into 1968. Professor Quan had continued his experiments to discover the genetic magic hidden within Elvis's hair. He sensed something elusive hidden within each helical DNA strand. In the meantime, Captain Lovins had been tracking the development of their first two test subjects, they had added a few more new subjects, and had started to collect samples from other significant people that Professor Quan thought might be useful to create a control group to compare with the Elvis sample.

"She grows strong," Professor Quan said. He sat back on his leather lounger.

"How do you know that?" Captains asked.

"I'm not sure," Professor Quan said. He took off his glasses. "It is an odd thing, sort of like having an evil twin, to know what someone is thinking that you've never met."

Captain Lovins stared down at his polished boots.

"Glad she's not in my head," Captain Lovins said.

"But I don't think she can read my mind," Professor Quan said. He pointed his forefinger forward. "Otherwise, she would have given us up long ago, but she knows I exist, she thinks of me and wonders where I am, and of those meteorites."

Captain Lovins sucked in a deep breath. He shook his head.

"Want to laugh?" Captain Lovins asked. He slowly released his breath. He pulled out a file folder.

"I need that," Professor Quan said.

"Our first subject, Bill, the bigger one," Captain Lovins said. He opened a manila folder. He folded back the top page. "He bought a 1967 Mustang, a convertible."

Professor Quan laughed and clapped his hands.

"Oh joy," Professor Quan said. "He is progressing."

"Yeah, Phi Beta Kappa," Captain Lovins said. He grinned. "Saxophone player, guess his IQ boost worked."

Professor Quan stared forward, immersed in thought. He crossed his spindly legs. He sipped his green tea from a paper cup. He clutched for his wooden kaleidoscope.

"Let me guess, our blond headed boy, the happy faced one," Professor Quan said. He studied through the kaleidoscopes eyehole. "He's not quite there."

"No, he's bounced a bit, but he is working to finish a degree in history," Captain Lovins said. He dabbed his forefinger on the tip of his tongue. He folded over the paper from the subject file. "But keeps playing his guitar, he's writing poems."

"An artist's heart at work, I sense that about him," Professor Quan said. "He just needs a little more time to learn his true talent, I know them both."

"I have not a clue what to think," Captain Lovins said.

"Random nature," Professor Quan said.

Captain Lovins stared over at his friend. He dropped the folders into his briefcase.

"You don't believe that," Captain Lovins said.

Professor Quan shifted back in the simple cushion chair. He stared down at his mesh-covered shoes.

"No," Professor Quan said. He set his kaleidoscope on the side table next to the chair.

"Then why? Why say that," Captain Lovins said. "Comforts me to lie to myself," Professor Quan said. He gazed over at this science stations. "I can go hide there, what I know, what I see, it scares me, actually, terrifies me."

"I can't do that, I need the truth," Captain Lovins said. He closed the file folder. "It's not in my DNA, not to."

Professor Quan wagged his forefinger over at Captain Lovin as he got up, and walked over to a science table.

"What?" Captain Lovins said.

"Do you have any idea what you said?" Professor Quan asked.

"Ah, not a clue," Captain Lovins said. He shrugged.

"You said, 'It's not in my DNA,'" Professor Quan said. He manically waved his hands in the air.

"What?" Captain Lovins said.

"No, don't you see?" Professor Quan asked.

"No," Captain Lovins said.

"Actually, it is in your DNA," Professor Quan said. He clapped his hands. "Seriously, it's how genes get turned on or off, but all the instructions are there, waiting."

"How's that?" Captain Lovins asked.

With his arms folded behind him, Professor Quan started to pace back and forth.

"It's right in front of us," Professor Quan said. He reached down for his kaleidoscope, he fidgeted with it, he paced faster back and forth. "I can sense it, the answer."

"Calm down," Captain Lovins said. He grasped his hands on his hips. "Going to give yourself a heart attack."

"That's the point," Professor Quan said. He shook his fore-finger at Captain Lovins.

"Man you're fired up," Captain Lovins said.

"Instructions, life choices," Professor Quan said. "Within that hair, genetic instructions whispered to Elvis that he could sing, and he should wiggle on the Ed Sullivan Show?"

"Instincts?" Captain Lovins asked.

"Yes," Professor Quan said. "But the problem, it's like picking through grains of sand along a foamy shore. I can isolate genes, I'm not sure which ones will-"

For some odd reason, Captain Lovins knew to keep quiet, and he simply sat back on a metal chair. He watched Professor Quan work and think. If it were not for the sounds of the electrical current coursing through the fluorescent lights, it was quiet enough within the laboratory he could almost hear his own heartbeat.

"I've been thinking of this the wrong way," Professor Quan said. He faintly smiled over at Captain Lovins. "It's just like when I created that genetic starter, it's not about comparing Elvis's hair sample with other samples, or even my sample, it's not about IQ, but there are other genes that-"

"Yeah?" Captain Lovins said.

"Think, lots of stupid smart people," Professor Quan said.

"I've met a few," Captain Lovins said. He leaned forward with his elbows on his knees.

"I want our subjects to sort of sense her," Professor Quan said. He scratched his clean-shaven chin. "If they sense her, they can fight her evil."

"Yeah," Captain Lovins said. "Only way to deal with a bully, have to step up, face them."

"It's deeper, than genes, amino acids," Professor Quan said. His hands stuffed in his lab coat. "It's guidance, perhaps an Angel gene? That hidden nudge."

Captain Lovins got up and took in a deep breath. He clutched the briefcase handle and slowly strolled over to set it next to his office door. As he walked back he shook his head, he shrugged.

"Hmm, you mean serendipity?" Captain Lovins said. He yawned.

"Yes, happy accidents," Professor Quan said. "But not-"

"Keep working," Captain Lovins said. He checked the security of the laboratory entrance. He tested the alarm settings.

"Not so funny thing, it's like when you're a child blowing a dandelion seed head, from far away, in a field it looks like a wispy planet," Professor Quan said. He tapped his lips with his fingers. "But up close, as each unique floret floats away, just depends on how the breeze bends, but is the breeze random?"

"Keep working," Captain Lovins said. He yawned.

"I will, it's odd," Professor Quan said.

"Yeah?" Captain Lovins said.

"Within out genetic structure, some get extra chromosomes, some have both sex organs," Professor Quan said. He shrugged.

"Hermaphrodite," Captains Lovins said. He crossed his arms. "Creeps me out."

"Yes, not their fault," Professor Quan said. He strolled through the laboratory. "Why?"

"That, I have never thought about," Captain Lovins said.

"Humans might be born with XX, or XY or XYY, XXY, even XXX," Professor Quan said. He shrugged. "Each has their own unique genetic structure, each has unique fingerprints, even their irises are distinct, but-" He tapped his shoe against the metal science table leg.

"But?" Captain Lovins said.

Professor Quan picked up his kaleidoscope. He handed it to Captain Lovins who crinkled his face at Professor Quan.

"Look inside," Professor Quan said.

Captain Lovins awkwardly gazed into the eyepiece. He twisted the cylinder back and forth with his fingertips.

"What do you see?" Professor Quan asked.

"Well, ah," Captain Lovins said. He continued to twist the cylinder for the kaleidoscope. "Crazy bright color, triangles, weird shapes-"

"Observer of beautiful forms," Professor said. He stared past Captain Lovins. "That's what kaleidoscope means."

"Sure," Captain Lovins said. He handed the kaleidoscope back to Professor Quan.

"Through the view finder, it might seem random, at first," Professor Quan said. He put another, larger kaleidoscope to his left eye. "But there is order, a beautiful predictable pattern."

"You've got that crazy look," Captain Lovins said.

"A pattern is right in front of me that is so simple I cannot see it," Professor Quan said. "It will change everything, it is the seed that will slowly eradicate her, simple answers are the best answers."

"Yet, you'll find it," Captain Lovins said. He winked at Professor Quan as he walked toward his office. "Just like breaking an encrypted code, right?"

"A code created from the dawn of man, not 1's and 0's?" Professor Quan said. He crossed his arms, and rapidly paced within the laboratory. "But something deeper than X's and Y's, past all of those amino acid instructions, there is a particle I need to discover, figure how to turn it on."

"By your look," Captain Lovins said. He clicked on his office lights. "Guess we need more DNA samples?"

"These will not be easy missions," Professor Quan said.

"What or rather who do you have in mind?" Captain Lovins said. He turned to face Professor Quan, he stood up straight, erect. His hands gripped his waist.

"I think I should create us a shopping list," Professor Quan said. He opened his experiment logbook. "What causes some people to act, while others do not?"

"I don't know," Captain Lovins said.

"That is what I need to find," Professor Quan said. He clicked a pen top thrusting the ink forward. "If I can discover that particle, I can use it with a genetic starter, all these samples will be quite useful. But, there has to be a common link. And then, we can share our discovery, and our dangerous girl will find her goals difficult to achieve, she will not have any advantage, she will be exposed, they will learn what she is thinking, and figure out how to stop her."

Captain Lovins shook his head in agreement with Professor Quan. He turned and set the files on his desk, he clicked off his office lights.

"Get your list together," Captain Lovins said. "In the meantime, I'm going to bed."

Chapter Nineteen

As Eddie drove his forest green jalopy on the left highway lane, and it past an eighteen-wheeler, he rolled his driver side window down. The spring breeze tasseled with his thick brown hair, as the chill perked him and he sojourned toward Memphis. A city named after an ancient Egyptian capital that had settled near the west bank of the Nile River. An interstate sign indicated thirty miles from his destination, Eddie glanced up and down at the road, he nervously pressed in Charlene's cell number and waited listening to the dial tone.

"Edward?" Charlene asked.

"Ah, Charlene?" Eddie asked.

"Yes, this is Charlene." Her voice was not a strange falsetto, instead, a smooth, intelligent baritone.

"Most people just call me Eddie."

"Mines Charles, but they call me, Charlene, so which shall it be?" Charlene asked. She lightly chuckled.

"Eddie," he said. He turned the car onto the right lane, and a chrome-invested hot rod pasted him in the left lane.

"Eddie, we look forward to your visit. But be warned, Raquel will likely call you what she likes. Do you have good directions to our place?" Charlene asked.

"I think so, I'll call if I get lost, there by seven or so. Is that okay?" Eddie said. His moist fingers gripped the hard steering wheel.

"Oh for heaven sakes, yes, we'll have a delightful dinner prepared, we welcome your visit. See you soon, Eddie."

The phone clicked silent. As Eddie stared forward, he tried to imagine Charlene. He crinkled his mouth. Uncertain how to achieve his perceived wacky goal, he would need luck, as in the Moirae sisters had spun him a golden thread shot through a serendipitous eye of the needle karma like good luck. He groaned, as if hypnotized by the freeway stripes passing by him like rhythmic reflective photon bullets.

"Jim Bob's done for," Eddie mumbled. He glanced at his reflection from rearview mirror. "An why am I doing this?"

Eddie drove his car south by southeast, the highway flowed as if a concrete river, he navigated along within the dense traffic, then he merged onto Interstate 40. There the highway forked off like an encircling protective moat around Memphis. The signage coordinated him toward the Poplar Road exit. There he proceeded east towards Germantown with a heading toward Anesidora Boulevard.

"Anesidora?" Eddie whispered. He stopped his automobile and studied the street sign. He looked down Anesidora Boulevard. It had a canopied dense forest of jagged hundred-year old laurel oaks distilling the golden sunset into single rays of light that reflected off the uneven red brick streets. Eddie parked his four-banger near the Turnbull's address. The early evening glow cascaded across the perfectly manicured lawn. The Turnbull's lived in high style, in an ante bellum, Greek revival mansion. It faced a southern perspective, with distressed winter white painted brick; and cobalt blue shutters flanked the windows. It had a recessed mahogany front double door. A weathered red brick wall surrounded the property, engrossed in blue sea green hued moss. With his head down, Eddie loped toward the front door with his duffle bag slung over his shoulder. A woman or he assumed a woman, emerged from behind the mansion's western side.

"Come this way," the woman said. She waved at him, she was about tall with a swimmer build, and she combed her dark brown shoulder length hair back. "Edward?"

"Yeah, Eddie's fine," Eddie said. "Are you Char-"

"No, inside, that's all well and good, but your mother named you Edward," the woman said. She marched up to Eddie. Her hands were on her thin hips. "I like the name Edward, it's an English king's name and Eddie makes you seem weak. I trust you are not a weak man."

Eddie slightly backed up and shrugged.

"I, ah," Eddie said.

"I'm Raquel." She held out her right hand.

Clevenger had described Raquel as attractive. Her beautiful face complimented her fit body. She tightly gripped Eddie's hand; she had the hands of a gardener. But it was her eyes; her dark blue eyes entranced Eddie. Her eyes could melt icebergs.

"Is that your green hornet?" Raquel asked.

"Ah, yeah-" Eddie said. He blushed.

"Well, park it on the left-hand side of our garage. Charlene will drive tomorrow," Raquel said. She waved him to follow. "In my college days, I had forest green six stroke love machine."

"Oh?" Eddie asked. He hustled along side Raquel.

"That's where I met Charles. I loved that love machine, kept the oil filtered, and had *a lot* of fun in it," Raquel said. She winked a hole through Eddie. She chuckled. "Sorry, Charles tells me not to have a potty mouth, I'll try to behave."

Eddie fidgeted with his right ear lobe that had turned burnt red orange.

"Okay," Eddie said.

"Enough of my collegiate reminiscing, hand me your bag. Just come on in the back door," Raquel said. They stood near the corner of the massive house next to a row of perfectly maintained azaleas. "I think you will like your room. I just finished decorating, you're our first test subject."

"Yeah?" Eddie said. He started to back away toward his car.

"In more ways than one, we don't have many house guests," Raquel said. She sashayed away with Eddie's bag. He wobbled over to his car like a decrepit palace chauffeur. He drove it up the lengthy brick, herringbone pattern driveway; he parked near the five-car garage. With his hands in his pants pockets, Eddie walked toward the recessed back door. The environment smelled of fragrant roses. He stepped up two blue slate stairs. Even though Raquel advised him to come in, Eddie knocked with the back of his left hand knuckles on the six-panel mahogany back door.

"Come on in." Raquel's voice resonated from inside the house. He opened the mortised lock door, and he shifted through the entrance. He peeked inside. After he blinked his eyes several times, his vision adjusted to the brightly lit kitchen. It had custom-built mustard yellow cabinets, and a blue gray soapstone countertop.

"Come on over here," Raquel said. She waved him over.

Eddie skirted past the butcher-block island with a cove ogee royal profile. To his left was a massive bay window that provided a panoramic view of the home's free form pool, backed by a trellised rose garden, and beyond a tennis court. A Spanish refectory table was parallel to the bay window, surrounded by eight Louis XV period chaises where the family sat. Raquel held her right hand out like a game show model featuring major appliances. She directed Eddie's eyes toward two thin-faced teenagers with sandy brown hair and pale blue eyes.

"I'm Charles, Jr., and I'll always be a Charles," he said. He stared past Eddie into the kitchen.

"My name is Samantha. You can call me Sam."

"Nice to meet you all," Eddie said. He thought the teenager's expressions were rather odd, as if trapped inside an electromagnetic bubble bouncing randomly in deep dark outer space. Eddie sensed someone behind him. He turned to find a lanky humanoid inspecting a plastic bag of food from a pullout refrigerator drawer.

"I'm Charlene," she said. She strolled over and firmly shook Eddie's hand. She had straight light brown hair, a five o'clock shadow wearing a fashionable purple paisley dress cut just below the knee. "Great to meet you-"

"Hi, I'm, ah," Eddie said. His cheeks flushed a ripe Georgia peach as all the hair across his body woke up. And the rim of his ears turned a lovely crimson hue.

"I trust your drive was uneventful?" Charlene asked.

Eddie thought her protruding Adams apple like a Boa constrictor squeezing down an unfortunate mouse. He connected with the teenagers' demeanors. As if two ice sculptors, both stared into space, begging anyone to end their suffering, to let them melt away into liquid time.

"Ah, they were, ah perfect," Eddie said. His eyes fixated on Charlene. She ignored Eddie's curious gaze.

"Terrific, I'm hungry. Hope you are," Charlene said.

"First, let me show you to your room," Raquel said.

After a few moments, they returned to the kitchen. Eddie sat across from Charles, Jr.

"Dude, golf tournament should be cool," Charles Jr. said.

"Yeah, hope so," Eddie said.

"You're from Nashville? That's such a wonderful city full of culture, music and higher education," Raquel said. She sat back and crossed her long, thin legs.

"Yes, well, actually Brentwood, just outside Nashville," Eddie said. Raquel's hypnotic gaze aroused him. He averted his gawk by glancing out the bay windows.

"Such a lovely part of Nashville," Raquel said. She followed Eddie's gaze. "You like my roses? I spend hour after hour pruning them. Do you enjoy gardening?"

"Oh, no, I just noticed how beautiful they are," Eddie said.

Raquel sat forward. She smacked her hands together.

"So, tell me about your people," Raquel asked. Behind her was the family room, there were numerous family photos and works of art atop a baby grand piano, the room centered by a well-used stone fireplace, now cold and empty.

"Mom lives there," Eddie said.

"And your father?" Raquel asked. Her tone was of a cross examining attorney.

"He passed away," Eddie said.

"Sorry," Raquel said. She studied his face. "Recently?"

"No, when I was thirteen," Eddie said.

"Thirteen? Tough age," Raquel said. "What did he do?"

"He was a plant manager, passed away at work from a heart attack," Eddie said. He sucked in enough oxygen to fill his lungs, and he slowly released the carbon monoxide.

"Hmm, thirteen," Raquel said. She stared up at the coffered ceiling and appeared to be looking for Charlene.

"Can I offer you a glass of wine?" Charlene asked. She gave Raquel a curious look.

"You were just a boy," Raquel said wistfully. She shifted and glanced over at her quiet children. "But, I don't think it really matters how old you are, once they're gone, there is a giant void inside, as if someone just pulled your heart out, put it in a box and hid it. At least that's how I feel."

"Sure," Eddie said. He looked back over at Charlene, as she had already poured the wine into a crystal glass. She set it in front of Eddie.

"Here you go," Charlene said. She stared over at Raquel. "Simmer down love."

"Thank you," Eddie said.

"I was an adult, eleven years ago, when my parents died, auto accident, they told me they died instantly. I doubt that, they just say things to keep you calm. I still pick up the phone to call them, and then I remember no one is at the other end," Raquel said. She clenched her jaw. "Sucks if you ask me, love can be cruel, snap of your fingers, they're dead."

Eddie stared down at the inspecting the table wood grains.

"I try to remember him sometimes, but it's hard," Eddie said. He gripped the crystal wine goblet at the stem. "Sort of a lonely feeling, I don't know."

"That sucks," Sam said. She tore apart some fresh bread; the she chomped it down.

Raquel sipped the deep cherry colored wine from her glass.

"They didn't just pass away. I think pass is too wimpy a word, or just as bad, lost them, I hate both," Raquel said staring at Sam and then over at Charles, Jr. "Sort of, like I dropped them off for an extended vacation, and I forgot to go back and pick them up at the airport. But, I know exactly where to find them, at least their carcasses."

"Darling," Charlene said. She set a bowl full of salad on the table, she shifted a tray full of sliced vegetables.

"Mom, you can be so after it," Charles Jr. said.

Raquel sipped her wine. She shrugged. She innocently looked over at Charles, Jr. and then over at Eddie.

"No, I prefer died, dead, killed. It makes life more cut and dried," Raquel said. She sliced the air in front of her. She glanced over at Charlene who had coughed to accidentally, on purpose clear her throat.

"Simmer, my love," Charlene said.

"Unfortunately, we're no longer on speaking terms with Charlene's family, so we do understand feeling lonely," Rachel said. She pursed her lips, and stared at Eddie.

Eddie readjusted his moist butt in the cushioned chair.

"You in college?" Eddie asked Sam.

Sam twisted her head. She sneered at Eddie.

"Cute, no I'm in high school," Sam said. She had the same alley cat instincts of her mother, Eddie thought.

"What do you think about my parents? Winning the three hundred million lotto was pretty cool from a last minute gas station ticket," Sam said. She wiggled her shoulders back, gripped her long ponytail, and rewound the holder. She glanced at her parents without moving her head. "We used to live in a house down the street about half this size, but then those six lucky numbers lined up. At least if I behave, you know keep quiet, I'll never be poor."

"Sam," Charlene said. She poured some wine. "Simmer down."

"That's cool," Eddie said. "I'm curious, Anesidora? Was that someone famous down here? Jazz or something?"

Raquel, Sam and Charles Jr. shrugged their shoulders and gave each other puzzled glances.

"Are you a fan of the classics?" Charlene asked. She had kind eyes, and a thoughtful gaze.

"Classics?" Eddie asked.

"What like old un-cool music? Makes me fall asleep," Charles Jr. said. He continued to eat with his mouth open.

Charlene chuckled.

"No my son, what I mean is Greek and Roman mythology."

"Pandora? Now I remember, Anesidora is a synonym for Pandora," Eddie said. He grinned over at Charlene.

"I love that stuff, everything has a deeper, metaphorical meaning," Charlene said. She held the wine bottle like a tall French waiter. "More wine?"

"It puts me to sleep, too," Raquel said. She cocked her head over at her children. They chuckled in surround sound. "Boring-"

"Laugh all you want wise-acres," Charlene said.

"She let all the evils into the world," Eddie said.

"Exactly, but what did she leave in the box?" Charlene asked.

Eddie crossed his arms, sat back and he looked up at the ornate ceiling. He thought his high school teachers would be proud that he actually remembered.

"Come on," Charlene said. They all stopped eating and stared at Eddie. After a few moments, Eddie stared over at Charlene. "You know it, it's in there."

"Hope," Eddie said. He thought about Ardee.

"Hope, you get an A plus," Charlene said. She paused for a reflective moment, she sighed. "I've tried not to lose hope." Charlene stared back across the table at Raquel.

"Sorry," Eddie said. He took a generous sip. The wine had a velvety texture, and tasted like intense blackberry jam.

"So Eddie, what's your job?" Sam said.

"I ah, work for Insurance Professionals. Your Uncle Clevenger's my boss," Eddie said. He shrugged.

"That's what I heard," Sam said. She grinned. "Sucks to be you, a seriously weird dude-"

Charles, Jr. elbowed Sam. A half-chewed piece of steak was stuffed in his mouth like a farmer chewing a wad of tobacco.

"Oh man, he's a really strange dude with all that Civil War crap. I have to turn away to keep from laughing in his face with that goofy looking goatee," Charles, Jr. said. He snorted.

"Charles," Raquel said. "I'm sorry about that."

"Enough Charles," Charlene said. She sliced into the steak without looking up. "Simmer, both of you."

"Oh, no worries," Eddie said. He choose not to add that Clevenger's halitosis made his eyes water.

"Well, a goatee is nothing, what do you think about our dad preparing to change teams?" Sam asked.

"I don't understand?" Eddie said. He gulped more wine. The acidity and conversation caused his skin to blush crimson. His scalp felt as though his head wrapped in one of Jim Bob's tin foil experiments.

"You know what Sam's asking. Our dad's getting his package replaced with chicks stuff," Charles, Jr. said.

Eddie sat deer hunter still, he thought he might teleport to another dimension via a nifty wormhole in the pine wood floor.

"Enough," Charlene said. Her voice sounded like an unseen thunderclap. The teenagers froze in their cushioned chairs.

"I loved Charles, but now I think I feel closer to women than I do men, I get the best of all worlds," Raquel said. Her gaze pierced through the children. Then she over stared at Eddie. "Is it so wrong?"

Eddie's vision blurred as if looking through hazy unfocused binoculars. He blinked rapidly. Charles, Jr. and Sam stared down at their partially eaten dinners.

"I ah, ah, not sure what to say," Eddie said.

"I guess you *did* get to be the test case," Charlene said. She reached out and tapped on the table. "I apologize, we're all grappling with unimagined, ah changes."

"No reason to apologize," Eddie whispered. He coughed.

Charlene tapped her thick forefinger on the table to get the teenagers attentions.

"I think it best you two finish dinners in your rooms. Say goodnight to Mr. Wilcox, time to skedaddle," Charlene said.

They glided past Eddie with their full plates, expressed their regrets, and headed to safe alcoves hidden on the homes second floor. The family tension replaced with silence but for the sound of forks and knives hitting the Flow Blue China.

Charlene sighed. She took in an exaggerated breath. She sipped the wine glass that reflected specs of light from the dimmed ceiling light fixtures.

"I know you find my appearance difficult to comprehend. In reality, it's just odd for everyone," Charlene said.

"I assure you we're not freaks, you won't catch any diseases, and his DNA is the same," Raquel said.

"I'm altering my appearance with a feminizing regimen," Charlene said. "The right pill, poof, you can alter *things*, modern science."

Raquel reached forward; she placed her warm hand on Eddie's right forearm.

"We hope you will accept us, not judge us," Raquel said.

Eddie's mind swirled from the wine and the bizarre reality. He had the distinct feeling he might black out, and wondered if he was dreaming, or had dropped down an electromagnetic wormhole into another dimensional reality he had read about from science fiction novels.

"I'm not, sophisticated about these matters. I do understand you care about each other, and I think that's the most important thing," Eddie said. He sucked in some oxygen. He glanced back and forth at Charlene and Raquel. "The one thing I always remember, my father always told me he loved me, he always called my mother, his love, I know that's what should matter the most," Eddie said. He shrugged. "Thank you for inviting me."

Charlene chuckled. She kindly stared at Eddie. She scratched her unshaven chin. She stared over at Raquel.

"You're being kind, sorry about all this heresy, I'll probably get to burn in hell," Charlene said. She paused for a moment and glanced out the bay window. "Regardless, we are pleased to have you visit."

"Yes we are," Raquel said.

"We'll have fun tomorrow, I promise you that," Charlene said. She stared back over at Eddie. "As you might imagine, the club membership just loves me."

Chapter Twenty

Captain Lovins marched into the laboratory with his backpack slung over his shoulder as if a paramilitary Santa Claus.

"Man, I'll remember '71, it has turned out to be fun year," Captain Lovins said. He lifted the backpack onto a wooden table. "I've got samples." He glanced over at Professor Quan who sat completely reclined on his back, splayed across his cushioned lounger aimlessly staring up at the ceiling. His bio-hazard smock haphazardly loose, his arms dangled over the sides.

"Hmm, indeed," Professor Quan whispered. He made a faint wave with his latex gloved forefinger over at Captain Lovins.

Captain Lovins stared over at Professor Quan.

"You okay?" Captain Lovins asked. He smacked his hands together. He pulled out a plastic bag from his backpack. "Man, I snagged that lefty pro tennis players wrist bands, it was a snap, that Australian just threw them at me."

Captain Lovins moved in closer to Professor Quan.

"Seriously, you okay?" Captain Lovins asked.

"Without question, hmm, nice going," Professor Quan said. He sighed. His tone was low, calm; his eyes seemed unfocused, lost, floating in a tranquil space.

Captain Lovins strolled over to in front of Professor Quan. "You look, well mellow, been getting happy here in the lab?"

Professor Quan took off his hood. He slipped off his latex gloves. He stared up directly into Captain Lovins eyes.

"I found it, or it found me, I'm not exactly sure," Professor Quan said. He shook his head. "I felt everything."

"What did you do?" Captain Lovins asked.

As Professor Quan wiggled forward, he held his hand out as Captain Lovins pulled him up off the recliner. He wobbled to his feet, his eyelids glazed with moisture.

"I know where it, ah, they hide, not sure," Professor Quan said. He tore off his garments and stuffed them into a container destined for incineration. "Life will never be the same."

"Okay, I know I won't get this," Captain Lovins said.

"For one, keep chasing down samples, I'll keep getting you a shopping list," Professor Quan said. He humbly smiled at Captain Lovins. "The most beautiful thing I have ever seen, but mostly, a complete sensation."

Captain Lovins walked over to Professor Quan. He carefully studied into his glazed eyes. But Professor Quan simply grinned, he bear-hugged him.

"Okay, I didn't expect that," Captain Lovins said. He backed up a few steps from Professor Quan. He crossed his arms.

"I now know how every gene works, how the amino acids, the protein instructions work, I've broken the code," Professor Quan said. He fiddled his fingers in front of his face. "We can fight her, she cannot overcome what I found."

"I knew you'd figure it out," Captain Lovins said. "But ah, going forward, I'm not the huggable type."

"I love you," Professor Quan said. He grinned.

"Whoa now," Captain Lovins said.

"No, no, not like that," Professor Quan said. He stared down at the terrazzo floor, and then over at the doorway to his gene therapy rooms. "It's so simple, yet, complex, pure love, yes, it has to be, love."

"Okay, I think, this is getting kind of weird," Captain Lovins said. He backed away from Professor Quan.

Professor Quan shuffled his eyeglasses up his nose. He put on his white lab coat. Then he leaned his elbow against a genetic analyzer encased in thick sheet metal.

"While you were out, I decided to take the Hope Diamond and instead of shooting energy through it horizontally, with it on its side, as I've done before," Professor Quan said. He opened his lab notebook. As he reviewed his experiment notes, he folded several pages over. "But this time, I set it beneath a tray of genetic material, mixed in restriction enzymes within a gel solution, a common practice. Then I inserted a radioactive probe but strung it down to the center point of the diamond. I placed the diamond on a three-prong copper pedestal with reflecting mirrors underneath at the center-most point between three high intensity thermal

UV lamps set in a perfect triangle, and with an electrode and magnet taped beneath the diamond conductor. I simultaneously fired the thermal UV lamps, and switched on the high voltage electrical current."

"Where do you come up with this?" Captain Lovins asked.

"I don't know," Professor Quan said. He shrugged.

"I did volunteer for this," Captain Lovins said. He nodded. "Right?" He gripped his waist.

"I did the experiment within a vacuum environment, inside here, like it's in dead black space, so I hooded it, to block out any visible light within the lab," Professor Quan said. He closed his notebook. He paused and wobbled a bit. "Nothing should be able to survive inside that environment."

"Hello, earth to you," Captain Lovins said. He snapped his fingers in front of Professor Quan's face.

"Sorry, sorry," Professor Quan said. He faintly grinned. "Thankfully, I had your welding mask on to block out the initial intensity inside the machine." He tapped against the machine's thick glass. He wiped away a tear from his eye.

"What did you see?" Captain Lovins asked. After Professor Quan scooted along, he followed in behind him, examined the glass panel for the genetic analyzer, and studied inside at the mobile rectangular tray that moved beneath a microscope with the viewfinders sealed outside the environment.

"I saw God," Professor Quan whispered.

Captain Lovins crinkled his face.

"Oh, God just popped up in here?" Captain Lovins asked. He tapped the glass with the back of hand. "Hi, I'm God."

"No, it's hard to explain, I guess I'd label it God," Professor Quan said. With his palms up in front of him, he shrugged. "I've never been religious, you know that, but, that's what I sensed, total love."

"Guess we're going to visit with the snake charmers down the hill?" Captain Lovins said. He crossed his arms, and then thrust his right hand up. "Yes, we shall be healed!"

"No, such the doubting Thomas, I will show you," Professor Quan said. He pointed at Captain Lovins. "I can set the experiment up quickly, then you tell me what you see?"

Captain Lovins twisted his shoulders back and forth, and moved with his thick neck to allow his spine to loosen. He studied inside the machine again and shrugged.

"Yeah, I have to see this," Captain Lovins said. He shook his head back and forth. He tapped at the machine with his forefinger. "God is not hiding in there, this is way too simple, and how will this stop that thing you created?"

And within short order Professor Quan replicated his experiment set-up. Then he draped the machine with a black sheet, Captain Lovins flipped the welding mask over his face, and he stared down into the vacuum environment. Professor Quan stood next to him and explained how the mechanism functioned.

"Flip this rubber switch," Professor Quan said. He pointed down to a plastic nob. "It will take a few seconds, the tray will slide forward, then it will seem as though a star exploded within the machine. But be patient, give it a few more seconds, then you can take off the mask, look into the microscope view finder, the lens illuminates at 200x, down at a Nano level, so watch along that tray, in it, you will note the dark strings, they are slices of DNA, okay? Examine them after they bond, the nucleotides, tell me what you see."

"The what?" Captain Lovins said.

"What will happen is the base pair, you'll have codon and anti-codons, a chain, positive and negative, ah," Professor Quan said. However, Captain Lovins flipped the mask up.

"The what?" Captain Lovins asked.

"Ah, never mind," Professor Quan said. "Just watch for the hydrogen bonding, you'll know it when you see, just be careful to let the intense energy stop first, that's the experiment, before you look into the viewfinder for the results."

"I can do this," Captain Lovins said. He quickly flipped the mask down over his face.

Professor Quan slipped from behind the curtain, and then he turned with his back to the machine.

"Whenever you're ready," Professor Quan said. He held his hands together in a prayer position. He closed his eyes.

And with little hesitation, Captain Lovins flicked the switch. Instantly, the thermal UV lamps and electromagnetic current fired through the Hope Diamond blasting from a single spark of pure energy. The diamond began to glow a burnt orange hue, then a beam shot up along the radioactive link up into the gel, causing an electrical wave to cascade across the genetic material. It immersed the breathless vacuum environment with a bright white interstellar luminosity as if Captain Lovins was observing an exploding Super Nova within deep space encircled by ever present, Dark Matter. Protected from behind the welding mask, Captain Lovins instinctively squinted with his eyes, and held his hands up to shield his face. Then he remembered Professor Quan advising him to wait for a few seconds, to be patient. After the initial shock wave dissipated, he carefully flipped up the welding mask. He leaned forward, and gazed into the viewfinder. The gel appeared as if sand after a summer time storm along a coastline, the foamy remains from along a sandy shore after crashing waves had dissolved back into the ocean. The gel material seemed to be cooling after the strings sequenced, bonding together as one. Then it happened, from each three-string intersection a golden orb rose from within the bound sequences. Captain Lovins thought it odd that the orbs appeared suddenly, as if tiny suns casting cosmic rays from one to the other. He realized they were in complete harmony. But Captain Lovins also noticed that for each Sun, there was an ever present dark spec orbiting its perfection. And at that moment, Captain Lovins sensed that each Sun seemed to simultaneously notice him. Although they were faceless, they seemed alive, and they welcomed his presence. They seemed to beckon him forward to absorb him into their light. And as they continued to burn, Captain Lovins sensed being embraced, his skin felt warm as if they had wrapped him within a baby blanket. He had the sensation that his life had mattered, a calm, content sensation that he was as important as any king who ruled over a vast empire. But as quickly as the singular fires had burned in unity, they disappeared into nothingness.

Captain Lovins slowly took off the welding mask. He huffed; his shaking hand pulled back the black curtain, and he saw Professor Quan waiting for him. He threw the welding mask down the lab floor like a bowling ball.

"I understand why you hugged me," Captain Lovins said.

"I've never felt perfect love, until now," Professor Quan said. He walked forward and hugged Captain Lovins.

"I don't know what happened, it's not just energy," Captain Lovins said. He leaned his hand against a science table.

"I do," Professor Quan said. He backed up. "God revealed to us the answer we have searched for."

"How so?" Captain Lovins asked.

"For ever more, for each child we chose, we must first listen to our instincts, and then chose the right gene instructions, we know this," Professor Quan said. The laboratory was still and as quiet as an abandoned chapel. "And from those instructions that we discover from our shopping list, with each there will be golden orbs that will bond with our new genetic starter. A whispered thought within their genetic structures, for them a thought as powerful as to encourage our subjects to seek their destiny. And for us, they will have the thought to seek courage in the face of evil. A simple thought, so simple I had missed it for years, you see, each life is important, they are not random, there is a purpose, and a reason-"

Captain Lovins stepped forward and put his hand on Professor Quan's left shoulder.

"I've got this," Captain Lovins said. He gently patted Professor Quan. "Love, that they are loved."

"Yes, the one universal feeling she is incapable of," Professor Quan said. His eyes misted over with happiness. "And we found it, she cannot vanquish love, if you love beyond yourself, you're no longer afraid of death, or evil."

"No, you found it," Captain Lovins said. "I just saw it, but most of all, you're right, I felt it."

"More like stumbled," Professor Quan said. He pulled the black curtain of the genetic analyzer. He adjusted his lab coat at the lapels. "Nucleotides, bond to form a codon, and an anti-codon, everything is in threes, remove one from three, it falls apart." He fidgeted with a kaleidoscope. "In perfect harmony, but the mystery for me is why does the structure become defective?"

"What do you mean?" Captain Lovins asked.

"A child is born with an obvious defect, for example, a cleft palate, so forth," Professor Quan said. As he paced, he clutched his hands behind his lower back, and stared down at the floor. "Perhaps a time released defect like heart disease, certain cancers, but for them to bond in the first place, there has to be love, that thing we both just saw under a microscope, what I called, God, it bonds together all our living cells."

"I don't know," Captain Lovins whispered. "I guess it's about not losing hope, to keep going."

"I don't know either, the more I learn," Professor Quan said. He tapped at the base of the genetic analyzer with his brown shoe. "The more questions I have, the more I realize I really don't know much."

Captain Lovins glanced at Professor Quan, for some odd reason, he stood reflecting on his life, his decision to seek a military career. The people he had left behind, the pretty girl he once loved. The family he never met, or the family he never created. But most of all, he wondered for the first time in his life what it would have felt like to be a father. The idea to love beyond reason, a feeling that has no words.

"Quite a day," Captain Lovins said.

"Indeed, I should pay more attention to the heavens," Professor Quan said. He peered into his kaleidoscope's eyepiece; he held it to the ceiling light and twisted it back and forth as if a sea captain searching for navigational points of light. "From beyond us, in the stars, something is trying communicate."

Chapter Twenty One

The high performance business jet with a passenger of one had scorched the transatlantic journey in less than six hours to burst beneath the bulbous dark grey clouds. Mr. Oppenheimer thought it like a fire-breathing black dragon swooping down from the darkness within the unsuspecting Nashville inhabitants. It landed and efficiently rolled into the empty executive airport hangar, where it stopped, began to gear down and within a few moments, Ms. Prosperina emerged. She was wearing her customary black sunglasses, he outfit a dark blue pants suit with a fashionable red scarf around her neck. Her blonde hair pulled back into a neat bun. She menaced her petite five-foot frame forward to square in front of Mr. Oppenheimer.

"Madam," Mr. Oppenheimer said.

"Do you have Dr. Yin?" Ms. Prosperina asked. He expression blank, unemotional as she looked up at Mr. Oppenheimer.

"Yes, Madam," Mr. Oppenheimer said. He reached forward to grab her computer bag. "He's in a safe location, as you instructed, it is an isolated area."

Ms. Prosperina faintly grinned.

"Good," Ms. Prosperina said. She glanced around the hangar inspecting back down the concrete runway and studied the outline of the downtown Nashville skyline. Her plane's pilot and crew silently exited into a nearby office to file the flight report that would not note her existence.

"Shall I take you to your accommodations, or shall we go visit Dr. Yin?" Mr. Oppenheimer asked. He opened the hulking black SUV's back passenger door. He set the computer bag onto the far passenger side on the rubber-matted floorboard.

"This human vessel I'm stuck in needs rest," Ms. Prosperina said. She stuffed her hands in her jacket pockets. She yawned. "I hate being weak, but I've learned to power through it, perhaps a black-eye coffee, then I want to meet this Dr. Yin."

"Yes, Madam," Mr. Oppenheimer said. With his right hand out, he guided Ms. Prosperina onto the back seat. He drove away from the executive airport hangar, and onto the nearby freeway. They traveled away from Nashville; he stopped at a Starry Eyed Coffee Hut for two espresso shots in a medium coffee for Ms. Prosperina. They continued their journey into a modest neighborhood, and drove in front of a storage unit complex. The line of dusty storage units had fake security cameras. A security guard did not staff the front gate booth. It had just a simple chain link fence that encircled the old facility. They drove inside and stopped near the back entrance, concealed by overgrowth and overhanging oak tree limbs that lightly swayed from the gentle southern breeze.

Mr. Oppenheimer pulled up the square metal unit door, and pulled down the light chain. Dr. Yin sat parallel to the door, gagged, blindfolded, and strapped to a cushioned folding chair with armrests. He blindly jerked his head side to side, and nervously wobbled in the rickety chair as Mr. Oppenheimer closed the metal folding door behind them. He placed a cushioned metal chair in front of Dr. Yin for Ms. Prosperina. She sat down, and crossed her thin legs. Mr. Oppenheimer loosened the blindfold, but kept the gag in place. Dr. Yin squinted to adjust to the pale yellow light; he swiveled his right hand as Mr. Oppenheimer plunged an 18 gauge peripheral intravenous line between the knuckles of his middle and index fingers.

"You must be calm, Doctor," Mr. Oppenheimer said. He powerfully gripped Dr. Yin's wrist, he tapped over the dangling line with a ported cannula to provide a secure injection site for Ms. Prosperina. She sat patiently watching Mr. Oppenheimer prepare Dr. Yin. She checked her platinum wristwatch for the time as Mr. Oppenheimer reviewed all the restraint straps, the injection site, satisfied, he then adjusted his shirt cuffs, and buttoned his jacket as he turned to face Ms. Prosperina.

"Madam?" Mr. Oppenheimer asked.

"Nothing, nothing else," Ms. Prosperina said. She waved him away like a common house fly.

Mr. Oppenheimer swiftly opened the storage door and closed it; as instructed, Ms. Prosperina could hear him click the lock shut. Dr. Yin jerked back from the sound. His eyes blazed with moisture and redness staring at the diminutive Ms. Prosperina. Her thick black sunglasses caused her face to appear like a blonde haired wasp. His breathing was erratic as he huffed continuously through his long nose, wondering if she had a poisonous stinger tail.

"Do you know who I am?" Ms. Prosperina asked.

Dr. Yin quickly shook his sweating head side to side. He pushed at the straps across his legs.

"Oh, yes you do," Ms. Prosperina said. She opened her computer bag and slipped out a rectangular tan leather case. "You've wasted a great deal of my resources, you know me, now don't you, don't be shy?"

Dr. Yin tried to gulp. He rapidly shook his head up and down. He tried to talk through the gag, but he only sounded like a dying elk in a cornfield shot with a 180-grain bullet just before the hunter humanely ended its life.

"I'm disappointed," Ms. Prosperina said. She opened the leather case to reveal two syringes with companion hypodermic needles. "Just so you understand, we are not going to have a conversation. I'm not going to kill you. I find that untidy and wasteful use of human resource."

Dr. Yin tried to talk. He wobbled on the chair.

"Now, now, you really should try to be calm, you'll give yourself a heart attack, panic is not a good human emotion, it releases all sorts of bad hormones," Ms. Prosperina said. He faintly grinned. "Besides, the door's locked, what are you afraid of little old me? Now, now, besides, you'd be of no good for me, or for your lovely family." Ms. Prosperina pulled out a flimsy manila folder and slipped out scanned photos of Dr. Yin's family. She closely examined them and then put the photos in front of Dr. Yin's face.

Dr. Yin moaned. He stared at the photos; he gulped and angrily gazed at Ms. Prosperina. A wrinkle snaked across his forehead and he bit hard on the gag.

"I sense you feel traumatized, set up?" Ms. Prosperina said. She half-smirked at him. "Amazing how easily the human body can be altered, trauma changes you, attacks your stress genes, but you know that, right? You are such the smart man."

Dr. Yin pushed his sweating shoulders back against the chair. He stared up at the rusting metal ceiling.

"Very well, this will not take long," Ms. Prosperina said. She examined her work products. "Good, good."

The lack of oxygen caused the storage unit to feel abnormally warm for Dr. Yin, but Ms. Prosperina appeared as though she was coolly sitting in a spa lounge inspecting her new manicure.

"Dr. Yin, you will nod if I ask you to respond, understood?" Ms. Prosperina said. She shifted forward on the chair, her elbows on her knees. "Let's try, can you nod for me."

Dr. Yin nodded; his eyelids lazily drooped over his eyes.

"Good, good," Ms. Prosperina said. She clutched from the leather case and the first syringe; she screwed on the hypodermic needle. She held it to the light. She lightly compressed the plunger to squirt out a minute amount of liquid tears that trickled from the needle tip over the tube.

Dr. Yin squirmed; he crinkled his face. He moaned as he fought with the restraints.

"Pity, I can always track down your family," Ms. Prosperina said. She questioningly gazed at Dr. Yin as she held back the syringe. "Shall I hunt down your daughters? Wife? You would agree they are quite photogenic, I think Mr. Oppenheimer found them to be quite lovely. But I can make their life miserable, if you wish to trade them for you? Nod!"

Dr. Yin nodded his head up and down.

"Good, you see, you should never love, love will only cause you pain, like now, see, that was unnecessary," Ms. Prosperina said. She plunged the needle into the ported cannula and compressed the contents into Dr. Yin's vein. He could feel the sting, then the liquid coursing inside his hand.

Dr. Yin sat still, quiet, and stared down at the dirty concrete floor. He closed his eyes.

"Since you are a molecular biologist, I think you will be quite interested, I injected into you a microorganism. A parasite, the parasite will swim through your body, as you are now quite aware," Ms. Prosperina said as she waved her forefinger in the air as if tracing through Mr. Yin's body. "Until it finds its target, which in this case is your pineal gland that you are aware is deep inside your brain." She dagger pointed at Dr. Yin's face. She unscrewed the hypodermic needle, and placed the empty syringe back into the leather case. "It will attach to your gland, and the surrounding tissue, and it will do what parasites do, I know you know, it will begin to feed, it has to grow, or it'll die, that would be a pity, I created it just for you."

Dr. Yin kept his eyes closed. He fought back his instinct to cry, to beg for mercy. Ms. Prosperina stood up; she leaned in close to Dr. Yin's face. He could feel her hot breath; He smelled her aroma of cigarettes and coffee. She sighed; she kissed his cheek, and then whispered in his ear.

"Ah, but my synthetic parasite is special. It has a dormant bacterial seed inside, that if you become a problem, I'll wake it up. The autopsy will only show you had a massive stroke, ah, must have been something you ate?" Ms. Prosperina said. She chuckled; she sat back down. The folding chair squeaked at the riveted metal joints. "Now, I want you listen to me. I think it unfair that I'm not motivating you in the proper way, so I need you to look at me, yes, look me in the eyes."

Dr. Yin slowly opened his eyes, and cautiously stared across the storage unit over at Ms. Prosperina, who seemed to sit like a cat about to pounce on its unsuspecting prey.

"Good," Ms. Prosperina said. She took off her sunglasses to expose her eyes. Her left eye had a distinct red coloration; her right eye had an almost black coloration. "Heterochromia, right? I think you told Mr. Screwtop is was nothing to worry about."

Dr. Yin clenched his jaw as he nodded forward. His breathing hard, irregular, his chest pulsed. Her abnormally large orbed eyes absorbed him; as if she had the eyes of a lethal carnivore.

"A defect usually found in animals, dogs, cats, and even little old me," Ms. Prosperina said. She unbuttoned her jacket. "My father had such the imagination. I suspect he is aware of my presence here in Nashville. He has that power over me. Hmm, regardless, I wonder, what do you see in my eyes?"

Dr. Yin averted his stare over to the ridged metal storage unit door. He could feel his heart muscle throbbing through his body like a flashing red stop sign at train crossing.

"Now, now, look at me," Ms. Prosperina said.

Dr. Yin hesitantly looked directly into Ms. Prosperina's eyes. At first, all he saw were red and black, but then her eyes seemed to clear, and a hellish picture show emerged. There were images of mass fish kills, the burning of crops, the slaughter of innocent baby seals, executions of political prisoners by lethal injection. And images of helical strands of DNA being altered that initiated human decay. Dr. Yin closed his eyes.

"Those are not pretty pictures," Ms. Prosperina said. She sucked in the filthy air. "I have gifts I don't think my father anticipated." She seemed to hiss her words. "Dr. Yin, close your eyes, then open them, tell me, what do you see now?"

Dr. Yin gazed back over at Ms. Prosperina. Immediately, he shook back violently. He tried to push back, to scoot his strapped feet back, and try to twist away from her. For Ms. Prosperina's head had molted into a King Cobra head, the vibrant colored face hooded as if it prepared to strike him. From the snake's mouth a long forked tongue poked out between white fangs, but Dr. Yin realized the snake's eyes were red and black, and it did not lose its controlled stare at him. And below the snake head, her body was the same. As the snake head hissed and snapped at him, she simply crossed her legs. Then the face molted back into the Germanic appearing Ms. Prosperina, as she interlocked her thin fingers. She adjusted her scarf, and pulled her cuffs forward.

"Are you a religious man?" Ms. Prosperina asked. She scooted the chair closer to Dr. Yin. Dr. Yin stared down at the dirty floor, shaking uncontrollably he nodded his head side to side.

"Ah, a non-believer, a scientist, right?" Ms. Prosperina said. She chuckled. "Hmm, I should show you another part of me."

And her face molted into a thick black haired boar head with a pronounced snout with dagger like white tusks pointing up. But with the same red and black eyes staring at Dr. Yin. It grunted and spat at Dr. Yin. She molted back into appearing as Ms. Prosperina. She laughed and smacked her hands to her thighs.

"I love that one, such a wild boar," Ms. Prosperina said. She stared down at her bespoke shoes. "As if I'm a hooved creature searching for truffles in a French forest? I can do that, but it gets messy." She lightly laughed. "I love truffles, they can be easily modified." But she sat back in the chair with her hands cupped over the ends of the armrest. "But then there are these two faces you might recognize."

And as Dr. Yin squinted his eyes to watch, Ms. Prosperina molted black wings, her hands twisted into sharp black claws, from her forehead emerged wide black goat horns. Her face was serpent like, but with the same red and black eyes staring over at Dr. Yin. The serpent face leaned forward as it dangled a black forked tongue past sharp fangs under Dr. Yin's exposed neck. The snake slithered back and the form of Ms. Prosperina reappeared.

"And I have another face, just for you," Ms. Prosperina said. Then just as easily, she molted into the face of an old man with pure white hair and kindly eyes. "Hello, Dr. Yin," the old man said. It was the face of his deceased father. Dr. Yin shook, his tied wrists rattled against the armrests. He screamed for mercy through the gag. Then Ms. Prosperina reformed back into her Germanic middle-aged appearance. She straightened her pants leg, and recrossed her legs. She buttoned her jacket, pulled out a cigarette pack, and tapped out a cigarette. She lit it with fancy silver lighter. She inhaled a few drags and puffed the smoke over at Dr. Yin.

"Dr. Yin," Ms. Prosperina said. She flicked away a particle of dirt with the back of her hand. "You cannot hide from me and now, I can read your thoughts thanks to that parasite feeding on your pineal gland. I did the same to your idiot friend Mr. Screwtop." As she filled the storage container with cigarette smoke, all Dr. Yin could see was the outline of her shape. "I love to smoke, it has no effect on my body, I guess it must be good genes?" She chuckled. She flicked grey ashes on the cracked concrete floor. "Interesting how the human body can be silently altered. I marvel at how much coffee consumed in this country, mind you not black coffee, no that would be too simple. But all those alterations, sugar, dairy, chocolate sprinkles, you name it, my companies can make it. A legal method that allows you to get your caffeine fix, right? Your girls love to hang out, study at the friendly, open 24 hours a day Starry Eyed Coffee Hut?"

Dr. Yin tried to breathe in just enough oxygen mixed with smoke to remain alive. His shoulder and arms ached. He pushed his bare feet against the hard concrete floor.

"Over the years, I discovered pharmaceuticals to be complicated, and other drugs and forms of numbing the human body riddled with government interference, taxes, regulations, so forth," Ms. Prosperina said. She casually waved her hand forward, and dragged on the cigarette and puffed a smoke ring. "Pity, drugs and alcohol block human productivity, but then I thought about my name, actually, what my father named my test tube, Kore, goddess of the springtime."

Dr. Yin thought he was having a nightmare floating within cold, smoky clouds, flying with an evil Archangel.

"Enough, I enjoyed the cigarette, sadly, we are done. Soon, I will have Mr. Oppenheimer open the door and allow you and the smoke to escape." Ms. Prosperina extinguished the cigarette on the concrete floor. She knocked on the metal door. Mr. Oppenheimer quickly slid the door up and open. The smoke plumed out like a storage unit within hell. Then Ms. Prosperina took the second syringe and plunged the needle into Dr. Yin. "A little narcotic for you, you'll forget most our conversation, and you'll just happen to wake up in your lab, clueless."

Mr. Oppenheimer swiftly untied Dr. Yin. He slung his limp body over his shoulder. Ms. Prosperina stood nearby watching her manservant work. She strolled behind him toward the back of the black SUV.

"But within your genetic structure, you will have found a new motivation to continue your experiments, but also, to help me find my father, Professor Quan," Ms. Prosperina said as she stared down at Dr. Yin stuffed in the SUV's cargo space.

Dr. Yin groggily nodded.

"Madam?" Mr. Oppenheimer asked.

"Take me to my hotel," Ms. Prosperina said. She brushed off the dirt from her pants suit. She examined up at the leafy overhanging oak tree, she stared at the line of storage units and got back into the SUV, she left the passenger door open. She did not turn to look back at Mr. Oppenheimer. "Return Dr. Yin to his lab. I'm certain my father knows I'm nearby, he and the Captain will likely take every precaution to avoid me."

"Yes, Madam," Mr. Oppenheimer said.

"Disappointing, but necessary," Ms. Prosperina said. She lit a cigarette as Mr. Oppenheimer shut the SUV door.

Chapter Twenty Two

The next morning, as Dr. Yin awoke in his lab, Eddie was startled awake as the crystal doorknob turned clockwise, it emitted a thump from the solid wooden doors brass mortise lock. Charlene pushed the door open; through the crack, her six-foot-two-inch frame backlit by the hallway light cast an ominous shadow into the bedroom.

"Edward, it's just past seven," Charlene said.

"Sorry, I'm awake," Eddie said. He stirred from under the zillion-thread count Egyptian cotton sheets.

"No need to apologize. I'll be downstairs in the kitchen. I think Raquel placed fresh towels in the bathroom. If not, let me know," Charlene said. She slowly shut the tall door.

Rubbing his eyes, Eddie sat up. He noticed the intricate carvings of the ornamental Tudor style four-poster bed. Rays of sunshine engulfed the bedroom's interior through the floor to ceiling French doors. He folded his arms over his knees, keenly aware that he had slept well. After he showered, he dressed; Eddie grabbed his duffle bag and loped down the back circular knotty pine wood paneled stairwell into the kitchen. A spread of buttermilk biscuits, fresh fruit and spicy sausages dotted the butcher-block counter top. Charlene was reading the newspaper; she snapped the wrinkles out of the sports section and took off her horn-rimmed framed glasses.

"Bacon?" Charlene asked. She wore a golf visor, periwinkle striped shirt, and mustard yellow crop pants. "Sausage makes me queasy, kids like it, I hate coffee, but I made some."

"I like it black," Eddie said. His appetite waned as he thought about his wacky secret purpose. But his instincts kept at him, nudging him into the dark unknown as he poured black coffee into a white mug.

"I must admit, I think the club members will be quite amused by us. I can almost see their faces now," Charlene said.

"I guess," Eddie said. He glanced around the quiet kitchen.

Charlene closely watched Eddie. She flipped the newspaper aside onto the nearby kitchen table. She crossed her long legs.

"Raquel's the taxi driver today. Charles Jr.'s off to soccer practice, Sam has a riding lesson," Charlene said. She smiled.

"Oh," Eddie said. He bit into a fresh baked biscuit.

"So, how's the guest room?" Charlene asked.

"Great," Eddie said.

"Raquel has just finished decorating it. I must admit, she did go a little overboard," Charlene said.

"It was nice," Eddie said. He shrugged.

"Well, it's a new day. A golfing adventure awaits," Charlene said. She adjusted the visor. "Time to test drive the new ride."

"Okay," Eddie said. He slugged down his last drink of black coffee and finished off the flaky biscuit.

The faux professional golf fans drove out from the estate's brick driveway, and glided along under a cloudless baby blue sky. Eddie thought himself a visitor from another planet next to his lanky transgender host in her convertible Bentley Azure. They sped along past dense, multi-colored foliage and under the oak tree's natural canopy over the narrow red baked brick streets. The cool morning air rustled across their hair, and puffed up Eddie's thick brown hair into a tangled pompadour.

"I'll buy you a hat so you don't get sunburned, you have Chia-Pet-like hair," Charlene said. She glanced over at Eddie. "You're so lucky. I presume your mother has beautiful hair?"

"I don't know, my mom does have thick brown hair," Eddie said. He smiled over at Charlene. "I like the top down."

"Cruising along without a care in the world - ha! - let them eat cake," Charlene said. She tapped her long fingers along the burley wood steering wheel. "This is my first adventure driving it, the car I always dreamed about."

"It's a cool ride," Eddie said. He rubbed his palms along the smooth hand stitched calfskin leather seat.

Charlene's eyebrows narrowed. A deep wrinkle split across her forehead, as she clicked off the radio.

"I'm so sorry about last night," Charlene said.

Eddie had assumed the prior evening hurricane quietly dusted under the cosmic family rug. He glanced over at Charlene.

"Oh, no biggie," Eddie said. He looked over at Charlene; the transgender issue did cause his mind to bend with the sunlight.

"No, I must insist. I'm sorry, my wife tends to be rather blunt," Charlene said. She winked at Eddie.

"I'm not sure I understand," Eddie said.

"Raquel's rather head strong, you might've noticed," Charlene said. She wiggled up her plucked eyebrows.

"Yeah," Eddie said. He nervously chuckled.

"Curious what happened?" Charlene asked.

"It's none of my business," Eddie said. He gazed out the passenger side at the stately homes with manicured lawns.

"She woke up one day and decided she preferred women. I didn't, I panicked," Charlene said. She shrugged. "I love her."

"You must love her a great deal," Eddie said.

Charlene dabbed a tear from her eye with her forefinger.

"Sorry, when you love someone, you'll do *anything* for them," Charlene said. She stared through the panoramic windshield. "I am totally lost, lost without her."

Eddie studied the side of Charlene's face. He wondered what love really meant, why an invisible sensation caused people to do crazy things. And for some reason, he thought of Ardee.

"You like Meatloaf?" Charlene asked.

"Not really, it's kind of bland," Eddie said.

Charlene chuckled. She orchestra conductor waved her right forefinger in the air as she hummed a familiar song.

"No, the artist, haven't you ever heard, "I would do anything for love, but I won't do that"? Charlene asked.

"I think so," Eddie said.

"I know. I'm no Frank Sinatra mind you," Charlene said. Eddie grinned at Charlene. "But, I did do *anything*."

"Yeah, I'm with you," Eddie said.

Charlene tightly gripped the steering wheel. She took in a deep breath and smacked Eddie on his forearm.

"Enough, just want minimize the ick factor," Charlene said.

"I'm not creepered out, to be honest, it was a little weird at first, but I'm okay with it," Eddie said. He glanced over at Charlene. It did not seem to matter to Charlene where he came from, or who his parents were. And it did not seem to matter to Charlene that Eddie did not win a gold medal at his mythical sperm Olympiad, and that he was not born to an important family with vast wealth and prestige.

Being an original equity member at TPG Memphis, Charlene flashed her badge and drove the Bentley past the first guard gate. She sped the noticeable automobile up to the valet station. A teenage male valet vacuously cocked his head in an arrogant stare, confused by the inconsistent visual message his brain attempted to process.

"Ah, yes madam, or is it ah, sir? Sorry, what's the last name?" the teenage valet asked. He tore off the numbered ticket and stuck it under the driver side window. He handed the stub to Charlene, and clicked his pen to write down her name.

"Turnbull, I'll spell it for you, T-U-R-N-B-U-L-L. Can you direct me to the inside the ropes gate?"

"Yes, over to the left of the main lobby, there's a service desk there," the teenage valet said. He pointed at the massive clubhouse. "They'll walk you through security,"

"Thank you young man," Charlene said. She tapped him on his head just enough to mess up his spiky hair-do.

"You're a pistol," Eddie said.

"A what?" Charlene asked.

"My dad, that's what he called funny people," Eddie said.

"I resemble that remark," Charlene said. "Therefore I be me." Charlene patted Eddie on his left shoulder and grinned.

They stood near the front of the austere, gentrified club entrance. Charlene's chest hoisted as she took in an exaggerated breath. Then she adjusted her visor. She stepped her right golf shoe on the carpet runner as if prepared to sprint forward.

"Here's the deal," Charlene said. She stared straight forward at the club entrance. She nudged at Eddie.

"What?" Eddie asked. He looked up at Charlene.

"Act like you own the place, actually I do own a part of it. But, whenever you're going into hostile territory, trigger your courageous and audacious gene," Charlene said. She nodded.

"Do what?" Eddie said.

"Trust me, I don't think there are such genes, but go with it," Charlene said. She nodded down at Eddie. "Look at me, you think I lack courage? And I think I've got the audacious thing down for now, right?"

"Good point," Eddie said. He gulped.

"So, Edward, if you ever want to get anyplace in life," Charlene said in a commanding tone. She dead stared down at Eddie. "Grab your package, or in my case, what's left of it. And jump in with both feet. Be courageous and strong. Not arrogant, not cocky, remember, confident, like you've got a secret inside your skin that causes you to feel quietly cool and Zen like."

"Wow," Eddie said. He scratched the top of his head.

"The trick is up right posture," Charlene said. She pushed her shoulders back. "Sort of like this, and most important secret, it's your eyes, look people square in their eyes. Lock in, as though they are the most important person in the world. And do not back up, regardless of what they say or do." Charlene pointed down at Eddie's tennis shoes. "You own that little spot wherever you are standing on this planet. Stage, board rooms, asking a hot babe out, wherever, got it?"

"Got it," Eddie said. He gulped. He glanced up at Charlene and nodded his head in agreement.

"Abandon all hope, he who enter here," Charlene said.

"What?" Eddie said.

"Sorry, a little Dante humor," Charlene said. She shrugged. "Let's go, tick-tock, tick-tock."

Charlene and Eddie marched up the salt and pepper specked granite stairs, through the clubhouse's stark white high gloss double doors. They strolled across midnight blue plush carpet, past groups of membership and visitors who milled about the dining and bar areas segmented apart by vast color-ful Persian rugs. They continued through the club's back doors. Charlene acknowledged several people as if she was campaign-ing for mayor. They strolled out the back doors, past the fed-eralist style colonnade, and into a dense crowd of spectators.

"Didn't I predict we would be the toast of the tournament?" Charlene said as she sneered at the club membership.

"I don't think they even noticed me," Eddie said.

"I think you're correct, but don't you find their perplexed look hilarious? Come on, admit it," Charlene asked. She chortled. She adjusted the golf visor. "When was the last time you ran around with a woman in training?"

"Never, but it's okay with me," Eddie stuttered. He stuffed his hands in his khaki pants pockets.

They walked past a line of professional golfers warming up on the practice range. Some stopped mid backswing to inspect the odd tall new golf fan with a young man in tow.

"Thanks, I needed that," Charlene said.

They arrived at the tournament service desk that was placed under a temporary tent, the course behind blocked by a long plastic white fence. Golf fans milled about the tent, some entered, some stood nearby waiting.

"Well, ah, hello Charlene, nice to see you again," Nimrod said, she was the club's assistant manager. She quickly waved them to follow her. "Let's get on out to the first tee, no need to stand around here." She nervously processed them through the security station; they vigorously patted Eddie down, but left Charlene alone. Then Nimrod escorted them out to the golf course toward the first tee box.

"You're quite the babbling brook, Nimrod," Charlene said.

"You're so lucky, Lionel will be teeing off very soon," Nimrod said. Eddie thought her eyes belied a combination of jealously and disgust for Charlene.

"I wouldn't miss this for anything," Charlene said. She stopped. "Oh, can you have someone get my young friend a white golf hat, preferably with the tournament logo on the front? Something tasteful, put it on my account, you know the number."

"Why sure," Nimrod said. She glanced over at Eddie.

"We didn't get by the pro shop," Charlene said.

Nimrod stared over at Eddie and then back up at Charlene.

"I'll be happy, too," Nimrod said. She puckered her thin lips. "Let's keep moving." Eddie and Charlene followed Nimrod through the enormous crowd.

"This is impossible," Eddie whispered.

"What's that Eddie?" Charlene asked.

"Nothing," Eddie said. His pale cheeks and ears flushed hot pink from his internal embarrassment at the absurdity of his quest, but he had the odd sensation that he was supposed to be here. Then Eddie noticed Nimrod stopped suddenly, she scratched at red bug bites on her cankles with her polished shoes.

"Oh, I almost forgot, because of the predicted bad weather for this afternoon, they've changed the pairings," Nimrod said.

"What?" Charlene said. She re-adjusted her visor.

"No, you'll never believe this, they've merged the pairings into foursomes, you know, to speed up play," Nimrod said. She exhaled. She clenched her jaw. "Lionel and Whaley are now paired with, ah."

"For Pete's sake," Charlene said.

"Wait, hold the phone, let me get out the new pairings sheet to be certain," Nimrod said. She held her thick hand up as if to divine her purpose from the heavens.

Charlene suspiciously glared down at Nimrod. Nimrod slipped out her pairing sheet from her folder, she over back the paper. She glided her forefinger down the lines of typed names.

"You must be the luckiest, man, I mean person in the world," Nimrod said. She nervously giggled. She gazed up at Charlene.

"Really?" Charlene said.

"Really, Lionel and Whaley are now paired with Jake Saint Nick and Billy Sikleston," Nimrod said. She stared at Eddie.

"You're kidding?" Eddie said.

"No, I'm serious," Nimrod said. She slid the pairing sheet back inside her folder.

"Eddie I think you're my new good luck charm," Charlene said. She gave Nimrod an uncomfortable hug. Nimrod backed up and appeared as though she wanted to take a hot shower.

# # #

Captain Lovins sat inside his lab office; a forty-two inch flat screen television cast a pixilated glow inside the dimly lit room. Captain Lovins drank some orange juice. He sipped bottled water, re-hydrating his lean middle-aged body. He had finished this morning's PT routine. Today was stamina day, which entailed a five-mile route up and down rutted hills, an hour of intense calisthenics, finished off with flexibility power yoga. His baldhead effused sweat from the overexertion. He sat at the center of the spartanly furnished room. He had his legs crossed American Indian style working on his flexibility.

He was watching the golf tournament thinking he might spot a weakness in Lionel's security detail. And recording the golf event would allow him time to review, and strategize. To date, he had not found anything from television, or in person, that would be a safe method to attempt an extraction. And not one of his independent contractors had gotten even close to him. If only he knew some of his girlfriends, but he thought that gross. He hit the pause button and left to ask Professor Quan if he thought it still would be worth him chasing down the professional golfer's sample. Captain Lovins thought the mission a useless exercise.

# # #

At the first tee box there was a dark green tent to the left of the grass-playing surface, where local volunteers, blue-jacketed tournament staff gathered, outside the roped off environment a kaleidoscope of colorful spectators swarmed up and down the first hole, drinking, smoking and snapping photos with their hand held cell phone tracking devices.

"Okay you two, be quiet," Brutus said. A ruddy faced volunteer, he wore a membership jacket and tan slacks. He pointed at an older couple standing next to Eddie. "Same goes for the Shea's."

"Hi, you look so dapper today," Charlene said.

"Oh, thanks-" Brutus said. He tried to ignore Charlene.

"Hey there Charlene," Chuck Shea said. A diminutive older man with perfectly quaffed grey hair, dressed in a blue starched golf shirt emblazoned with the club logo on the breast pocket.

"I'm sorry, I didn't see you all, hey there," Charlene said.

"I think you know my wife Charlsey," Chuck said.

"Hi Charlene," Charlsey said. Equal in height to her husband, she had grey shoulder length hair back in ponytail.

"Why I do," Charlene said. She leaned forward, held Charlsey's hands and kissed her left cheek.

"This is my new friend Eddie. He's from Nashville, works for my cousin, the Civil War guy," Charlene said. She grinned. "Pray for him."

"Hey there son," Chuck said. He twisted to present his wife.

"Hi, it's Eddie?" Charlsey asked.

"Ah, yes, Eddie's fine," he said.

Charlene gripped her hands on her hips.

"I asked him the same thing Charlsey," Charlene said.

Charlsey took off her sunglasses.

"You know my father named me, he was sure I'd be a boy," Charlsey said. "My mother told me years after I was born, they just altered my name from Charles to Charlsey."

"I know something about that," Charlene said.

Mr. and Mrs. Shea held hands, and nudged close together.

"Yes, Mrs. Shea," Eddie said. He backed away from the group.

Charlsey elbowed her husband. He nudged at her.

"Sorry, I'm not a Mrs. Shea, I'm Charlsey," she said. She smiled at Eddie. "My father raised me like a boy. I play golf. I hunt. I fish, can field dress a deer, I'm all my man needs."

Chuck slinked toward Eddie. He wrapped his left arm on Eddie's shoulder. Eddie thought he smelled like bourbon.

"She's not kidding. I've been married to her for over forty years. I can't figure her out, you'd think I was gay," Chuck said. Then he stuck his tongue out over at his wife.

"I'm almost a man," Charlsey said. Her hands gripped her hips. "Sorry, I can't go all in get a dangling worm."

Charlene crossed her arms. She tapped her golf shoe.

"Amateur," Charlene said. She half-heartily grinned. "Eddie, never mind these two, Chuck won the sperm Olympics. His daddy hit the mother-load in the oil business. He has never worked a day in his life. And as for Charlsey, don't arm wrestle her."

"Okay," Eddie said. He had the sudden onset of dry throat syndrome. He coughed and stuffed his hands in his khaki pants.

Chuck sheepishly shrugged his shoulders.

"True, guess somebody's got to be Fauntleroy," Chuck said.

"But you're my Fauntleroy," Charlsey said. She gave her husband a soft kiss on his tanned forehead.

"Simmer down over there," Brutus said.

"It must suck to be him," Eddie whispered.

"You're right," Charlsey said standing close behind Eddie. "I don't think he has good DNA, just unlucky I suppose."

The crowd began to part, from within the human tunnel Jake and Billy emerged, close behind them marched Lionel. The throng ooh, aah, and they began to loudly clap and cheer. Lionel had a blank, unemotional expression. But Jake Saint Nick took off his cap, and waved to the crowd. He wore a light blue sweater over a white golf shirt and black slacks. He shifted over, shook Billy's hand, and then shook Lionel's. Billy slipped off his visor. He acknowledged the crowd. He glanced at Charlene. He asked his caddie to verify he had not started to see things as they both stared over at Charlene.

"Good one Eddie," Charlene said.

"It's weird, everybody's looking at them, yet they don't seem nervous," Eddie whispered. "Bet Lionel's a good poker player."

"I think he's done enough poking," Charlene said. She covered her mouth with her lanky hands. "Did I say that?"

"Ouch," Chuck said. He shrugged. "Hush."

"I'm in for Vegas, although I'm beyond Cougar status," Charlsey said. She patted her husband on his butt.

Not long after Lionel, Jake and Billy were ushered on to center stage, their playing companion Juan Whaley emerged.

"Sorry fella's, had to take a piss," Juan said. He wore a multi colored checkerboard-patterned outfit, sort of like a court jester warming up the crowd before a queen's beheading.

The professional golfers exchanged scorecards. Eddie noticed the network television cameras were adjusting their shots; one in particular was hoisted up on a small crane in a metal basket.

# # #

Captain Lovins and Professor Quan stood inside Captain Lovins office watching the television; he had fast-forwarded through the commercials. He hit play and the telecast began.

# # #

The voice over of the television cast was the host, Jimmy Pants, with melodic music as the network rolled through live televised shot after shot of Memphis, Beale Street, Graceland, then the golf course and then the professional players practicing and preparing for competition.

"What a glorious day here in Memphis, today is the second round of the St. Judith Classic. Springtime is in full bloom and Mother Nature bursts at her seams creating an ideal playing condition for today's competition. Hello there friends, I'm Jimmy Pants; we are pleased to bring you complete eighteen-hole coverage with a minimal number of commercial interruptions. We will focus much of our telecast featuring future and current hall of fame players, Lionel Forest, Billy Sikleston, the irrepressible, Juan Whaley, and perhaps best of all time, Jake Saint Nick," Jimmy said. Then the television shot showed Jimmy Pants and Flick Valdo, both wearing blue jackets, sitting close together behind a made for TV desk. "Now, I'm pleased to bring in my announcing partner, Flick Valdo, six-time major tournament winner, and former world number one to provide us with his expert analysis. Flick, what are your thoughts for today's round? And what do you expect my friend."

Flick had a faint, gravely East-Anglia English accent. "Scoring conditions are marvelous with the course near perfection for now. We will see what happens tomorrow after the rain comes. But, me thinks the lads will do themselves well today. I think it'll be steady-as-you-go for Lionel, Billy will be, well, Billy. As for Long Juan, he might keep us all in stitches with his wild-and-free-spirited nature."

"It's unusual for the tour to have a foursome," Jimmy said.

"Indeed, sort of like a blue moon over the PGA to have foursomes, must be an unusual event," Flick said. He laughed.

"I guess Jake is the catalyst?" Jim said.

"Absolutely, and to be honest, I'm honored to be a mere spectator to watch Jake play one more time." Flick paused. "He's what a man, a father and a professional should be, I'm not fit to polish his shoes given what he did for all us professionals."

"I think you're being a bit hard on yourself my friend," Jimmy said. He lightly chuckled.

"Not really, but I will say this," Flick said. He shrugged as he nervously chuckled. "This foursome would make a great Labradoodle."

Jimmy paused for a moment. He nudged at Flick.

"Not sure I follow," Jimmy said.

"My new wife wants one of those designer pups, its part Labrador retriever and part Poodle, she calls it a Labradoodle," Flick said. He tapped at the booth counter top.

"Sort of designer golfer then?" Jim asked. He lightly chuckled. "I suppose with all the bad genes removed?"

"No, no, you leave all that in, all those flaws just make us more interesting," Flick said. He grinned at Jimmy. "I hate vanilla, I love everything swirled together as one."

"I like vanilla," Jimmy said. "But with sprinkles."

"How interesting would golf be if all these lads did was hit the ball down the middle every time, knocked it on the green and two putted for par?" Flick asked. He held his big left hand on Jimmy's shoulder.

"Not very, a bit to Byron Nelson," Jimmy said.

"Yeah, Iron Byron, but all the wisdom flowing through their veins from their fathers teaching them how to play as boys, and then their coaches, can't prevent them from making mistakes," Flick said. He elbowed Jimmy. "On or off the course-"

"Yeah, very true, my friend," Jimmy said. "Quite the philosopher today-"

"Oh, now you've done me in," Flick said. "All I'm saying is they all have learned how to get out of the messes they make and still win tournaments, that's what keeps people watching? Right, right, it's what made Arnie so special, and Trevino."

Jimmy Pants twisted and grinned at the camera lens.

"Flick Valdo designer golfers, now on sale," Jimmy said.

"Think of it, you've got Jake, Lionel, Billy and Long Juan, if you could mix their DNA all together, know what you'd have?" Nick asked. He chuckled at Jimmy going off script.

"I can only guess," Jimmy said. "A LionelBillyJakeWhaley?"

"No silly, you'd have an Arnie Palmdale," Flick said dryly. "Now that's what I call inspired science."

Jimmy grinned at Flick and into the camera lens.

"Well played my friend, I'm sure wherever Mr. Palmdale is, he's smiling," Jimmy said.

"It's good to be the king, of course here in Memphis they had the kang of rock and roll," Flick said.

"Quite true, perhaps we'll go pay our respects over at Graceland," Jimmy said.

# # #

Captain Lovins pressed the pause button on the remote control to allow the telecast to record ahead so he could then skip through the commercials.

"That was weird," Captain Lovins said. He set the remote control on a side table.

"Are they always like this?" Professor Quan asked. He leaned against Captain Lovins' wooden desk.

"I don't know," Captain Lovins said. He shrugged.

"I could have explained some things," Professor Quan said.

"Are you sure about golfers?" Captain Lovins asked. He crossed his arms. "It's not really a sport."

Professor Quan adjusted the frame for his glasses. "I don't know, instinct I suppose," Professor Quan said. He scratched his smooth, shaven chin. "I came across a name, I was reading the sports section."

"You?" Captain Lovins asked.

"I don't know," Professor Quan said. He stuffed his hands in his lab coat. "I noticed a name, you should research him."

"All right, give it to me," Captain Lovins said. He picked up the remote control; he fast forwarded through the commercials, and then pressed play.

# # #

After they drew numbers from a hat, Lionel had the honor of teeing off first. He leaned over and teed up the white golf ball with his symbol printed underneath the manufacturers' symbol. Initiating his normal routine, he previewed the shot from behind the ball. He intently stared down the green-carpeted fairway, as if unaware of the lines of spectators were six people deep. He blinked his eyelids several times; he exhaled and appeared to visualize the desired result.

The talkative golf patrons were silent, as if frozen within the stillness of an empty church cathedral field. A slight southern breeze rustled the leaves of a yellow tulip poplar. Perched near the end of a bent willow tree limb, a lone red cardinal chirped.

"It's like a grand wizard has cast a spell," Eddie whispered to Charlene.

"I know, weird," Charlene said.

"Simmer down," Charlsey said.

With precise timing, Lionel transformed into a human lever. His forearm muscles bulged as he twisted his thick athletic shoulders, and he rhythmically turned his back to the target line. Then he reversed the sequence, hands a nanosecond in front of the club head. He released immense centrifugal force down on the motionless white orb. The metal driver against Thermoset *clinked after the compression.* A shock wave rippled across Eddie, Charlene and the crowd as the ball took off like a tiny Lear jet on a one-dimensional string scorching into the pale blue sky at instant cruising speed. It crested at altitude, glided back to Earth, and landed three hundred yards away within the fairway's closely cropped zoysia grass.

"Cool!" Eddie said as he leaned sideways to watch the ball.

Lionel ignored the ball flight. He picked up the dislodged tee, stuck it in his pants pocket. He tipped his hat over at Eddie.

"Why don't you just go kiss his ass next time," Chuck said.

"Wrong team," Charlene said.

"Then, I'll take one for the team Eddie," Charlsey said.

"Sorry honey, I think that's a long train," Chuck said.

"Choo, Choo," Charlsey said. She pulled down her arm with a fist. "Don't steal an old lady's thunder."

Juan followed Lionel. He performed a similar action. But his swing unique, rapid in quick process and timing around a pear shaped frame. The result similar to Lionel's, but the ball position appeared more random, and his routine quick and less methodical as he left the sisters of fate to decide the result.

Billy adjusted his visor up and down allowing his long brown hair to flap in the light breeze. He stood behind his tee ball and took a few short practice swings. Left-handed, he positioned his ball on the opposite side of the tee box. Near the ball, he kept moving his golf spikes in a marimba like movement. Then he stopped dancing, twisted his shoulders, and returned the club head to square. The ball soared at maximum speed but with a steep right to left attack pattern. His finish was a bit unsteady, for he swung hard enough to lose his footing. He danced a jig to regain his balance. Nevertheless, the ball landed safely down the left side of the fairway just past Lionel's ball and scooted forward to its temporary resting spot.

Jake had watched the younger men perform; he trundled out to left side of the tee box. He gingerly leaned down to tee his ball; father time had caused his limp from the years and years of effort to perfect his craft. Then he moved directly behind the ball. He wistfully thumped the golf club along on the teeing ground, adjusted his cap and coughed. He glanced up into the stands at the many patrons.

"I guess I'm the short knocker today," Jake said. The crowd applauded. The other three golfers lined up down the right side of the tee box with their respective caddies. They all stared back at Jake wondering when father time would tap them on the shoulder. He stood behind his ball. He blinked his eyes as he envisioned his goal. He followed the same disciplined routine golfer, after golfer, after golfer had copied from him. After all, he was the creator of the movement.

Jake walked astride his ball, his chin turned just to the right of center. His left arm straight, he shifted his weight onto his right instep. His right hip moved back and his shoulders turned away from the ball. His turn not as pronounced, or as fluid as the younger players, but he returned the club head to square, and the ball glided slightly left back to the right, landing dead center of the fairway, but twenty yards behind his playing competitors.

Without conversation, the players strided down the first hole with their caddies close behind. Flags and placards with last names emblazoned in block letters provided signage for the patron army to follow. The fans followed close behind as if a Roman Legion-like mob marching in lock step mass, with each player appointed scribes to document their battle movements.

# # #

Captain Lovins dangled the remote control in his right hand.

"This is a waste of time," Captain Lovins said.

Professor Quan adjusted his glasses, he moved closer to the television screen. He pointed at the image of Charlene.

"What's that?" Professor Quan asked. "Pause it."

"That, I do not know," Captain Lovins said.

Professor Quan turned to stare over at Captain Lovins.

"Keep an eye on that," Professor Quan said. "My skin feels on fire, as if I just stuck my finger in electrical current."

"Really?" Captain Lovins asked.

"Yeah," Professor Quan said.

Captain Lovins pressed the play button, and closely watched the television screen with Professor Quan.

# # #

"The players seem to be off to a good start," Jimmy said. Both he and Flick noticed the rather odd, tall person dressed in periwinkle. As the on-course camera crew kept their shot on Charlene, the director unable to roll to the next shot.

"Yeah, they must both feel satisfied not to have let distraction prevent them from focusing," Flick said.

"Perhaps we can all agree that this unique foursome seems to bring out the most unique crowds," Jimmy said. He seized the moment with deft announcer skill.

"Dear me, this will sure be a gender bending round," Flick said. "I thought my Labradoodle was unique."

# # #

Captain Lovins with the remote control clutched to his fingertips, he pressed the pause button. He shifted close to the television screen.

"Right there," Captain Lovins said. He tapped the screen with his forefinger. "Edward."

Professor Quan and Captain Lovins stood close together examining the television screen. They could almost breathe on the glowing television screen as they studied the face of Edward.

"I'll be," Professor Quan said. "Still a waste of time?"

"No," Captain Lovins said. "He's right there."

# # #

Eddie and Charlene followed behind the golf foursome. Hole-after-hole, the players stroked the golf balls into strategic dimensional positions within their space and time. The television announcers acclimated to the transgender following the group. The players made the outward nine turn, and then they prepared to begin the tenth hole and turn for home.

# # #

"Flick, so far Lionel and Billy are two under par, Juan's hung in at even, but the big surprise is Jake, three under, harkening back to another time," Jimmy said.

"Simply marvelous, he's chipping and putting like a mad demon," Flick said.

"Tell me about the next hole, the tenth?" Jimmy asked. As the network showed a prepared birds-eye view along the hole from tee box to kidney shaped green.

"Ten is a rich hole that often entices players to take a risk. Flabby Cellar designed the hole as a dare," Flick said.

"How so?" Jimmy asked.

"It's short enough to bait a player to challenge the dog leg left and cut off the hole, then you're left with a easy approach shot to back right pin, but that little innocuous stream has been a watery grave for lads a bit too frisky," Flick said.

"Which player do you think this hole favors?" Jimmy asked.

"None really, but I'll be curious how Long Juan approaches his tee shot, he's a gambler at heart. I doubt the others will be baited into making a poor tactical decision at this point in the round," Flick said. "Besides, sorry to say, but Jake can't get there anymore, so the stream doesn't come into play."

# # #

Eddie watched as Juan had knocked in a treacherous birdie on the ninth hole, which earned him the honor on the tenth teeing ground. Juan quickly teed his ball, and smacked his drive over the hazard. He missed the stream by a perilous few feet. The ball bounded down the shaved fairway to an ideal position.

"Nice shot," Jake said.

"Thank you Mr. Saint Nick," Juan said. He pulled out a cigarette packet from his golf bag.

"I could do that," Jake said. He snickered with his hands resting on top off the club grip. "In 1978-"

Lionel ripped the head cover off his driver and flipped it at his caddie after the gallery, ooh and ah, after Juan's bravado, flicking on Lionel's super-sized competitive-gene. Lionel repeated his normal routine with an exact whirlwind movement; he smashed his club into the ball, the ball flight torched into the sky, targeted to land just to the left and slightly longer than Juan's result. The crowd exploded in delight from witnessing Lionel's powerful show of force. His face responded with a satisfied confident expression. He began to twirl his club in his fingers like a high school band majorette. However, a freshly planted pin oak sapling with fragile limbs barely tangled into the sky, clipped Lionel's ball. It inflicted a premature fall from grace. The ball dropped with a thud next the stream's east bank, and it disappeared, nestled in four-inch high Kentucky bluegrass.

# # #

"Oh gracious, Lionel's a bit unlucky there, all those little branches and twigs can reach out and even bite a Lion," Flick said.

"What do you think Lionel will need to do next?" Jimmy asked with a low, hushed tone.

"It appears the ball has nestled down in that thick fescue, fortunately he's out of the water, but Mr. Lionel's a righty. So, I think he either hits one of those backward chips to the fairway, or pulls up his knickers to step into the *what-tree* breach," Flick said.

"Either way it would seem to be a tough shot?" Jimmy said.

"Oh, without question, he'll be lucky just to escape," Flick said. His voice was off camera, as the next television image showed Billy grimace and then snag his driver.

# # #

"Let's give it a go," Billy said. After his swing, he almost fell down backwards. His ball flared right to left and crash landed directly on the west bank, parallel from Lionel's result. Billy frowned. He handed the club back to his caddie. He shrugged over at Eddie.

# # #

Professor Quan tapped at the television screen.

"Something's about to happen," Professor Quan said.

"Yeah, I get that too," Captain Lovins said. They both appeared to be in a trance staring intently at the colorful pixels from the glowing television screen.

# # #

"Dear me, I think Lionel and Billy need to switch balls for a moment," Flick said off screen. The television crew had hurriedly moved down the fairway to show the audience where the balls had landed.

"Hard to believe," Jimmy said.

"Righty needs to be a lefty, lefty, now needs to be a righty," Flick said. He chuckled.

"But, they'll not be gender bending," Jimmy said cryptically.

# # #

Eddie strolled a few feet behind Lionel as Lionel kicked away dead tree branches. He stuffed his hands in his tan pants pockets; he noticed Eddie nearby and simply shrugged. They approached the meandering stream. It appeared shallow, with little jagged rocks and boulders smoothed by the constant friction of the tributary's current. Lionel and Billy crouched down to examine their golf balls; it was the sensible thing to do, Eddie thought. They inspected above the ball, behind it, testing the grasses depth with their feet. They huddled with their caddies and calculated their next shot. After brief discussions, each committed to stroking their golf balls while standing in the shallow stream. Juan and Jake stood nearby watching the escapade; their white orbs resting on finely cut resplendent green grass. Eddie, Charlene, and the Shea's stood nearby listening to the competitors discuss their strategy.

"Lionel, I count one hundred twenty nine yards to the pin, one hundred thirty, and one hundred twenty eight the green's front right," his caddie advised.

"Nine iron, I need to compensate for the uphill trajectory and the humidity is down, so I think I can close the face on a nine," Lionel said. He tightly gripped his golf glove.

"I agree with a solid nine," his caddie said, he hoisted the golf bag shifting the metal clubs shifted, "the flag is nine feet in and ten feet from the false-front."

Chuck elbowed Charlene with his left arm.

"Sort of like watching this through a weird window," Chuck said. He looked up at Charlene.

"Yeah, they both seem to be doing the exact same thing," Charlene said. "But opposite."

Eddie stood near the on-course camera crew, standing whisper quiet with hands in his khaki pants pockets.

# # #

Captain Lovins pressed the pause button.

"He's right there," Captain Lovins said staring at the television screen, "within what? ten feet, just amazing."

Professor Quan sat on the corner of the desktop, his arms crossed with his right hands fingers tapping against his lips.

"You and your instincts," Captain Lovins said as he twisted to look back at Professor Quan.

# # #

Lionel slipped off his white golf shoes and gently stepped into the stream. He kept his spongy socks on to minimize the shock from the water's frigid, springtime temperature. He kept the golf club hovering above the grass; he took dead aim at his target. He blinked his eyes to lock in the thought. With practiced timing, he struck the exact blow down on the ball. He dislodged the offending sphere, and shot the white orb through the cobalt, cloudless sky. It crested, bounced forward and rolled within ten-feet of the cup.

Eddie and the crowd burst into applause. Lionel flipped the stiff shafted club back at his caddie. He tipped his cap with his fingers. He smiled over at Eddie.

# # #

"My gracious, what an incredible shot, only a *Lionel* can do that," Flick said. He chuckled.

"Indeed, quite the Houdini," Jimmy said.

# # #

"Man, nice shot," Juan said. He dragged on his cigarette.

"Thanks," Lionel said.

"Man, he does that crap all the time, must be in his DNA or something," Juan said over at Charlene.

"You hit a perfect shot too, Juan," Charlene said.

Juan glanced up at Charlene; he took in a deep drag, and released a cloud of smoke from his lips. He turned to act as if he was deciding which club to use.

"I think he's afraid he might turn into salt," Chuck said.

Jake ignored the episode. He quietly stood next to his caddie within a Zen like plasmatic bubble.

Billy, who had already taken off his shoes and socks, rolled his pants legs up to his knees. He dipped his feet into the cold stream. He danced, and then performed a similar shot to Lionel's. But his ball flew left to right, bounced just short of the green, bounding several more yards to stop nine inches from the cup.

The crowd exploded in awe. Billy sheepishly grinned back at over at Lionel. He shrugged. He tipped his visor to the crowd.

"Why am I even here?" Juan said.

"Juan, we're just too boring, hitting our shots in the fairway," Jake said. He kindly grinned over at Eddie.

# # #

"I guess those are good results?" Professor Quan asked. He hopped off the desk. He walked over next to Captain Lovins.

"I guess," Captain Lovins said. "The announcers are impressed, crowd seems happy, I guess getting out of trouble is what makes them special, and why people watch."

"Yeah, that squares with the announcer," Professor Quan said.

"Why on our shopping list?" Captain Lovins asked.

"I am never 100% certain, but I think we just answered our question," Professor Quan said. He sat down on the nearby couch.

"What?" Captain Lovins asked.

"A gene not for golf, but for being imaginative," Professor Quan said. "Smart risk taking, is my guess, it's not brute force, you have to think and then act."

"Like a sniper," Captain Lovins said as he nodded his head; he tapped at the television screen. "And Edward is right there."

# # #

As Lionel stepped out from the watery shallows, he collapsed to his knees; his hands plunged onto the dense grassy bank.

"Crap," Lionel growled. He whispered a few choice expletives.

"What's wrong?" the Caddie asked.

"I stepped on something, think I'm bleeding," Lionel said. He slowly pulled his feet out of the water.

His caddie nervously unzipped a pocket in Lionel's golf bag.

# # #

"What seems to have happened to Lionel?" Jimmy asked.

"Ah, I hate that. I have done it me self. Oh my, I guess Poseidon must have stuck his hostile trident into Lionel. Well, he's human after all," Flick said.

# # #

Lionel sat on the smooth grass with his knees bent against his chest. He picked at his bleeding foot. He noticed Eddie.

"Hey buddy, can help me out," Lionel said to Eddie.

Charlene nudged at Eddie to walk over to Lionel.

"Sure?" Eddie said. He walked over to Lionel.

"Can I use you for balance? I don't want to get more mud all over, as I get this sock off," Lionel said.

Lionel leaned against Eddie and he peeled off his white cotton, water-soaked sock. It emitted a red, nickel-sized dot within the fibers.

"The things you do," Lionel said. He balanced on one leg and against Eddie's shoulder.

"Great shot, sorry you got cut up," Eddie said. He looked down at Lionel's foot.

"Yeah, whatever, you're a real life saver," Lionel said.

"What's up?" Billy asked. He had strolled back to the other side of the stream. He, Juan and Jake all converged near Lionel.

"Ah, I stepped on something," Lionel said.

The caddie barged back with a bandage and clean socks.

"How random is that, I took my shoes and socks off and didn't get a scratch," Billy said. He leaned forward inspecting Lionel's foot. "I got lucky."

"You okay?" Jake asked. He patted Lionel on the back.

"Yeah," Lionel said. "I'll get it together."

# # #

Captain Lovins leaned back and stared up at the tiled ceiling. He slowly blew air out of his lips.

"He got nothing, not even an autograph," Captain Lovins said.

"Be patient," Professor Quan said. He bit on the curved tip end of his eyeglasses. "Something, it's coming, I can feel it."

# # #

"Thanks," Lionel said, as he got his shoes back on.

"No worries," Eddie said. He felt a weird electrical rush that caused the hair on his neck to spring up. As the foursome dispersed toward their next shots and Eddie, Charlene and the Shea's started to stroll forward. Suddenly, out of the gallery, a thin young woman, with strawberry blond hair, perhaps in her mid-twenties scampered bare footed toward them.

"Take me, take me," she screamed at Lionel. She tore off her 'I Love Swingers' t-shirt to reveal her bountiful naked upper torso. Lionel comically stared at her and started to back away.

"Oh crap," Lionel said. He put his face in his golf cap. "I'm cursed." As he twisted away from her behind a wall of security guards, the guards, golfers and fans appeared mesmerized by the bouncing beauty. But Eddie noticed with the revelation from the late morning sunshine, the sparkle of a thin blade tucked underneath her right hand fingers. She jerked her hand up above her head to reveal the knife. Eddie instinctively tucked his head down and plowed his left shoulder into her rib cage like a football cornerback stopping a wide receiver from catching a game winning pass. The shrieking woman folded over Eddie's shoulders, as she dropped the knife. She collapsed and splashed head first into the shallow stream. Then the security guards woke up, charged forward and yanked her out of the stream. Then they tackled her to the ground. The crazed woman screamed at Eddie and moaned as if demon possessed.

Eddie huffed and stared at the woman as he got up from all fours after landing on the bank of the stream. He gulped. His palms and knees of his pants blotched with moist fudge brown mud, with green grass stains and moisture.

# # #

"That was a miracle, that young man stepped in just in the nick of time," Jimmy said. He nervously whistled.

"Gracious, my heart is pounding," Flick said. "Almost like that tennis player, life is so random, so fragile, oh that was so close to a tragedy."

"Yeah, ah, let's take a commercial break, so we can gather ourselves," Jimmy said. "Yeah, life is so fragile."

# # #

"What?" Captain Lovins said. He squeezed the lifeless remote control in his muscled hands.

"Simmer down," Professor Quan said. "It's out of our control."

"Yeah, I hate commercials," Captain Lovins said.

"I think you might want to drive to Nashville," Professor Quan said. He put his eyeglasses back on. And about that time, his pet dog Waldo raced into the room, her face crinkled from sleeping in her den, her furry tail wagged.

"Waldo, you missed all the fun," Captain Lovins said. He bent down to pet her. She innocently gazed up at him, with her seal brown eyes, her pink tongue waggled out.

"You need to meet with Edward," Professor Quan said.

"Of course," Captain Lovins said.

"He got something, but look him in the eyes," Professor Quan said. He crossed his arms. "I'm curious what you will see, he should not, be whatever he has become, I think something happened to him, a trauma of some sort."

# # #

Down on the tenth fairway near the meandering tributary, Eddie tried to slow his breathing; his cheeks had flushed a ripe Georgia peach color, his face splattered with brown mud.

"Hey dude," Lionel said. He patted Eddie on his back. "Man, that was cool, didn't see that coming."

"Sure," Eddie said, his voice a pre-pubescent boy octave.

"You okay?" Charlene asked. She brushed clumps of grass and dirt off Eddie's shirt.

"Brave thing to do son," Chuck said.

Charlsey whisked over, and patted Eddie on his left shoulder.

"Gracious," Charlsey said. She hugged Eddie. "I can't get my pulse to slow down, man o man."

Jake, Billy and Juan and their caddies hesitantly walked over toward Eddie. They quietly stood nearby watching him.

"Well done young man," Jake said. He stepped forward with his right hand out. He stared directly into Eddie's eyes.

"Same here," Billy said.

"Ditto for me," Juan said. He patted his chest, fished into his pants pockets. "Need a cigarette?"

"No thanks," Eddie said. He glanced back and forth at them. His mind swirled with being the center of attention.

Jake pursed his lips. He shrugged his shoulders. After a brief moment of reflection, he took off his golf cap.

"Does anybody have a pen?" Jake asked. He glanced around at the other players, and spectators.

A nearby official handed a blue ink pen to Jake. He signed his name in cursive across the brim.

"This isn't much, but on short notice," Jake said. He handed Eddie his golf cap. "You didn't just defend Lionel, you defended us all, and that could've been tragic, thank you."

"Thank you, I'm not sure what to say," Eddie said. He shook Jakes hand, and held the cap. "Ah, thank you."

"Hand me that pen," Billy said. He signed his golf glove. "This is from me and my family, we forget how vulnerable we all are, so thanks." He patted the awe struck Eddie on the left side of his shoulder.

"Hey, I'm in on this too," Juan said. He signed his sweater vest. "Man brother, I never realized, scary man, take this, it's kind of valuable, sell it on WePay or what not." He patted his chest for his pack of cigarettes. He huffed. "Man, I need a cigarette, wish they had coffee out here."

"I don't know what to say," Eddie said.

Jake, Billy and Juan all shook Eddie's hand one more time and headed back toward their respective shots. Eddie held the cap and gloves in his shaking hands. Startled, by his good fortune, but then Lionel unfolded his arms and strolled back over toward Eddie. He slipped past the television crew; he inspected the spectators, and stared directly down at Eddie.

"People always seem to want *something* from me," Lionel said. He scowled. He shook his head in disbelief.

"It's cool, just what you do," Eddie said.

"I don't think you care, here, I signed my golf glove," Lionel said. He shrugged.

"Thanks, it's no big deal," Eddie said.

"Not sure about that," Lionel said. He stared blankly across the rolling green grass golf course.

"Yeah," Eddie said. "Weird day-"

"Life's weird, I think people just assume they know me, since they see me on TV," Lionel said. He sighed. "Judge us from the comfort of their living room. I just love golf, I love the competition."

"Yeah," Eddie said. He thought someone else had emerged from behind Lionel's brown eyes, his angst from childhood, his secret thoughts that went unshared, and the guarded feelings hidden from view behind the scar tissue earned from living a public life in front of the ever-present camera eye.

"Wish I could hide sometimes," Lionel said. He pensively studied the gallery and the odd transgender. "I know this is weird, but for some reason, here take my socks. I bet people will think they're cool, I guess, this is as much of me as I can give." He shrugged his shoulders, sighed, and then smiled. "Thanks man, I'm not sure what else to say, sort of put stuff in perspective, golf's just a game."

"I still don't know what to say either," Eddie said. He stared down at the blood stained socks as his dirty hands shook. He thought had dropped into a weird time warp that had predetermined the sequence of his life.

"Got to go," his caddie said. He shook Eddie's hand. "Thanks dude, camera crews getting antsy."

Lionel smacked his hands together. He waved to the crowd.

"Yeah, see you later, dude, thanks," Lionel said. He nimbly twisted and limped up the fairway toward the bent grass green. He disappeared within the penology of security guards, police officers, reporters and professional camera operators.

# # #

Captain Lovins pressed the play button in time to see Lionel walk away from the group where Eddie was standing. He could see Eddie clutched several items. He and Professor Quan played the scene back and forth in slow motion.

"Unbelievable, that little nerd just stood there," Captain Lovins said. He tapped his boot on floor.

"Guess it was meant to be," Professor Quan said. He petted his dog behind her floppy ears.

"Yeah, guess I'm heading to Nashville," Captain Lovins said.

"Be extra careful, our girl decided to pay Dr. Yin a visit," Professor Quan said. He leaned down to pick up his pet. "And some sap named Bertrand Screwtop, lawyer I think."

Captain Lovins curiously stared over at Professor Quan.

"She decided to get nasty?" Captain Lovins asked.

"Yes, she knows I know, she didn't even attempt to hide her thoughts," Professor Quan said. He gently hugged the dog. "And her manservant is loose, roaming Nashville."

"I'll figure out who this Screwtop is," Captain Lovins said. He clicked off the television. "And you have a name for me?"

Professor Quan lightly kissed Waldo on her ruby furred head. He put her down on the simple earth tone carpet. He pulled out a clipped out section of newspaper. He handed it to Captain Lovins who set it on his desk, next to his computer screen.

"Jose Hernandez, Jr.," Professor Quan said. He tapped on the newspaper scrap. "He interests me for some odd reason, and I think Edward has provided me the samples I'll use."

Chapter Twenty Three

Ms. Prosperina stared out the smoked glass windows from her perch above downtown Nashville. Her magnificent suite took up the top two floors within the exclusive boutique property. She was the only occupant. The house staff was only allowed to enter the suite with Mr. Oppenheimer. He knocked on the front double doors before he entered.

"Madam?" Mr. Oppenheimer asked.

Ms. Prosperina turned from the windows, he hands behind her.

"I've decided to terminate Mr. Screwtop's services," Ms. Prosperina said. She tightened her warm white housecoat.

"Yes, Madam," Mr. Oppenheimer said. "I'll take care of it." He started to back away from her.

"No, I've taken care of it, I let the bacteria loose inside his brain," Ms. Prosperina said. She waved him to stay in the expansive room and to sit down. "I want you to search his home office, his desk, the lower right drawer, it will be locked."

"Something specific?" Mr. Oppenheimer asked. He unbuttoned his black jacket. He sat forward on the blood red leather chair.

Ms. Prosperina paced across the Persian carpet over to the fully stocked bar. She found some top shelf bourbon in a crystal decanter. She poured a shot of the auburn colored Kentucky nectar into a highball glass. She sipped it and admired its intense flavors. She slithered her tongue across her lips.

"Quite nice," Mr. Prosperina said. She examined the reflected light from the crystal highball glass. "Mr. Screwtop is addicted to this stuff, it causes him confused thinking, like his preference for mixing alcohol with erectile medication. Pity, soon his current partner will suddenly feel all limp inside."

"Madam," Mr. Oppenheimer said.

"He is having a private dinner for now," Ms. Prosperina said. She set the glass down on a cherry veneered sideboard. "You have about an hour before she screams at his dead crossed eyes."

"Yes, Madam," Mr. Oppenheimer said.

Ms. Prosperina put her forefinger up as she paced.

"He added security since your last visit, he changed the security codes, the new code is on your hand held device," Ms. Prosperina said. She stopped pacing.

Mr. Oppenheimer pressed his PDA, he confirmed receipt from her encrypted email.

"I have them," Mr. Oppenheimer said. He stuffed the cell phone back into his front breast pocket.

"Pushed to the back of the drawer, a locked metal box, inside you will only find a thumb drive," Ms. Prosperina said.

She strolled back to the sideboard and grabbed the highball glass. She sipped the bourbon. "I do like this. He thought he was being sneaky, researching into my past, asking his government contacts about me. He just asked too many questions, it would be untidy to leave that information behind."

"Shall I dispose of it?" Mr. Oppenheimer asked.

"No, I'm curious what he discovered," Ms. Prosperina said. She sipped the bourbon. She stared up at the custom dentil molding above the marble faced fireplace. "I think I will visit his firm's general partner, a Mr. Lewis, it would give you a reason to be seen in the building, so the cameras pick you out with me. And I can discover if Mr. Screwtop had a big mouth, and confided his information with this Mr. Lewis."

Chapter Twenty Four

"Well, that doesn't happen every day. You know Eddie, you might want to put those socks in a plastic zip top bag," Charlene said. She dug inside her purse. "Oh wait, I know, I just picked up a Summa Binder bag, by Aquinas and you know to get through airport security. It'll be perfect so you can protect it, and most importantly not mess up my ride."

"Not sure I've an issue taking lipstick onto a plane, but yeah, seems like a good idea," Eddie said.

"Geez, Charlene, you're all in," Chuck said.

"I've never done anything halfway," Charlene said.

"You might even be able to sell those socks on WePay," Charlsey said. "Someone might want it for a paternity test."

"You know, I think my wife's got a point," Chuck said. He smoothed back his hair. "All those slugs picking at the boy, bet they'll do about anything to get into his wallet."

"Yeah," Eddie said.

"As if they didn't know what they were doing?" Charlsey said.

"No doubt, Genie Bean," Chuck said. He kissed his wife's hand. "Those boys get chased after by them wenches digging for gold, there are no Virgin Mary's left these days."

"Gold will not fill up their hearts," Charlene said.

Eddie blushed as he examined his new treasures. He could barely hear them talking. He was completely transfixed, thinking about the Wish List.

"Yeah, but I think I'm going to keep them," Eddie said. He cryptically smiled. "At least for a while-"

After the momentous events on the tenth fairway, Eddie and Charlene decided to leave the course. They waved goodbye to Chuck and Charlsey. As they rode away in Charlene's luxurious gas powered modern chariot, Eddie basked in his halo of glory, as if a triumphant Caesar. He thought he had magically collected enough personal stuff to bail Jim Bob out of prison.

"I bet you never imagined this would happen?" Charlene asked.

"My brain's spinning," Eddie said. He glanced up at Charlene.

"That took courage Eddie, real courage," Charlene said.

"Thanks, but it all happened so fast, I didn't even think," Eddie said.

"You listened," Charlene said.

"Sorry," Eddie asked.

"You didn't need to think," Charlene said. She turned off the radio. "You listened to your instincts, they told you what to do, it's all about listening."

"Never occurred to me," Eddie said. He fumbled with the golf glove, closely examining the signature.

Charlene glanced over at Eddie. She grappled with the steering wheel at nine and one o'clock. She shook her head.

"I can't figure you out," Charlene said.

"Why?" Eddie said. He looked up at Charlene.

"You come all the way down here last minute to a golf tournament, you're not really that interested in," Charlene said. "And now you've got this epic golf memorabilia, how random is that? Amazing-"

"I just wanted to do something different," Eddie said.

"I don't think so," Charlene said.

"Why?" Eddie said. He faintly gulped. He stared forward as they whizzed past the security gate. And she turned the car onto the main road, and past lines of parked cars.

"Like I said, instinct, I never question my instincts," Charlene said. She waved her right hand in the air. "Forget that, we favor you, Clevenger should thank his lucky stars."

"Not sure I follow," Eddie said. He stuffed the gloves into his pants pocket.

"You didn't make rash emotional judgments about us last night," Charlene said. She winked down at Eddie.

"No worries," Eddie said.

"It's not what you said, it was your expressions, your body language," Charlene said. She rocked back and forth smiling. "Thank you, I needed a happy booster shot." The sun's golden rays flooded all that was visible. The odd couple coursed past the golf course littered with a human menagerie of hopes and dreams walking across the non-lethal battlefield pock marketed with brown turf scars. "My inner core is the same." Charlene said. She shifted back on her leather hand stitched seat.

"I see," Eddie said. But he was curious about the glint of sadness in Charlene's eyes.

"I doubt that, it's hard for my family to accept this," Charlene said. She paused for a moment and randomly stared at the Germantown boutiques and quaint restaurants crowded with Friday afternoon shoppers. "I'm a thousand percent certain of only one thing. You can never truly understand another person, unless you *see the world through their eyes*."

Eddie leaned his left forearm along the center console studying Charlene's face. He thought she was one of the kindest people he has ever met. She had everything money could buy, but nothing of value in return to ease her pain. The pain from hopelessly loving someone that didn't fully understand love.

"I guess I'm the perfect example of walk-a-mile-in-my-shoes," Charlene sang a bit like Elvis. "I chose women's shoes."

"Sorry?" Eddie asked. Eddie fidgeted with Jake's cap.

"Old Elvis song, 'before you abuse, criticize and accuse, walk a mile in my shoes," Charlene said. They reversed their path from the golf club driving down the bumpy brick roads canopied with oaks and red maples. "I'm allowed to sing like Elvis, it's part of my Memphis DNA."

"Did you ever think you'd win the lotto?" Eddie asked. He chuckled at Charlene.

"Never, total fluke. I never used to waste money gambling or buying lotto tickets, but, we saw the massive number and

Raquel and the kids goaded me into spending a dollar, then lightning strikes and here I am."

"Dumb luck works," Eddie said.

"Oh, for sure, money or not, you need luck, like you had today," Charlene said laughingly.

"Yeah, I guess so, but I think all those golfers, they got lucky in life. They all won the sperm Olympics, gold medalists for sure," Eddie said. He closely examined the plastic bag with Lionel's blood stained sock.

Charlene glanced over at Eddie. She let the high-powered sedan coast down the street.

"Not sure I agree. I'm sure they are all blessed with tremendous God given gifts. But my sense is they all sort of make their own luck," Charlene said. She half-smirked as she watched a couple strolling on the concrete sidewalk.

Eddie scratched the top of his head.

"Really? I think they all got predestined, lucky people," Eddies said. He held the sweater vest open. He shook his head. "Right family, born at the right time-"

"Do you really believe that BS?" Charlene asked. She glared over at Eddie. She took off her visor and stroked her hairline with her fingertips.

"Why?" Eddie said.

"If I hurt your feelings, I'll apologize. I suspect you've never had someone tell you what they think," Charlene said.

Eddie anxiously shrugged his shoulders. He slid down in the seat. He crossed his arms.

"Okay," Eddie said. "I think."

"Ever taken a risk everybody thinks insane?" Charlene asked.

"I don't know, maybe," Eddie said. He stared forward.

"Wrong answer, if you did, you'd know exactly what I'm saying" Charlene said. She tapped the steering wheel. "Life's what you make of it, like it or not, you need to be self-reliant, practice your craft."

"I hear you," Eddie said.

"I don't think so," Charlene said. She shifted the convertible into the left-hand turn lane bisected by a row of yellow tulip poplars and dogwoods. She mashed on the gas pedal and sped past the lackadaisical traffic.

"I do feel lost, not sure why," Eddie said, "Numb, I guess."

"I'm not surprised," Charlene said. She paused for a moment as they waited for the streetlight to turn green. "Let go of that negative cynicism, that sperm Olympic garbage."

Eddie closed his eyelids.

"I just think some people are lucky," Eddie said.

"How do you think those golfers felt today?" Charlene asked.

"Like they're supposed to be there," Eddie said.

"Fair enough, how do you think Billy felt the first time he played in a tournament?" Charlene asked.

"I don't know, maybe a bit nervous," Eddie said.

"I bet he was nervous today. Playing with Jake, Lionel and Juan, intimidating bunch, big crowd, television, but he has practiced enough now, that he has taught himself to overcome his nerves."

Eddie refolded his arms across his chest.

"Okay, positive thinking, I get it," Eddie said.

"No, I don't think you do. Ever watch Biff Soxworthy or Stephano Martine?" Charlene asked.

"What? Sure, those guys are hilarious," Eddie said. He looked at Charlene with a puzzled expression.

"Do you think they were nervous the first show they did?"

"Yeah, I would think so," Eddie said.

"Okay, think their families thought being a comic was a good idea?" Charlene asked. She smiled at Eddie.

"Never thought about it," Eddie said. "No."

"That, my 'chia-pet-haired' friend, is what makes all the difference. It's the fork in the road, as the poem goes," Charlene said. "Courage, audacity and a lot of hard work-"

"What?" Eddie said. "I don't understand."

"Courage, some people have the courage to face failure," Charlene said. She tapped her fingers along the steering wheel. "It's not like winning the lottery, you have to have audacity to try something you believe in. To try, but fail, maybe fail miserably, but keep trying, and failing, and keep trying, until one day, BANG, everybody says you make, IT, look easy."

"You're serious?" Eddie said.

"Yep, that's that - it thing - I think, some people have a voice inside their brain nudging them," Charlene said. She grinned over at Eddie. "Ever been in love?"

Eddie scrunched even further down in the handmade leather seat. His heart somersaulted over the image of Ardee's face. He paused for a few minutes and stared out at the rows of rosy red and pale white brick houses, some had blue-gray slate roofs.

"I don't know," Eddie said. He readjusted the golf cap on his head. "But I think I know what you are about to say."

"Wrong answer again, a name, a face should flash inside your brain," Charlene said. She smacked Eddie on his leg. "I remember the girl I had puppy love for when I was thirteen, never forgot her. Raquel's face the day we got married. I think love is the biggest risk, to feel pure love, to love someone more than yourself, now that takes courage."

"That's sweet," Eddie said. "But I think love's over rated."

"Come on, that's what life's about," Charlene said. "I think love is part of our DNA."

"All right, I hear ya," Eddie said.

"I don't think you truly understand true love or faith for that fact, until you've lived through hell. Had your heart broken, and pieced your life back together," Charlene said. She huffed. "I refused to lie down like dog and die, I got back up."

"I hear ya," Eddie said. He shrugged.

"Besides, a winning lotto ticket solved all my problems?" Charlene asked. She slowly breathed through her mouth. "Right?"

"I'd like to take a turn," Eddie said.

"It just magnified them. All I ever wanted in life was to find true love, why I worked so hard," Charlene said.

"But you found Raquel," Eddie said.

"Yes, I'm thankful to God. But I sometimes wonder at what cost," Charlene said. She stopped the car at a red light. Several shoppers gawked at them as they strolled past. "Look at them, they can't help themselves, standing over there judging us from a safe distance. They've never met us."

"It's weird," Eddie said. He watched them.

"Don't be afraid to face life, if you make mistakes pick yourself up, and just keep going forward," Charlene said. She snapped her fingers. "Time gets by-"

"I here ya," Eddie said.

"I hope you do," Charlene said. "I pray you'll find love and you find someone who loves you as much in return, just do me a favor, stop hiding."

Charlene maneuvered her flashy ride up the curved brick driveway at her palatial estate. They recounted all the minute details from their golf adventure with Raquel and Charles Jr. and Sam. Then Eddie said his good-byes.

The late Friday afternoon sunlight splashed through the oak trees creating a kaleidoscope of cascading heart felt light. Eddie glanced at his rearview mirror at the peculiar family's reflection. They stood huddled together waving good-bye. Eddie turned the car wheel and drove off the estates driveway and onto Anesidora Boulevard.

Chapter Twenty Five

As Captain Lovins and Eddie converged toward Nashville, Mr. Oppenheimer crouched down near the back servant's door at Bertrand Screwtop's mansion. He adjusted his latex gloves for a snug fit, flipped open the security key pad and pressed in the code. He quickly picked the dead bolt lock, and the knob lock. Covered in a form fitting black outfit, he slithered his tall sinewy body inside the laundry room, careful not to step his lightweight black mesh boots on the innocuous appearing pressure pads placed on the exterior red brick landing, and just inside behind the door. He grinned down at the basic security devices, but appreciated the thought behind the easily obtained commercial measures. He crouched down below the Blue Bahia granite counter top, and next to a deep farmhouse sink. He flashed a light spectrum beam to detect any infrared light. He quickly detected the photoelectric security beams that crossed waist high at the entrance into the massive custom kitchen. He had detected the same security system profile in the estate's back yard as he had approached the main house. He thought Mr. Screwtop had spent a great deal of money to prevent his unannounced visits. But he was a professional, he was one of Ms. Prosperina's creations. She had used her genetic material to form him, and several other organisms from one of her laboratories. But for some reason, he was the only human organism she trusted. He understood his purpose and he knew she could read his every thought. She had trained him from his odd birth to always be on guard because it was vitally important not to get sloppy, for inattention to detail guaranteed the end of his usefulness and then his existence. And in a few moments, Mr. Screwtop would pay the ultimate price for defying Ms. Prosperina's commands.

As he easily defeated the motion detection system by starving it of electrical power, he noted Mr. Screwtop had taken the cheapest option by not installing any energy detection system with the motion detection system. And as typical for a cheapskate lawyer, the security cameras were fake. He shook his blond head in disapproval. If he had an unhappy client like Ms. Prosperina, he would have spared no expense. He shrugged; at least it would have created a temporary challenge for him.

After he efficiently made his way toward Mr. Screwtop's office down a wainscoted hallway, he crouched down on the Brazilian cherry floorboards to pause and listen. He took out his small flash light and checked the long hallway in front and behind him. Then he carefully inspected the thick six-panel yellow oak office door and wooden frame. He sprayed a mist over the ornate brass doorknob, and across the half-inch gap at the bottom. He found the magnet for the simple security device and waved a demagnetizing wand across the top and below the door as he watched the security beam die. He picked the brass lock and pushed the door forward, and stared into the dark office centered by the outline of an ornate desk. But down the hallway, toward the front doors he heard a woman's panicked voice. Checking his digital watch, he quickly pulled the office door almost closed; he twisted to scamper down the hallway back toward the kitchen to investigate the disturbance. In the formal living room, he crouched down next to a walnut Louis XIV period antique sofa, he spied into the custom kitchen. But Mr. Oppenheimer glanced away after seeing two naked middle-aged wrinkled pasty white bodies. He shut his eyes as he leaned back against piney wood paneled walls.

"Bertrand, honey what's wrong," she asked.

"I'm on fire, I can hardly see," Bertrand said.

"Oh honey, your pulse is racing," she said.

"My head is cracking open," Bertrand said.

Mr. Oppenheimer heard her bare feet flop nearby him, as she snagged a throw pillow off the couch. He thought Ms. Prosperina would have enjoyed watching Mr. Screwtop suffer.

"Lie down, put your head on this pillow," she said. She yanked open the icemaker. She opened and closed cupboard drawers until she found some plastic bags. She rapidly stuffed them with ice. "Bertrand, can you hear me?"

"Ya," Bertrand said slurring part of the word.

"I've got to cool you down, try to hold this to your face," she said. She grabbed more bags of ice; she shoved them next to his shivering body. She smashed them under his blushing, wrinkled neck. Then she added more bags of ice on each side, and down his body. Then she went back and poured several glasses of water. "You need to hydrate, drink this honey." As Mr. Oppenheimer watched, she left, and scampered from the kitchen. He snuck over to the living rooms far entranceway as she ran into home's front reception area. Through the floor to ceiling windows, the full moon cast a bluish glow over her as she scaled the front marble stairs. Mr. Oppenheimer ducked down on his hands and crawled forward across the cold marble flooring, down a short hardwood hallway back to his insertion point to observe Mr. Screwtop. He could see Mr. Screwtop's bare feet, and bags of sweating ice bags. Then he heard the woman return, she sprang past the doorway.

"Open your mouth," she said, "swallow these, they're aspirins." On her knees holding Bertrand's wrist, she had grabbed her cell phone and was contacting emergency services. Mr. Oppenheimer was well within striking distance, he considered killing them both, but Ms. Prosperina would consider that untidy, particularly after a call to EMS. And if he were caught in Mr. Screwtop's office, or on the property, it would not take long for the authorities to connect him back with Ms. Prosperina. Left with only one option, he deftly escaped from the mansion. And as he drove toward downtown, he was quite aware Ms. Prosperina already knew what had happened. He would accept her decision; he had accepted his fate many years ago.

Chapter Twenty Six

O ut of the Turnbull's sight, as Eddie drove back toward Nashville, he wondered if he would ever meet them again.

As he glanced over at his glove box he thought about the autographed items, Lionel's socks, he felt energized by his good luck. But his emotions were entangled from meeting Clevenger's cousin and her family, that just the day before he had stereotyped as freakish, and out of line with normal society. But now, human beings he had a strange eternal bond. "What a weird day," Eddie whispered. He blinked his eyelids several times, as he tried to focus on the concrete road. Driving back along the freeway as darkness overtook the day, Eddie considered his precious life and the perceived treasures in his glove box. He wondered if pure evil had nudged him to help Jim Bob, and to try selling something as sacred as another human beings DNA. Or was this all pre-destined, was he doing what a cold, calculating higher power had already mapped out for his insignificant life. Eddie was quite aware he did not have much of a life; he thought he was just another grain of sand along the beach. And what kind of life could he offer to Ardee? He thought it better not to fall in love as he thought of his lonely mother. And the tragic moment he lost of his father. He would not wish that feeling on his worst enemy, but he would have to get one first. He felt a sharp wound reemerge as his stomach churned from his memory thinking about Raquel's comments. His father was dead, and not lost, as if Eddie were out searching for him. Raquel's comment was a cold hard truth. He quickly wiped away a tear with his forefinger. He clenched the steering wheel, and then clicked on the radio turning it up to ear splitting volume.

# # #

Later in the evening, Eddie returned to his apartment complex. Concealed within the darkness, Captain Lovins watched him lope past the white panel van were he sat behind the steering wheel. He waited for Edward to enter his apartment, turn on a light, then he got out, and strolled over toward Edward's jalopy where he marched to the rear passenger side. He pulled out from his jacket pocket a tiny tracking device pasted to a magnet; he crouched down and stuck the monitor under the rear wheel well. He got back up, checked the area for anyone watching, and returned to his van.

Back inside his van, Captain Lovins flipped open his wireless computer. He tested the tracking device, it blipped motionless within the mapped screen, assured it operated properly; then he shifted his attention to contacting Edward.

# # #

Eddie meandered inside to his old world apartment. Skimming the interior painted wall with his left palm up, he flicked the light switch to turn on a lamp set across the room. The worn furniture seemed to be in place, his couch still pushed against the bisecting interior wall. Eddie clicked the deadbolt lock shut behind him. He stuffed the autographed golf cap, glove and sweater vest inside a kitchen cabinet. The plastic bag with Lionel's bloodstained socks, he held with his fingertips like soiled underpants. He closely examined them, he shrugged, and then he dropped them into the empty refrigerator freezer, not sure why, he figured it was what they would do on CSI. After a deep breath, Eddie retrieved his laptop computer out from under the bathroom sink, hiding it from thieves, as if a criminal would have targeted his low rent abode. He thought if Jim Bob could do this, it could not have been rocket science, and not to mention, if these people were dangerous, Jim Bob would be dead. And the last he checked Jim Bob was safely housed inside Dorian-Hyde Federal Penitentiary charged with not paying his federal income taxes.

"I can do this," Eddie said at his computer screen. He pressed the on button. He opened his web browser. The screen glowed across Eddie's blank face as he navigated to WePay.

# # #

At the same time, Captain Lovins sat inside the van scanning for Edward's wireless internet access; he locked onto it, and pirated Edward's unique IP address. The easily obtained software blocked any nearby inbound internet traffic or suspicious return pings. The encrypted communication software would swipe Edward's computer clean after the dialogue, the digital fingerprint as if Edward were simply having a conversation with himself.

"I'm a huge golf fan." Captain Lovins typed. He waited for Edward to respond, then he would be able to shadow Edward's computer screen.

# # #

The instant message blipped open on Eddie's screen. He read the message. Eddie crossed his arms and stared out the apartment window into the darkness. Jim Bob's contact didn't mess around, but then he realized they likely saw him on television.

"What about WePay?" Eddie typed.

"We need to discuss terms." Captain Lovins typed.

Eddie's skin-flushed crimson. He paused. He folded his arms across his chest. He paced his apartment. He stopped and walked back over to his computer.

"How can I trust you?" Eddie typed. He wiped perspiration from behind his ear.

# # #

"You can't." Captain Lovins typed.

Simple responses go a long way, Captain Lovins thought. He could almost visualize Eddie squirming after he read his response. Then he typed the release valve. "No harm will come to you. Perhaps you will get more samples from our list."

# # #

Eddie closed his eyes. After a deep breath, he responded.

"How do we do this?" Eddie typed.

"Be in your parking lot in thirty minutes." Captain Lovins typed. "Stand on the walkway near the mailbox station. I will be in a white van. When you get there, if you want to continue, raise your right arm high in the air."

Eddie bit his lower lip. He backed away from the computer. He wondered how they knew where he lived. He wandered through his apartment, fidgeting with the pillows on his couch, readjusting a lamps position on a side table and running his fingertips along the kitchen windowsill for dust. He took in a deep breath. He faced his computer screen.

"How do I know you won't kill?" Eddie typed.

"This is business," Captain Lovins typed. "We are not the mob. And I know where you live, you'd already be dead."

"Good point." Eddie typed. He coughed. His scalp tingled.

"Thirty minutes?" Captain Lovins typed.

"Yes." Eddie typed. He stared up at the starless textured ceiling. He interlocked his fingers on his head.

"This is insane," Eddie said. After twenty minutes, Eddie wobbled into his bathroom. He studied his sunburned face for some mysterious courage hiding behind his eyeballs.

Meanwhile, Captain Lovins had parked the van at his predetermined position. From experience, if anyone noticed, they would likely be ignored thinking it just another ho-hum harmless drug deal. As Eddie splashed cold water on his face, he thought, Jim Bob and his half-backed schemes. He grabbed the items; he pulled out the bloodstained sock from the refrigerator freezer. He marched outside. He descended to the ground floor landing and stood astride the complex mailbox. The temperature had cooled. A thunderous roar shook the ground underneath his tennis shoes. As if a wooden Italian marionette on a puppeteers string, up his right arm dangled. He stared over at the white van parked perhaps twenty feet from him. Captain Lovins relished the pressure packed transactions. He got out and stood next to the van. His hands gripped his hips. Eddie gulped. His throat constricted, as a menacing bald headed man emerged from the driver side of the van, his shadow crept toward Eddie by the parking lots halide lamps.

"Okay, keys are in my left hand," Captain Lovins said.

"I've seen you before," Eddie said nervously.

"Perhaps, here are the van keys," Captain Lovins said. With tactile precision, he threw the van key at Eddie's feet.

Eddie stared down at the shiny silvery keys.

"Okay?" Eddie said. He hesitated.

"Hey Bambi, I'll not harm you, I'll walk over there," Captain Lovins said. He pointed in the opposite direction from his van. "Take the keys, open the van side door, leave the items in the basket. You walk back to there, I'll slowly walk over, I'll inspect them. You can watch me the entire time, okay?"

"Okay," Eddie said. He tightly clutched the golf memorabilia.

"Let's get this done," Captain Lovins said. He glanced back and forth for any nosey neighbors. He marched away from the van.

"Okay, okay," Eddie said. He expelled his breath. Without any hesitation, he ran toward the van, he slid the side panel door open. Inside, an eighteen-inch rectangular wire basket encased within a solid metal frame. A neat and clean interior, it had three large black suitcases placed in a perfect horizontal row over the rear axle. In reality, the suitcases contained Captain Lovins negotiation funds, a few well-maintained weapons, and a refrigerator/freezer. His most important piece of equipment kept safely with him. Concealed in his right front pocket of his black camouflage pants, his Proteomic-Asscher-Loop, a device Professor Quan invented. It appeared similar to a jewelers magnifying loop, a simple device for Captain Lovins to use to verify living genetic material existed on the samples he collected. They did not waste resources searching for dead dinosaur eggs or decaying DNA.

"Okay, I put a bunch of stuff in there" Eddie said.

"Good, now move back," Captain Lovins said.

"Okay," Eddie said. He poked his head in the front of the van's quarter panel. The man had not moved. Eddie slinked back to his assigned post. He closely watched the man march toward the van where he slipped on latex gloves. He carefully opened the plastic bag containing Lionel's bloodstained sock.

Captain Lovins began his basic analysis. Within seconds, he determined the sock held not just blood, but also retained dried sweat, and a few black hairs with the cuticle, likely from Lionel's foot and ankles.

This item will get Professor Quan's juices flowing, Captain Lovins thought. He smiled. He clasped the PAL to his dominant eye, and held the lens close to the bloodstain. The verification protocol was initiated after he pressed a pimpleish looking knob on the loop surface. It emitted a blue laser beam of xenon light through the aperture. It reflected off tiny mirrors, into a single beam shot through the genetic material. Within the Nano-world, Lionel's helical shaped DNA strands vibrated like foamy dancing ladders. He examined Jake's golf cap, then Juan's sweater vest and then Billy's golf glove. Each item was packed with genetic material.

"Excellent," Captain Lovins said. He expanded a black rubber drum he had concealed under the passenger side seat. He carefully placed each item in a clear vacuum-sealed bag; he took out a black magic marker and wrote in a white panel the sample name and date collected. Then he poured a solution over them to instantly flash freeze them inside the septic drum. Then he sealed the container with a sticky glue film. He was certain Edward would take his offer, and he dared not risk further contamination from the polluted environment.

Captain Lovins smirked. Now was the time to look Edward dead in his eyes, and figure out what was wrong with him. He efficiently walked in front of Edward.

"Please don't kill me," Eddie said. He held his hands up.

"Pipe down Bambi," Captain Lovins said. "A truly remarkable achievement, Edward." A thunderous rumble pierced through the ghostly night as a thunderstorm approached. The parking lot started to smell earthy, and the temperature was dropping.

"Thanks, I don't know how I did it," Eddie said.

"Look me in the eye," Captain Lovins said.

"Dude, I'm nobody," Eddie said. He squinted with his gaze looking at the fit man. "I just got lucky."

"Well, perhaps you'll help Mr. Calhoun, rather unfortunate situation," Captain Lovins said. And he stared directly into Eddies eyes. He saw the pain he had seen many times before in the eyes of countless children. For he had learned the eyes connect to the essence of the soul. Captain Lovins instinctively understood Edward more than Eddie understood himself. The pinprick glint from trauma stirred Captain Lovins to sadness and anger aware life can be cruel, unfair and seemingly random to those unaware how nature worked.

"What do you want? Eddie said. He backed away. He stared down at his untied tennis shoe.

"In as such, we are offering you three hundred thousand dollars. I have the money nearby," Captain said. He blankly stared forward.

Three hundred thousand dollars, Eddie thought. He wobbled back, as Captain Lovins quickly walked over to his van.

"Holy biscuit eater," Eddie said. He did not move his shoes, but watched Captain Lovins return. "I accept."

Captain Lovins threw forward the black duffle bag full of Federal Reserve Notes.

"Cash is inside," Captain Lovins said, as an unwelcome breeze rustled through Eddie's thick, mangy brown hair.

"If you like, count it, bathe in it, if you happen to obtain another item from our *Wish List*, you know how to contact me," Captain Lovins said. He glanced behind him and up into the dark dense sky blocked out all forms of celestial light. "Storms brewing, so I suggest you disappear, see you soon."

The eight-cylinder engine roared a noxious exhaust cloud that engulfed Eddie. The wraithlike vehicle disappeared into a wavy curtain of light rain. With his eyes shut, alone with enough U.S. currency a Latin drug lord might blush. A claustrophobic sensation engulfed Eddie. He lifted the duffle bag, but it was dead weight heavy. As he dragged it up the stairwell, halfway up to the first landing he had to stop. He huffed as his lungs stung. His shoulders strained. His biceps twitched as he trudged up the stairs fighting Newton's Law of Universal Gravity. At his apartment door, Eddie's sweat soaked hands shook as he attempted to open the metal door. He glanced behind him and over at his neighbor's apartment door. He imagined groups of Ninja warriors waited nearby for him with sharp swords strapped to their backs, about to descend and slice him into sushi-sized pieces. The swirling mists shifted into a full out tempest. A lightning bolt struck near the complex and lit up the night sky as if Thor was curious what Eddie had in the duffle bag.

"Breathe, don't panic," Eddie whispered. After a measured inhalation, enough oxygen cycled from his lungs to his brain to calm his nervous system. He wiped moisture off his eyebrows; then he turned the silver key. He collapsed inside clutching the fabric strap as he embraced the suitcase in a non-sexual pose. "What have I done?"

Chapter Twenty Seven

Ms. Prosperina glared over at Mr. Oppenheimer. She had taken her sunglasses off. Mr. Oppenheimer simply stared down at the finely stitched Persian rug. He sat up straight on the high back leather chair with mahogany wood carved eagle claw feet.

"Lucky," Ms. Prosperina said. She dragged on her cigarette, the tip end lit up the room like a sizzling red lava rock. She stared out the expansive bank of windows down at the quiet downtown. "You made the correct decision, we had more to lose than to gain, and that is the only reason you are alive." She extinguished the cigarette. "Speak."

"Yes, Madam," Mr. Oppenheimer said.

"Is that all you ever have to say?" Ms. Prosperina said. She walked toward the suite's bar. "Perhaps some bourbon?"

"I am thankful you spared me," Mr. Oppenheimer said.

"Spare?" Ms. Prosperina said. She blankly stared up at the ornate ceiling. "What does that mean?" She poured some bourbon into a crystal highball glass.

Mr. Oppenheimer closed his eyes. He expected death.

"Ah, you had mercy on me, Madam," Mr. Oppenheimer said.

"Hmm, hardly," Ms. Prosperina said. She set the highball glass down on the bar. As she strolled toward Mr. Oppenheimer, she morphed into the form of a black winged serpent, her black forked tongue shot out like a bendable two-tipped spear. But just as quickly she reformed into her petite middle-aged body profile. "Weakness, speak or die, or I'll scramble your brain like Mr. Screwtop."

Mr. Oppenheimer gazed up at Mr. Prosperina's glowing red and black eyes. He did not move his head, or shift in the chair.

"I fear you, but I am not afraid of death," Mr. Oppenheimer said. He clenched his defined jaw. But for a brief moment her eyes radiated as if black holes, absorbing him into oblivion.

"Then you don't fear me?" Ms. Prosperina said. She snarled at Mr. Oppenheimer. The she hissed like a King Cobra. "Your humanity gets the best of you, someday I will shed this vessel I'm trapped in, then you will see, if you are still living." She suddenly stopped. She turned her head; she focused her attention toward the suite's double doors. He hands draped behind her back.

"Madam?" Mr. Oppenheimer asked.

"Dr. Yin has been active," Ms. Prosperina said. She stared over at the fireplace. "He knows Mr. Screwtop's situation, he called, the woman picked up."

Mr. Oppenheimer stood up. He buttoned his jacket.

"We must be very careful, I cannot allow myself to think about what he knows," Ms. Prosperina said. She sensed

Professor Quan channeling inside her mind. "As I have always suspected, he is not far, but I must quiet my mind."

"Yes, Madam?" Mr. Oppenheimer asked.

"In a few days, we should pay a visit to Mr. Screwtop's firm, this Mr. Lewis," Ms. Prosperina said. "That is what I sense."

"Yes, Madam," Mr. Oppenheimer said.

"Now go away, I need quiet," Ms. Prosperina said.

Chapter Twenty Eight

Agent Machiavelli and Agent Prince sat waiting in a late model pickup truck parked along the busy residential street, just outside of Eddie's apartment complex. As the storm raged, the white panel van driven by Captain Lovins sped past them, Agent Prince switched on the windshield wipers.

"I knew it, Calhoun's friend," Agent Prince said.

"I thought this was a waste of time," Agent Machiavelli said. He checked the security of his government issued service revolver. "Let's follow, try to keep a safe distance."

"No telling where, got a full tank," Agent Prince said. He smashed his wool cap down over his ears. Then he shifted the standard transmission into drive. "The rain should help conceal us, I think."

"Yeah," Agent Machiavelli said. He pointed forward. "Drive."

# # #

Unaware that the Federal Agents followed, Captain Lovins traveled east, on ignored state and county roads across western

Tennessee, and then drove north over the unguarded Kentucky state line. After driving thirty miles into Kentucky, he turned the van onto winding roads snaking toward the heart of eastern Kentucky. As the husky raindrops transformed to particles of mist, darkness withdrew Captain Lovins drove past the lush sea of green hillsides overgrown by broad leafy kudzu, and the densely treed landscape permeated with the constant sulfur scent from burning coal. He traveled through the rock-quarried Three Pagodas Pass, exited the van off the old state highway, and drove down a dirty two-lane blacktopped road blanketed with a dense fog layer. He slowed the van, and maneuvered it in front of the working gas pump for a dingy two-pump gas station. The other gas pump wrapped in dark garbage bags duct tapped together, a paper sign taped on both sides – Out of Order. He sensed a pickup truck coast past him, and he heard it roll onto the gravel roadside hidden just past the corner of the cinder block station. Across the road in the front yard of a tin roofed house, white and black feathered roosters pecked at piles of grain devouring their breakfast.

# # #

Agent Prince clicked off the yellowish headlights, but as he compressed the brake pedal, the brakes squeaked louder than a nest of hungry baby chicks. Agent Machiavelli shoved at Agent Prince.

"Idiot," Agent Machiavelli said.

"Sorry," Agent Prince said. "Think he heard?"

"You woke up that cemetery," Agent Machiavelli said as he pointed toward a fenced in family plot of headstones littered across a modest clearing. "Let's hope he's tired, distracted, and ignored us."

# # #

As the milky haze swirled, Captain Lovins heard the truck's brakes loud squeak. He knew that random pickup trucks do not magically park near this gas station. Captain Lovins did not flinch as the gang of roosters reacted with their own morning hackles. He squeezed the cold metal gas pump handle as the black and white metal numbers added up the totals. He had frequented the same gas station for decades, he knew the attendant, he knew the attendant's family, some of them he employed at their diamond drill bit facility. Captain Lovins continued to pump gas as he studied the steaming woods behind the gas station.

"Amateur," Captain Lovins said. He shrugged. He finished pumping gas. He pressed the keyless remote to lock down the van. He strolled inside the gas station. He acknowledged the attendant. He studied a shelf of teenybopper magazines, and turned right toward the restroom sign. Then he ran through the building and out the back door. He scratched up the wet, wooded hillside that abutted behind the gas station. Captain Lovins scaled across as he put his arms up in front of his face to block the sharp thicket, shoving his boots through piles of leaves, as he scooted between burley barnacled trees. At the hill's crest, he crouched down. His breathing controlled. He saw an agent slowly getting out of the passenger side of the truck. The other agent on the driver's side appeared unsteady, as he kept checking his cell phone for text messages.

# # #

"He has to take a piss eventually, I'm thinking now," Machiavelli whispered. He stood next to the open passenger door. He checked his PDA's camera. "Let's see if I can get a few pictures, doubt his tag will pan out, you never know."

"I don't know, sir. He's awfully dangerous," Agent Prince said. He yanked his cap down over his ears. He checked his cell phone. "I don't have any cell coverage, are we in the US?"

"Grow a pair, maintain silence," Agent Machiavelli said. He shrugged. He checked his weapon. "Besides, he's old." He carefully shut the truck door. He walked away from the truck and acted as if a drifter strolling along the lonely curved highway. But Agent Machiavelli was unaware there are no stray drifters or homeless in eastern Kentucky. The owner of the roosters sat on his front porch watching them and sipping his morning coffee.

"He's not *that* old," Agent Prince said. He stared down the road carved through the steep mountains searching for anything and everything; he twisted around to watch through the truck's back cab window as Agent Machiavelli stopped. He looked back to acknowledge Agent Prince with his forefinger across his lips. Then he walked toward the cinder block gas station and disappeared past the building's corner.

# # #

As he observed the distracted agent with his knees on the bench seat monitoring the other agent, and constantly checking his cell, Captain Lovins descended in front of the truck. He clawed forward like a black crab. He sprang past the truck's front headlights. He slithered to the driver side door, from below; he edged up to observe the agent, he grinned. Then he stood up and tapped on the driver side window with the butt-end of his spider knife as he swung open the truck door with his left gloved hand. As Agent Prince instinctively twisted back around, Captain Lovins slammed Agent Prince just above his nose with his right elbow. Agent Prince huffed out all the air in his lungs, he grabbed for his broken, bleeding nose. He wobbled, hazily blinked, and flopped back on the bench seat. Captain Lovins climbed inside the cab, he leaned Agent Prince upright behind the steering wheel. He locked him in place with the seat belt. He patted him down, found the cell phone, and took his holstered weapon. He did not find a weapon under the seat.

# # #

Finding the van temporarily unattended, with his cell phone, Agent Machiavelli had taken several photos of the van. He stared inside the gas station searching for Captain Lovins. The gas station attendant ignored him and continued to watch his small color television and eat corn chips. Agent Machiavelli crept behind the service station tow truck. Crouched under the dangling tow hook, he was pleased to have taken the photos, collecting evidence, and thought Dr. Yin would be quite pleased to have these after they apprehended Captain Lovins.

But in a ghostly manner, Captain Lovins had glided in behind Agent Machiavelli. He tapped him on his shoulder.

"Lost?" Captain Lovins asked.

"Wha-" Agent Machiavelli said as he twisted his shoulders around. His expression confused, then stunned, and then frightened. He put his left hand up and tried to shove Captain Lovins back. But Captain Lovins with the base of his thick right hand, jabbed forward into Agent Machiavelli's throat. Then he recoiled and rapidly popped the agent on the bridge of his nose.

"Tell our girl hello," Captain Lovins said as he punched Agent Machiavelli in the mouth with his left hand. The final blow stumbled Agent Machiavelli backwards, his head smacked against the cast-iron hook. He dropped his cell phone on the oil stained concrete as he crumpled against the back of the truck. Then he fell forward onto his knees, he wobbled, his arms flapped and he flopped like a bag of sand dropped near a concrete mixer, sideways against the truck's hard rubber retreads. Captain Lovins bent down, grasped the agent by his jacket, then slung him over his right shoulder, and trudged back to the truck as the roosters cackled in approval. He shoved him inside the passenger side, and he clicked the seatbelt back across Agent Machiavelli. He took his weapon.

After he snagged the cell phone from the concrete, he took out the battery, and the sim card. And just to be nasty, he pulled off their shoes and tossed them across the road into the cock-fighting pens. Then he slashed their back tires with his spider knife.

"Hmm, stranded," Captain Lovins said at the unconscious agents. He sprayed them in the face with one of Professor Quan's unpatented memory erasing mists. He returned to his van. He took his time, he checked the wheel wells for a transmitter, or underneath the van, or inside the hood. He inspected the engine, closely examined the tires. He was certain they had not gotten inside. He marched into the station, gave the gas station attendant cash for his gas, extra for his troubles and a little for the neighbors. Then he sped off down the county road and disappeared within the morning dew.

A few miles down from the gas station, he turned the mud-splattered van off the two-lane blacktop road and onto an unmarked gravel and dirt path concealed with dense emerald foliage. The vans shock absorbers constantly squeaked bouncing along the narrow road over potholes filled with ground surface water. He voyaged deeper and deeper within the heavily canopied forest. Though exceptionally trained, his meticulous plan mandated patience after any detection. After he drove the van the predetermined half-mile down the mud-caked road, he stopped at a spot marked by a bent southern crabapple limb. He lightly pushed the brake pedal. And he clicked off the van engine. Night vision goggles now strapped to his forehead, he clicked the viewfinder down, and then got out with a M4A1 Carbine with a thermal sighting device. His boots squished in the mud as he marched behind the van. A viceroy butterfly emerged from the morning gloom now interspersed with rays of sunshine. It crested upon the gun barrel. He gently shooed it away as he crouched down near the vans hot tailpipe. The moist woods smelled of sulfur dioxide and the earth. White tail deer rustled through mounds of leaves, as crickets chirped and a red-cockaded woodpecker hammered against a pine tree. After he timed with his wristwatch forty-five minutes and one second, Captain Lovins was satisfied that nothing wicked would come his way. He got back inside the van and continued on his journey.

Captain Lovins maneuvered the van past massive American chestnut trees interspersed by mountain maples. September elms twisted their limps toward the grayish sky. Under the natural canopy, a tiny Kentucky warbler emitted its loud two-syllable song, a bobcat with tawny fur and dark spots crouched underneath a hawthorn tree, as fox squirrels foraged for seeds.

After he ventured three miles into the sylvan, Captain Lovins braked in front of the pinewood paneled shotgun style refuge. A tin roof cantilevered over an angled front porch, floored with a concrete textured slab. Captain Lovins pushed his shooting glasses over his eyes, he flipped a laser-sighted device over the left lens, and he twisted the tube to open the aperture. He waved a magnetized wireless access card past the eyehole and from within the house a laser beam locked onto Captain Lovins. It radiated within the device scanning his retina, past his blood vessels, and matched his genetic markers with his sample. The beam stopped. The porch began to slide back; it folded underneath the roofline, and exposed a dimly lit cargo cage. He drove the van over the concrete porch, and onto a shiny textured metal floor. He turned the engine off, and clapped his hands. The shotgun shack, reinforced by a steel skeleton, ingested the van and the elevator began its journey down into their lair. The powerful hydraulic motor's mechanical hum ceased as the elevator door pulled apart on the opposite side of the cage. Captain Lovins drove the van out of the mineshaft elevator, and steered left around the primary load-bearing member, a massive light grey painted column. He parked next to Professor Quan's spotlessly maintained 1957 Buick Roadmaster. Captain Lovins retrieved the drum containing the genetic merchandise. He marched toward the entrance to the laboratory; he stopped next to the door for another retinal scan, and to verify his DNA sample matched with the scanned information. After it stopped, he heard a metal thump as a five-inch diameter steel rod released the three-foot thick stainless steel door.

Professor Quan sprang up from a leather strata lounger. He released his pet dog, Waldo. His shoes covered by surgical socks. He rested his kaleidoscope on a nearby table and stood at the center of an Oriental rug with dark yellow pattern on it within the massive silo-like laboratory painted military grey. Waldo bounced over and sniffed at Captain Lovins' boots.

"He lives," Professor Quan said.

"Yeah, with our newest samples," Captain Lovins said.

"An amazing discovery," Professor Quan said.

"Yeah, but we have a problem," Captain Lovins said. He hoisted the septic drum onto the science table.

"How so?" Professor Quan asked. He examined the drum's seal.

"Caught a couple of agents trying to sneak up on me, while I was getting gas," Captain Lovins said. He took off his black skullcap. "I think they had Edward's apartment staked out, they used an old pickup truck to follow me, I got sloppy, I should have lured Edward to a better location."

Professor Quan put his glasses on as Waldo pranced behind his every movement within the lab. He stopped and leaned down and picked up his pet.

"She's in Nashville, she almost killed her lawyer, Screwtop, scared the hell out of Dr. Yin, literally, but it was all for show, to show me how powerful she has become," Professor Quan said. He ran his fingers through the dog's soft fur.

"Show of force to intimidate," Captain Lovins said.

"*It* is a relentless beast. And *it* is becoming desperate," Professor Quan said. "She has her shadow world in place, but she needs the meteorites, I guess she figured out her DNA is a jumbled mess, this girl wants purity, alien purity."

Captain Lovins shook his head.

"Then I think we should put Edward on the back burner," Captain Lovins said. He put on some latex gloves. He unsealed the ribbon around the drum top. He lifted each item out, and placed them inside a refrigerated antiseptic basin.

Professor Quan sighed. He hugged his dog and set her down on the worn couch. She curled in next the armrest.

"No," Professor Quan said. He stared past Captain Lovins. "It's interrelated, Edward, it will become aware of him, we will need to act fast, I fear."

Captain Lovins felt his skin flush. He thought of Edward's terrified face. He remembered Edward's happy baby face staring up at him the night he snuck into the Wilcox's home.

"I have to protect him," Captain Lovins said.

Professor Quan crossed his arms. He glanced across the laboratory at his gene therapy rooms.

"Let me think about it," Professor Quan said.

"Sort of makes all this rather unimportant," Captain Lovins said as he pointed over at their newest DNA samples. "Don't you think? I mean, it time to prepare for battle."

Professor Quan perked up and smiled.

"Oh, no, no," Professor Quan said. He waved at Captain Lovins. His pet sprang off the couch, she barked, and panted at Captain Lovins. "Oh Waldo, yes we need to keep our minds focused on love, he knows that."

"All right, I followed precise protocol, the PAL worked like a champ," Captain Lovins said. He smirked. "We got not just Lionel's sample, but Jake Saint Nick, Billy Sikleston and Juan Whaley samples, I checked them out, in that world, they're well known, it seems they just handed the stuff over to Edward."

Professor Quan wobbly leaned back against his lounger. He blinked his eyes rapidly and stared over at Captain Lovins.

"Ah, exceptional work," Professor Quan said. He sighed. "I just thought we got, I don't know, not this much."

"It's the find of our lifetime," Captain Lovins said.

"Yes, yes," Professor Quan said. He happily shook his head. He grinned at Captain Lovins. "Sorry, you ran across a few snoopy agents, but this is amazing."

"I used one of your concoctions, they'll be lucky to remember their names," Captain Lovins said. He chuckled. He coughed with his left-hand fist over his mouth. "About, ah, Edward-"

Professor Quan stared down at the floor. He frowned.

"And tell me about our prodigal one," Professor Quan said. He crossed his arms behind his back.

"I did exactly as you asked, I looked him square in the eyes," Captain Lovins said. He paused.

"And what did you see?" Professor Quan asked.

A deep stack of horizontal wrinkles squished across his forehead. He leaned his back against the science table.

"At first, bewilderment, fear of me," Captain Lovins said. He wagged his forefinger in the air. "But then, a sadness, it was the look you only get from someone who lost what they love."

"Trauma, right?" Professor Quan said.

"Yeah, I figured it out, he was thirteen, his father died suddenly from a massive heart attack," Captain Lovins said. He snapped his fingers. "Just like that, he lost his will."

"I can barely remember my parents," Professor Quan said.

"Like someone blew out his pilot light," Captain Lovins said. "He's lost hope."

Professor Quan moved over and hugged Captain Lovins. He reached down and he pulled his dog up and hugged her.

"I've suddenly become a bit of a hugger," Professor Quan said. He shrugged. "I don't know why, thank you."

"Yeah, I noticed. Ah, I gave Edward a huge sum," Captain Lovins said. "Figured it was the least I could, I know what it's like to see death up close, it changes you."

"Indeed, but no worries, we keep selling diamond drill bits," Professor Quan said. He angrily shook his fists. "I feel so stupid, love, what if you lost that? But focus, right?"

"Yeah, so, what's up with this Hernandez kid?" Captain Lovins asked. He slipped off the latex gloves. He stuffed them into a biohazard trashcan. "Good news at least, he lives in Nashville."

"Oh, with this bountiful collection," Professor Quan said. He stared over at the new golf professional samples. "Come on!"

"Just point me in his direction," Captain Lovins said.

"All right, the molecular synthesis needs to start, the specimens need time to thaw in the molecular cooler. I'll run them through genetic analysis tonight," Professor Quan said. He clapped his hands together. "I may not sleep for three days."

"Sorry," Captain Lovins said. "Not much help."

"This is my passion, not to worry, my secret is how I manipulate the chromatin, play with DNA and RNA associations,"

Professor Quan said. He shook his head at Captain Lovins. An expression, as if he caught the tail of a comet. "How it all gets bound together, ha, Jose Jr., will never know what hit him."

Chapter Twenty Nine

"Dr. Yin?" Agent Machiavelli asked. He stood in his brown socks outside the dusty gas station; he glanced around, he scratched the top of his head, he shivered, he stared up at the smoky Appalachian hills.

"I don't recognize this number?" Dr. Yin said.

Agent Machiavelli stared through the grimy gas station window over at the station attendant who frowned back at him, and shook his head. He sipped his coffee cup, set it down on the glass counter top and then stared down at the local newspaper.

"I had to borrow some money to call," Agent Machiavelli said. He pulled at the silver cord tethered to the side of the rectangular block pay phone bolted to the side of the cinder block building. "The number, old fashioned pay phone-"

"Yeah? Whatever, I'm waiting," Dr. Yin said.

"Someone took our stuff, we're, ah, stranded," Agent Machiavelli. He shut his eyes. He leaned against the building.

"Where are you?" Dr. Yin asked.

"Not sure, somewhere in east, Kentucky, I think? I'm not sure how we got here," Agent Machiavelli said. He stared across the concrete lot dotted with oil and gas stains at the sleeping Agent Prince splayed across the pickup truck bed.

"Moron, Lovins nailed you two bumbling fools," Dr. Yin said.

"Who? Sorry sir," Machiavelli said. He twisted his neck and rubbed his hand against his forehead because he had a pounding headache and his lips had ballooned. "Yes, Lovins-"

"Never mind, I'll send someone to collect you two, is Prince alive?" Dr. Yin asked.

"He's out, in the back of truck, he's breathing," Agent Machiavelli said. He rubbed his forehead with his fingertips. Across the road the roosters waltzed and laughingly crowed at him as their master feed them grain.

"Fine, stay there," Dr. Yin said. "That place sounds like a barnyard, I'll trace the number."

# # #

After Dr. Yin angrily replaced his office phone back into its cradle, he wrote down Agent Machiavelli's phone number. His cell phone started to rattle on top of his desk. He snagged the phone, but the phone number was blocked.

"Yes?" Dr. Yin asked.

"Dr. Yin, you have information for me?" Ms. Prosperina asked.

"Pardon?" Dr. Yin asked. He pulled the phone away from his pointy ear. "Who are you?"

"Pity, you don't recognize my voice?" Ms. Prosperina asked.

"No, who is this? What do you want?" Dr. Yin asked. He could hear the woman lightly chuckling. He thought she was smoking from the sound of her puffing near the phone's microphone.

"Well, you have accepted a great deal of my money," Ms. Prosperina said. "Does that help?"

Dr. Yin froze on his office chair. He stared out into the busy laboratory that Ms. Prosperina had funded. He thought she did not actually exist, he thought the money came from hidden government resources. And he thought locating Professor Quan for the original formulas was an exercise in futility. He was an old doddering fool by now, he thought. He shrugged. Then they hired Bertrand Screwtop to supervise his work, and the search for Professor Quan had intensified. Since then, he knew the clock had started to tick inside his mind.

"Ah, yes," Dr. Yin said.

"So sad to hear Mr. Screwtop fell and hit his head," Ms. Prosperina said. She sounded like she was purring.

Dr. Yin scratched at what appeared to be a bee sting on his hand. But he didn't remember getting stung. And he was surprised how fast news had traveled to this woman about Bertrand being in the hospital, after suffering a stroke.

"The doctors, from what I'm told, think he had a stroke, or aneurysm, that's all I know," Dr. Yin said. He shrugged.

"Hmm, pity, what else do you know?" Ms. Prosperina asked.

Dr. Yin had an immediate claustrophobic sensation, as if Ms. Prosperina was sitting near his desk, staring at him, having a direct business conversation. He hated to tell her bad news for their first conversation. Her reputation frightened him. And the fact Bertrand had suddenly become ill caused the hair along his neck to spring to life.

"Well, we almost caught my former bosses' protector," Dr. Yin said. He held his breath.

"Good, you told me the truth," Ms. Prosperina said. "It is unfortunate that Mr. Screwtop had a tendency to hold back."

Dr. Yin picked up his office telephone and examined it. He checked the corners of his office for a camera, he inspected the lamp set on his credenza.

"How?" Dr. Yin said without considering who was on the other end of the cellular phone conversation.

"I didn't bug your phone," Ms. Prosperina said. She sighed.

"I just," Dr. Yin said.

"Always be truthful, my one commandment," Ms. Prosperina said. "Now, I think you need to understand, although it might be useful, I do not care about the Hope Diamond, or any of his silly formulas for synthetic diamonds."

"Oh? I was told," Dr. Yin said. "But my research?"

"He has some other items, I need them to improve my processed foods, help feed the children," Ms. Prosperina said. "Obviously, I intend to make profit, but, I must feed future generations. I'm sure you can appreciate my approach."

"He's weird," Dr. Yin said. He set the landline back in its cradle. "Man's a kook, or was, he might be dead given his age."

HE could hear Ms. Prosperina take a drag from a cigarette. Then she puffed close to the microphone.

"No, he is quite active," Ms. Prosperina said.

"How can you be so sure?" Dr. Yin asked.

"It would be good for you not to question me," Ms. Prosperina said. "Have you met Mr. Oppenheimer?"

Dr. Yin shifted on his swiveling office chair; he sat up straight. He loosened his shirt collar.

"Sorry," Dr. Yin said. "Of course-"

"He has collected some important samples, modified them," Ms. Prosperina said. "Let's just say, he likes to make things from organic material, things that will help me, help this planet. But he is not inclined to share his thoughts with me, likely thinks I'm just a greedy business woman, hmm, pity."

Dr. Yin got up from behind his desk. He shut his office blinds and he locked his office door.

"Body parts? Has he figured it out," Dr. Yin asked.

"Oh, I sense I have your complete attention," Ms. Prosperina said. "If someone found his laboratory, they might find secrets that could make them rich, perhaps powerful, and diamonds are a mere minor part."

"Yes, he is rather self-absorbed," Dr. Yin said. He tapped at the desktop. "He's a, kook."

"I just want a few of his organic samples, for my cause, you understand, but you can have the rest," Ms. Prosperina said.

Dr. Yin paced back and forth. Hanging on the office wall nearest the lab, he adjusted to square his gold framed degrees.

"Maybe go down there," Dr. Yin said. Then he scooted to the far side of his office, he scanned through the windows at the parking lot, then he shut the blinds. "Inquire at that drill bit company, guess I'll take Monday and maybe, Tuesday off."

"My, my, you read my mind," Ms. Prosperina said.

"One man wouldn't get noticed down there," Dr. Yin said.

"Brilliant, simply brilliant," Ms. Prosperina said. "I'd go look for myself, or perhaps Mr. Oppenheimer, but given my eyesight, as you are aware, they'd gawk at me."

And Dr. Yin remembered Bertrand's description of Ms. Prosperina. He could see an almost picture perfect image of her within his mind's eye, her red and black eyes, her blank expression and then she morphed into the head of a King Cobra. He shook. He blushed. He sucked in air. He blinked to clear the image from his mind.

"Yeah," Dr. Yin said. He gulped. "I see."

"I'm sure you do," Ms. Prosperina said.

Chapter Thirty

After several restless hours, Eddie awoke Saturday morning. He clutched the duffle bag packed full with money. His sympathetic nervous system scorched, as he had to vomit several times through the night. His cheek rested against the cold porcelain goddess, he had the stale aroma from sleeping in wet clothes. He wiped his gooey mouth with the back of his hand; he huffed. He laid his back on the cold bathroom floor with the duffle bag snuggled in close.

A few moments passed as he stared up at the starless textured ceiling. He concluded his best option was to hide half the cash in his car trunk, the other half in his mother's deep freeze. If they wanted their money back, who would suspect his 1984 junker had one hundred fifty thousand dollars in cash stuffed inside its trunk, or his mother, a conservative middle-aged widow, had stumbled onto the old U.S. Congressmen, frozen money in the freezer trick. He massaged his scalp with his palms. His legs stretched out over the tile floor. Eddie glided his fingertips through his thick mange. A haircut might provide a little distraction, he thought. It would give him a reason to leave, to take the duffle bag, and time to think. He flipped open his cell phone, and decided to call his childhood friend Chris.

"Christopher Clayton Originals, this is Jill Marie," she said. "How may we be of service?"

"Hey, ah, Jill Marie, it's Eddie," He said. He wiped the corner of his eyes with his shaking forefinger.

"Mr. Edward? How are you sweet thing?" Jill Marie asked.

"Fine, Chris have any, ah, free time for me?" Eddie asked. He grabbed the duffle bags cushioned strap.

"Are you kidding? Honey, the boy's booked solid for the next three years, but come on over," Jill Marie said. "You know he loves for you to visit, besides, he could use a friendly face."

"Cool," Eddie said. "See you soon."

"I'll alert the media," Jill Marie said. "See you honey."

As Eddie quickly lathered in a hot shower, he kept pulling the shower curtain back to monitor the duffle bag. He dried off, dragging the duffle bag along with him as he dressed. He dragged the bag down the apartment's stairs; he averted eye contact with anyone nearby as he stuffed the bag on the passenger side. After he coasted through the burger joint drive-thru for a bacon cheeseburger, hangover elixir, he cruised with his silent duffle bag friend into a fashionable, artsy section of Nashville.

#

After his tracking device alarm went off, Captain Lovins sat inside his office watching Eddie's movements. He wondered why Edward had decided to visit an expensive salon. The decision did not match with his profile.

# # #

Eddie parked as close the salon door of Christopher Clayton Originals as he could. He monitored the mostly female shoppers combing through quaint boutiques, and enjoying conversation on the patio section at a Starry Eyed Coffee Hut. He opened the passenger side door, and hoisted the duffle bag on his shoulder using the cushioned strap as if he had all his gym gear inside. He got the trunk open, and stuffed the bag inside. He starred down at the duffle bag, and admired its waterproof fabric. Then he quickly smashed the trunk lid down. He quadruple checked the trunk to ensure it stayed locked. With the keys crushed inside his moist palm, he walked toward the salon.

As Eddie quietly entered the salon, it was warm, dimly lit and smelled of lavender with hints of roses. Calm sedate environmental music played in the background of the open floor plan. The boutique had only two cushioned styling chairs.

"Well, if it isn't our little Nashville tramp," Christopher Clayton said. He mischievously grinned at Eddie. Chris had two employees, Jill Marie, a slinky, naturally curly Pippi Longstalking redhead woman who played the salon's gatekeeper. And Pedro, a nickname, because his given name Chris could not pronounce. A diminutive Indian man, middle-aged with short-matted black hair, he was Chris' primary assistant and off-hours yoga master, who demanded Chris remain fit and trim.

"I know, always such the fashion plate," Jill Marie said.

"Edward," Pedro said. His English was spoken with a blended accent from tribal colonial India. He had intense brown eyes. He wore a cream-colored Nehru jacket, and he was bare footed.

"How is your lovely mother?" Chris asked. His bushy Elvis like side burns shaved into a distinct point. A dyed sunshine yellow pencil thin mustache and goatee concealed a nasty scar under his chin from an elementary school playground fight with Bobby Humperdinck. As always, he wore his signature, eight-panel Gatsby cap.

"I think she's been dating someone, creeps me out, but I guess it's been long enough since dad passed," Eddie said. He stuffed his keys in his pants pocket. "Or should I say died?" Eddie briefly thought about Raquel Turnbull.

"Really? My, my, who is the lucky devil?" Chris asked.

"Not sure, I got suspicious when she started making snack cakes. Used to make them for dad," Eddie said. He walked further inside the salon. "Called them his, treats, for good behavior."

"If she makes him fried chicken, I'll know she's in love," Chris said. His powder blue eyes gazed at Eddie's hair. "God help me, I do love your hair."

"Come, Edward," Pedro said. He guided Eddie to the left sided salon chair. He rolled over a sink with a concave, curved lip on the front. Chris had invented the state-of-the-art sink from a dream. The idea sprang from his subconscious dislike of shifting his high-end clients from the traditional bank of shampoo sinks, where Pedro washed and conditioned hair, and then trudged his hair dripping clients back to a salon chair. He thought the traditional process made his patrons feel uncomfortable. He thought the negative vibe messed with his artistic flow.

His expensive solution, he had installed hydraulic styling chairs similar to a luxuriously padded transatlantic first-class lounger. Underneath the chair, concealed from the client's view, the tile work slid back to reveal plumbing receptacles coupled and locked in place to a flexible water tube connected under the shampoo bowls drain. Ingeniously, instead of porcelain, Chris chose a material similar to a spongy mouse pad that ergonomically molded to each client's particular neck and shoulder profile. The sensation their head set was on a form-fitting pillow.

As Pedro shampooed and scrubbed Eddie's hair, his scalp tingled as Chris strutted next to Eddie.

"Well, I hope she finds a nice man to live out her days with," Chris said.

Eddie thought if Chris had not chosen to be a hair stylist, he could have easily been a fashion model and sashay half-naked up and down a Paris catwalk.

"Excuse me," Jill Marie said. Her hands shook as she handed Chris a note. Then they giggled like prepubescent teenage girls.

"Exciting news, guess who had her publicist inquire about our little salon?" Chris asked. "Three snaps and you'll never guess, that petite little thing, Regan Fryingpan." He snapped his fingers three times and tangoed with Jill Marie. Eddie followed their reflections via the salon mirror. Pedro crossed his arms behind him as he coolly studied over at Eddie.

"He is not sane," Pedro said.

"Really?" Eddie asked.

"Ah, yes, really," Chris said. He twirled Jill Marie and released her back toward the reception station. "I simply cannot get over myself, my reputation grows."

"I say no evil," Pedro said. He covered his mouth with his hands. He continued to study Eddie.

Sedated from the expert shampoo and conditioning massage, Eddie could only muster a queer glance back at his reflection as he thought of a name on the bald headed dudes list. The name was fifth one down, after, Henry James O'Rahilly, Jr. and above, Cando Hillary Grain, the name on the creepy list was, Fryingpan. The same list that had Lionel's names another two lines down.

"This can't be happening," Eddie whispered. He shook his head. He intently stared forward.

Jill Marie and Chris followed Pedro's constant stare, then they investigated Eddie's expression. They happily pointed at each other. Pedro continued to study Eddie's eyes.

"Are you hiding from something?" Pedro asked.

"Look at him, he can't move. I think Mr. Edward is getting aroused," Jill Marie said. She slinked in next to Eddie with her long finger on her bare knees. She wide toothed smiled at him through the mirror's reflection. "Little miss cutie-pants will swoosh her perfect behind on this seat."

Eddie simply stared back at her in disbelief.

"Oh god," Chris said. Behind them, he clapped his palms together; he twirled in merriment inside the silk taffeta curtain with Parisian pleats concealing the salon chairs.

"God?" Pedro asked.

"Edward, a star gazer?" Chris said.

"No, I'm not," Eddie said. He crossed his arms and legs.

"Oh, yes you are," Jill Marie said. She pointed at Eddie. "Look at yourself, been reading Page Six?"

"There is much to learn from the stars," Pedro said.

"If I had only known, I'd let you hang out in the corner," Chris said. He chuckled. "You could fill up your autograph collection. I know, snap not so secret photos, then sell them to those goobers on television, you'd make a fortune."

"That's a great idea," Jill Marie said. "You two always need new help."

"I know, you can be Pedro's assistant," Chris said.

Pedro covered his ears with his hands.

"I do not listen to evil," Pedro said.

"Are you serious?" Eddie said. He blushed.

"I don't care, they seek me like I'm a wise man," Chris said. "You might find the whole thing underwhelming."

"I was not aware of this," Pedro said at Chris.

"Chris?" Eddie said.

"Oh, I don't get it, most are lost in their own snow globes," Chris said. He smiled, as he; air pulled with his fingertips from above his head down to his waist a half-circle shape.

"I think neediest call the paparazzi, tip them off that they are coming," Jill Marie said. She winked at Eddie. "Sad."

"You know, I'm very selective," Chris said. He adjusted his shirt collar. "I don't need the drug addicted, whoring crowd, and no time for un-Kool-Aid karma."

"Uncool aid karma?" Pedro asked. He quizzically stared at Chris. "That cannot be."

"You know what I mean," Chris said to Pedro.

"Spoiled DNA," Jill Marie said.

"There are no such things," Pedro said.

"Pedro, chill," Jill Marie said. She patted Eddie on his head. "You'll ruin Eddie's fantasy."

Pedro covered his eyes.

An odd grin emerged across Eddie's face.

"She's a few years older than us?" Eddie asked.

"I think you're right. That little thing has sure taken what God gave her, got the most out of it," Chris said. He twirled snapped his fingers. "She has magic DNA, good coffee karma."

"Perhaps, coffee karma?" Pedro said. "How do you know?"

Chris' expression changed, as he touched Eddie's head with his fingertips. His eyes appear rapt with Eddie's thick brown hair. He stopped chitchatting, lost in his artistic world, with manual dexterity of a vascular surgeon started to trim Eddie's hair.

"Jill, honey, why don't you give Eddie a penciled in appointment," Chris said. He half-grinned without looking at Eddie. "You'll need to be light on your feet."

"Why not," Eddie said. He held his breath.

Pedro studied Eddie's eyes, as he stood near the chair handing Chris instruments, a towel draped over his arm.

"What are you seeking?" Pedro asked.

"I cannot wait to see your expression," Chris said.

Pedro shook his head. He gazed up at the starless black painted ceiling as Chris tamed Eddie's Chia-Pet-like hair into a sensible style that belied the expert touch to a casual observer. But if any professional hairstylist closely observed his haircut they would know it was Christopher Clayton's work.

"Oh, that will be worth saving," Jill Marie said.

"All done, now give Jill Marie whatever you want. I expect to see your charismatic self back here," Chris said.

"I wonder if she is as good looking in person," Eddie said. He tried to ignore Pedro. He wobbled off the cushioned chair.

"I never know," Chris said. He shrugged. "Some are just butt ugly without makeup."

Jill Marie crinkled her perfectly waxed eyebrows, as she waved Eddie away as he tried to pay her. He stuffed his hands in his pants pockets. He twisted to look over at Chris.

"Perhaps I really should be Pedro's boy? He can order me around," Eddie asked.

Chris cackled. He swirled inside the silk curtain.

"Ha, that will make all the more fun," Chris said.

Pedro crossed his spindly arms. He stared at Eddie.

"I am worried for you, Edward," Pedro said. He gently touched Eddie's left arm. He pulled his hand back as if burned by fire.

"What now?" Chris said.

"Edward, you must be careful," Pedro said. He stepped back from Eddie as if his bare feet danced on hot lava coals.

"Pedro, take your meds," Jill Marie said.

"No, listen to me, take great care, be aware," Pedro said.

Eddie just stared intently back at Pedro.

"What'd I do?" Eddie asked.

"Darkness, I sense darkness," Pedro said. He stared down.

"Pedro, stop molesting my oldest friend," Chris said. He cackled. "You can have our friend Jim Bob."

Jill Marie slinked in next to Pedro.

"Let me guess?" Jill Marie said. She dramatically acted as though she cast a witch's spell. "Eddie is the spawn of?"

"Satan," Chris said. He intensely pointed at Eddie.

"Yes, Eddie is the evil one," Jill Marie said. She walked around Eddie sniffing his neck.

"We'll stop, sorry, Eddie," Chris said. "I don't think you're capable of being evil."

Pedro stared at them and turned to face Eddie.

"Yes, if that is what you call it," Pedro said. He put his hand on Eddie's chest. "I cannot see it, but I sense it. Edward you must take great care, pure evil seeks you."

Eddie thought about the weird list he had, the money he got last night that he had stuffed in his car trunk.

"Chris, I did tell you Jim Bob got arrested?" Eddie asked.

Chris crossed his arm and leaned to the side.

"How am I not surprised, he ain't right," Chris said.

"Yeah, I'll tell another time," Eddie said. He shrugged.

"Edward, do not forget," Pedro said.

"Pedro, calm down," Jill Marie said. "Eddie, we'll call you."

Eddie played with car keys and remembered the duffle bag.

"Okay, think I'll go visit mom," Eddie said. "I'll tell her you said hello."

"Oh, please do," Chris said. He waved by at Eddie. "Tell her not to be shy, I'd welcome her here, tell her she's loved."

# # #

After Eddie checked his car trunk for his duffle bag, and as Captain Lovins' tracking device blipped his movements, he drove to a Piglets & Giblets grocery store where he purchased packages of frozen hot wings, a box of black trash bags and a bag of cinch ties. Then he drove his rust bucket toward his mother's house. His plan was to use the back door key to sneak inside, where he would briskly assemble the money, and then stuff half inside the double stuffed plastic bags. Then hide the cash under the hot wings within her deep freeze. She never removed items from her deep freeze, she only added bags of frozen vegetables, and his mother hated hot wings; and she thought that spicy hot wings demonic inspired. Besides, Saturday was pre-church day, so she would likely be gone to a warm-up prayer luncheon. If she were home alone, she would likely be sitting in his dad's den on his father's worn recliner watching spiritual television. If he showed up, after a few pleasantries, she would examine their formal family photo, tell him he was such good boy, and his father looked so handsome. Then she would focus on the television. She might even forget he even stopped by.

The afternoon sky was a resplendent powder blue with streaks of burnt orange and canary yellow glazing the horizon. The clouds rolled and twisted as if young lovers lost in a moment of passion as Eddie's car crested a top a smooth hump along the blacktopped two lane residential street. Below, he could see his mother's house. A two story red brick with five windows across the top floor, four windows across the ground floor, and centered by a six-panel door painted forest green. And bolted above the two-car garage door rested his rusty basketball hoop. He considered the years that had slipped past him without his father, as quiet as an early morning snowfall.

But Eddie stopped his car, because he immediately realized danger lurked. Littered outside her house were several nondescript four-door sedans. It meant one thing, her turn to host Methodist Ladies Prayer Group. His initial instinct was to flee. Then he thought the MLPG ladies a perfect diversion.

Without knocking on the front door, he entered to a high-pitched gaggle of conservatively dressed women, with boring hairstyles, all simultaneously gurgling about other peoples' lives. The front parlor whiffed of a dense perfume odor, strong enough to compete with Clevenger's cockroach killing halitosis. His petite, beautiful mother wisely sat on the center cushion of her living room couch that she had taken off the plastic covers for the event. She noticed Eddie and she got up and softly hugged him.

"Did I forget something? If so, I'm so sorry," Sophia said.

"No, mom, I just wanted to see if you'll let me store some food in your deep freeze," Eddie said. He thought it best to not mention the hot-wings, if she discovered them, worst case she would call him to remove them. She would not touch them.

"Oh, heavens, yes, but go through the garage door that way you don't have to be bothered us?" Sophia said. She waved him to move along, and pushed away an uncooperative sting of gray hair.

"If you don't mind, okay," Eddie said. He hugged his mother. He averted any direct eye contact with any of the double chins or other flightless human foul as he skipped out the back door. He suspected his mother quickly immersed herself into conversations reminiscing about past Thanksgivings, dead cousins third removed, and what had Mildred Humpsickle been thinking wearing bubble gum pink to big church on a Sunday morning. They would all conclude it was the work of the devil.

Eddie ran back to his four-cylinder car, snatched the hot wings, and set them on the concrete curb. He hoisted the duffle bag onto the passenger side seat. He stood up and suspiciously inspected for anyone watching. He crouched down. He quickly guessed he had half the money separated, and he zipped closed the duffle bag and stuffed it back in the trunk, then he triple cinch tied the garbage bag, slung it over his shoulder, and grabbed the bags of hot wings. He casually, but with purpose, strolled toward the garage. He pressed in the security code, and the garage door folded up and back. Inside the quiet garage, he walked between his mother's sedan, and his father's truck. It had not been started in decades; he looked inside the driver side window as if into a time capsule back to his childhood. He shrugged, and moved to stand in front of the freezer chest. He studied the deep freeze for a brief moment remembering he had helped his father deliver it a long since forgotten Saturday afternoon using the now dated truck. He lifted up the top. The stale smelling frozen environment was full of his father's favorite, mint chocolate chip ice cream. Eddie dug a space near the bottom. He stuffed in the warm bag of cash, and then covered them over with the bags of hot wings. Additional frozen food bags filled over any potential gaps that might reveal his non-consumable addition. Satisfied with the decision, Eddie fled from the garage. He walked across the concrete driveway.

"Eddie," Sophia said in a loud voice. "You don't have to leave so soon."

Eddie stopped at the end of the driveway, his right brown shoe on the curb. He turned to see his mother waving at him near the front door. He fiddled with his car keys as he walked back toward the house.

"You don't have to leave so soon," Sophia said. She fidgeted with her fingers, a glint of a tear in her eyes.

"Mom, ah, I'm not really into," Eddie said. He shrugged.

"I want to introduce you to my, ah, companion," Sophia said.

"Companion?" Eddie said. He started to sense the need to back away from his mother. "Mom, I don't think it-"

From inside the house, an older man emerged. He wore a two button navy blue blazer, underneath a crisp white button down.

"Eddie, this is, my friend, Simon. He and I," Sophia said. She looked at Eddie's shoes. "I feel it best I introduced you two." Then Sophia carefully studied Eddie's face. Her thin arms folded. She pursed her lips.

"Hello, I'm Simon Lewis. Nice to meet you," he said.

Eddie shook Simon's hand. His voice sounded soothing and genteel. Perhaps he was just north of six-three, with square shoulders, kind eyes and a distinguished appearance.

"Simon and I met at church. It is such a coincidence that you stopped by today. It's just meant to be," Sophia said. She nervously laughed. She clenched her jaw.

"I guess so," Eddie said. He glanced down at his shoes.

"Ah, well, perhaps, what is your line of work?" Simon asked.

"I work at Insurance Professionals," Eddie said. He shrugged. "I do the underwriting for professional liability submissions."

"Oh, I know that family. Clevenger? I knew his father," Simon said with a sheepish grin. "Civil War buff, has a bushy goatee?"

"Yeah, reenacts battles," Eddie said. Simon smiled at Eddie. Simon might be okay, Eddie thought.

"Why's that funny?" Sophia asked.

"Nothing mom, and what do you do, Mr. Lewis?" Eddie asked.

"Now, call me Simon. I'm a lawyer. Hope you never have to fool around with the likes of me," Simon said. He chuckled. He shrugged at Eddie's mother.

Eddie's mother intently stared at him. And Eddie realized his mother had not moved her blue dress shoes since Simon had walked outside. She averted her gaze; she stared down at the manicured hemlocks along the path to her door. Then she cautiously gazed over at her son. Eddie realized his mother was searching, hoping for her son's approval. Eddie blushed. He instantly understood what she did not say, it was all said with her eyes. He nodded; he smiled at his mother, and told her he loved with his eyes, with his slight grin. Sophia lightly smiled back. She wiped away a sneaky tear; she nodded.

"Oh, a lawyer?" Eddie said. He coughed. "What kind of practice?"

"I defend folks that get into tax trouble and such," Simon said. He breathed in. He waved his long fingers toward Eddie. "Commercial transactions, some internet commerce, rather boring life I suppose."

"Really?" Eddie said. He shook his head, his spine tingled with the sensation he had been tasered. "What are the odds?"

"What? I don't understand Eddie," Sophia asked. She turned her head with a puzzled expression gazing down at Eddie.

Eddie backed up, he thought he was simply an actor in his own life, and each new scene, just a predestined part of the story.

"Well, this might be a strange thing to say, but Mr. Lewis," Eddie said. He coughed to clear his throat.

"Now, now, call me Simon."

"Okay, sorry, Simon, I've an old friend, Jim Bob."

"*Jim Bob*? Such an odd fat boy, but he's been your friend for a long time," Sophia said. She gazed up at Simon. "Oh my lands, sad story 'bout his parents, killed in that unfortunate accident. You know, they were *drinking* at the time." His mother arched her eyebrows. She put her fingers in front of her lips, as if to sift out speaking ill of the dead.

"Yes, go ahead," Simon said. He patted Sophia on her left shoulder, his eyebrows furrowed. "Eddie, it's fine."

"Well, he's gotten himself thrown into jail down at Dorian-Hyde," Eddie said. He inspected a nearby oak tree limb.

"Dorian-Hyde? Oh my lands that's, this is serious," Simon said. He crossed his arms. "That's for federal cases."

"I went to visit him last Friday evening, federal agents suddenly raided his house," Eddie said. He waited for his mother's reaction. He thought it best to get it out of the way.

"Edward! You could have been killed! Was he drinking? Did he get you involved with some illegal pornographic website?" Sophia said. She wiggled her right forefinger into the sky as if asking the celestial being for lightning to zap Jim Bob. "Pastor Emerson preached about that just last Sunday."

"Mom, let me finish," Eddie said. His hands up in front of his body like an invisible force field. "Jim Bob was selling athletic memorabilia online, he knew some ex-football stars. They signed jerseys and other whatnots for him, and then he sold them on, WePay. He collected the money but didn't pay the tax, that's what I was told."

Simon turned to assure Sophia.

"Now, now, I can handle this," Simon said to Sophia. His gaze narrowed and he glanced over at Eddie. "Perhaps you can visit me at my office Monday afternoon. I have court at eight, however, here take my card. Call my assistant, she'll schedule a time."

Eddie was certain Simon realized there was much more to discover from Jim Bob Calhoun versus the United States of America as his mother rapidly tapped her dress shoe.

"I knew that Jim Bob was no good, I must say, I'm not surprised. You know his parents were *drinking* Baptists. Nope. Not surprised at all." She shook her head. "I think his mother grew up Catholic, or Jewish, or was it they worshipped the Sun?"

"Mom, they were Baptists, not Catholic nor Jewish or what-not. Besides, he needs my help. You always taught me to assist those in need." Eddie said. He could not resist twisting the whole affair into missionary work. "Right?"

Sophia uncrossed her arms as she smiled down at Eddie. She approvingly nodded.

"Yes, you're such a nice young man. I must go inside now and gather with the girls. We will add Jim Bob to our prayer list. If you will please excuse me boys," Sophia said. The spirit had moved her. She marched back inside the house to gather with her spiritual troops. Simon acknowledged her as she walked inside. He stepped down off the front porch.

"I'll help you, don't worry," Simon said. He gave Eddie an encouraging glance. He stepped forward. The sun's yellow haze, partially blocked by the black singled roof pitch, caused an eerie hallow to cast above his head.

"I know this is crazy," Eddie said. He fidgeted with his car keys, he stared down at a row of freshly planted petunias.

"I'm quite fond of your mother and have great respect for her," Simon said. He kindly nodded at Eddie.

"Thank you," Eddies said. He shrugged. "She makes amazing fried chicken, my dad loved her fried chicken."

Simon chuckled. He patted his modest belly.

"Oh my lands, had to walk a few extra miles," Simon said. He reached over and shook Eddie's hand. "I'm sure your father was good man. He cannot ever be replaced."

"He was," Eddie said. He nodded. "Thank you."

Simon shook his head. He stepped back; he crossed his arms.

"I am quite familiar with folks getting involved with hiding income, and getting incarcerated. I think you said his name was, Jim Bob?" Simon asked. He gently touched Eddie's left arm.

"Yes, Jim Bob," Eddie said.

"Very well, we can look up the case," Simon said. He looked down at Eddie with a sheepish grin. "There is a lot more to this? I suspect, right?"

"Yeah," Eddie said.

"I suspected. But we'll talk Monday, I better get back inside before your mother pulls us both in." Simon winked at Eddie.

"Thank you, I'd like to get Jim Bob out of there."

"Oh, for heaven's sake, that's what I do," Simon said. He waved his hands forward as if to encourage Eddie to escape. "I look forward to you visiting my office. Now take care."

"Oh, no kidding," Eddie said. He scampered toward his car.

Chapter Thirty One

Early Sunday morning before sunlight, beams had begun to pierce the forest floor. At the beginning of the dirt path into their habitat, Professor Quan closely watched Waldo prance and circle near dense foliage before she finally pooped her business. Captain Lovins sat inside his white panel van with the window down. He sipped some coffee, glanced down at their pet dog as she rapidly scratched the earth with her rear paws.

"It was weird, I think it's what happens to artists," Professor Quan said. He yawned. "I couldn't stop."

"I couldn't stop thinking about Edward," Captain Lovins said. "But at least I had a good night's sleep, I'll need it."

"Yes, our time is short," Professor Quan said. He tapped on Captain Lovins arm. "Find him."

"What's Yin thinking?" Captain Lovins asked. He sipped his coffee thermos as steam escaped past his face.

"I don't know, he's all out of balance," Professor Quan said. He patted his hands together. "Come Waldo, stay here, I'd lose you in the darkness, and there are mean creatures out there."

Captain Lovins started the van. He shifted it into drive.

"It's time, okay, I'll hide these evil things first," Captain Lovins said as Professor Quan handed him the lead draped metal box. He set it on the passenger seat. "Few things make more nervous than this stuff, but with Yin, better to be cautious."

Professor Quan bent down to pick up Waldo. The pet licked his face, and gave him a happy smile with her paws apart.

"Last place she'd be caught dead in," Professor Quan said. "No kidding," Captain Lovins said. He patted his chest pocket. He pulled out a plastic bag with what appeared to be a simple package of chewing gum. "And this is for Jose, Jr.?"

"It was like a dream, give him the gold foiled one," Professor Quan said. He rubbed his pet's soft belly. "It was so simple, the golfer's genes were almost the same, but ever so slightly different in how they solve problems. I marveled how they all bonded together into one. And then I realized, just give a kid some chewing gum."

Captain Lovins smashed the black skull cap down on his head.

"I'll go find him, not sure how I'll get him to chew the gum, but I'll find him," Captain Lovins said. He sucked in a deep breath. "You sure you don't want me to follow Yin around?"

"No, he'll find nothing, just lots of eyeballs, and maybe diamond drill bits," Professor Quan said. He coughed. He nodded for Captain Lovins to go. "Now, Godspeed-"

"Yeah, he'll probably trigger another audit," Captain Lovins said. He winked at Professor Quan as he rolled the driver side window up. Then he drove the van down the dirt path and it disappeared into the hazy wilderness.

# # #

Captain Lovins drove the white panel van out of the forest and down a quiet single lane blacktopped road that wound up and down through the densely treed hills; he was just three miles from Professor Quan's laboratory. If Captain Lovins had hiked, the trail would have taken about the same amount of time, but he needed his van for the next phase of his Sunday mission. As he drove past a bend in the road, he switched off his headlights, and slowed his van down to below five miles an hour. He benefited from the clear sparkling night sky and the pawkmarked moon's lunar phase being just short of a full moon, and then through the tree limbs a pie shaped clearing emerged. But he drove the van onto a partially concealed side road he had marked with a blooming honeysuckle dotted with yellow and white blooms. He thought it best not to be seen driving onto the gravel parking lot. After he clicked on his night vision goggles, as he got out of the van, he smelled the sweet honeysuckle fragrance blending with the shy whip-poor-will's sad song. It was the common nighttime sounds of life and death within the active forest. He grabbed the metal box lined with a thick layer of lead. The lead layer blocked out Ms. Prosperina's satellite constellation from locking onto the two meteorite's unique radiation signal. But the box could not completely conceal their radiation fingerprints. He had timed his insertion down to the second; he needed to focus.

Captain Lovins tightly clutched the box, he marched across the road and down into a meandering creek bed that meandered behind his destination. As his waterproof boots stepped into the clear stream, he heard a creature lapping up water, then it stopped, he heard a low growl form behind him, he saw the yellow glowing eyes of a white wolf. The animal did not move, but appeared curious as it sniffed the cool air for Captain Lovins.

Captain Lovins did not flinch; he did not fear the wolf's eyes, the eyes were not red or black, he turned and strode along the creek bed careful to dodge the smooth, slippery rocks as the wolf stalked above him along the grass bank. He completed the quarter mile journey, and then he scaled the moist mud embankment as he snuck in behind a modest white chapel. At the front, the sole security light focused on the sanctuary's front double doors. Captain Lovins had purchased the wooden plank property years earlier after the old minister had passed on and the members no longer tithed enough to keep the faith active. He thought it was perfect for hiding the diamonds and in particular, the meteorites coated with Ms. Prosperina's organic material. The property and grounds maintained to appear as if the church was still open for business. And from time to time, his drill bit company employees or the locals knew they could use the chapel free of charge for family weddings, funerals, or gatherings.

The wolf sat back on its hind legs just beyond the illumination zone. Its almond shaped eyes glowed within the shadows, curiously watching as Captain Lovins snuggled a fabric strap around a downed oak tree trunk. He tightened the strap and slowly pulled the huge log back from the rock foundation. Then he clutched the strap over the edge of a thick boulder that he dragged back to reveal a square solid lead hatch. He took off his black fabric gloves, and wiped sweat from his face and hands. He checked his watch; he was within the margin. With a small flashlight between his lips, he simultaneously stuck his thumbs inside a tubular receptacle bolted to the hatch, then his thumb-prints triggered on a blue beam that scanned his left eye. After the locking mechanism verified his sample with the scanned data, the hatch popped up. He snuggled his gloves back on, and slid the hatch off, he flashed the light down inside the square galley style opening and then over to find a solid iron ladder.

As he descended into the darkness, he had hooked the box to his belt using a climbing carbiner and utility cord. With the aid of his night vision goggles, he stopped at the third rung; he looked up, then reached for the hard plastic nob, and slid the hatch back over the opening, and locked it tight from the inside. He checked his watch; he had made it with time to spare. He continued down the ladder another twenty feet; he stepped off the ladder onto a rubberized floor. He took in a deep breath from within the musty environment with his hands on his knees.

Captain Lovins turned around, at first the reflected light appeared as clusters of stars in a night sky. But as he walked into the square room, trays and trays of diamonds emerged, from tiny ones the size of grains of sand to large ninety-nine carat paragons. There were several exact copies of the Hope Diamond, or other known well-known stones. Each made from pure carbon, but they were all fakes. But the black meteorites in the metal box he unhooked from his belt that were devastatingly real. Captain Lovins pulled back a corner section of the rubberized floor. He waved a demagnetized security card across, and a large lead lid popped up. He opened the lead box he unhooked from his belt; he stared down at the menacing meteorites. He quickly closed the lid, slid the box inside the custom-made container, and pushed the top down locking it in place. He sealed over the opening with lead tape, and pushed in the rubberized floor section, he hoped it blended with the rest of the flooring, and prayed the room would never be found. He got back up, he carefully inspected the integrity of the vault.

After Captain Lovins emerged past the vault hatch, he skillfully locked the lead hatch, he repositioned the bolder, the oak tree log and tried to create an undisturbed appearance to the back of the chapel. As he expected, the white wolf had not moved, it sat back waiting and watching.

And as Captain Lovins retraced his steps down the creek bed, the white wolf followed close behind. As Captain Lovins crossed the road the wolf stopped, and remained in the darkness panting, with its tongue waggling out the side of its jaw. Captain Lovins took off his night vision goggles; he wanted to see the wolf with his bare eyes. As he stared across the simple road, the wolf sat back on its hind legs, its yellow eyes seemed to ask its master for instructions. Captain

Lovins would not insult the white wolf with food. It ate pity. It only respected truth. Captain Lovins got back in the van; he drove off, heading toward Nashville to find Jose, Jr. and to seek Edward.

Chapter Thirty Two

Later Sunday morning as Captain Lovins drove his van toward Nashville, and Dr. Yin was driving toward eastern Kentucky, Eddie's vibrating cell phone disturbed him from his death like slumber. "Man," Eddie mumbled. His throat packed with morning mucous, he rapidly blinked his eyes as sun light blazed through his bedroom window. He clasped the cell phone.

"Hello?" Eddie said.

"Wake-up sunshine," Chris said.

"What? I'm awake," Eddie said. He blinked his eyelids rapidly. He shook his head.

"You have a new part-time job. This Monday, Regan's appointment is set up for six sharp, cut and color," Chris said.

"What?" Eddie said. He sniffed; he crinkled his face. He stared over at his dirty clothes hamper remembering where he had stuffed his rain and sweat soaked clothes. He figured he better do some laundry soon. He sucked in some oxygen. And he better check on his new duffle bag.

"Pedro has never had a man slave, so he expects you to show up for work." There were whispers, static, as Eddie heard the sounds of people arguing and tugging for the phone.

"Edward, I will not harass you," Pedro said. "I do not do such things. I am not part of that caste."

More static and whispers erupted over the phone line.

"Get a sense of humor Pedro, you there?" Chris asked.

"Yeah, sorry," Eddie said. He leaned back on a couple of pillows he had shoved behind him. He thought he heard odd sounding music in the background.

"Are you still interested in being Pedro's man servant?" Chris asked. He giggled.

Eddie wiped the corners of his eye, to get the sleep goo.

"Yeah, I think so, what time?" Eddie asked. He glanced over at his walk-in closet. "Hey, what's that music?"

"Oh, Pedro's sitar music, part of his yoga practices," Chris said. "You need to come over, it looks simple, but I am exhausted and exhilarated at the same time, it's like sex."

"I think that's the point," Eddie said. He put his hand over his face. "What time?"

"Hmm, let's say 5 o'clock? That should be plenty of time for us to scheme," Chris said. "Seriously, next time you get it on, I swear that is what yoga feels like, is that dirty?"

"I'll take your word for that, ah, but I'll be there," Eddie said. He shifted forward. "Got to go, see you tomorrow night."

"See you then," Chris said. He giggled.

Eddie set his cell phone on the nightstand. His bare feet stepped onto the carpet, his toes dug into the fibers. He walked over, and he separated the metal window blinds and scanned the full parking lot. He thought his car appeared secure with all the other modest, late model modes of transportation. But he thought he should check the trunk. He hoped the duffle bag spent the night unmolested. He turned around; he stared up.

"Simon?" Eddie whispered. He picked up his crumpled khaki's from the floor. He found Simon's business card in his front pocket. He sat down on end of his bed. The name Simon harkened an image of someone wearing a seersucker suite drinking lemonade after Sunday morning church. He grabbed at some dirty clothes; he slipped on a t-shirt and a pair of dirty blue jeans. On his bare feet, he hustled out of the apartment and down the concrete stairs. He tried to minimize drawing attention to himself from any of the other non-church going backsliders. Tiny goose pimples traversed his exposed arms and neck. He did an inspection of his well-used auto. He scanned up at his apartment windows. Then he unlocked his trunk, the now half-full duffle bag set quietly, rumpled across the spare tire. He shut the trunk, and for some reason, he scampered back into his apartment. He snagged his cell phone.

"Hello?" Ardee asked.

"Ah, it's Eddie," he said.

"Oh," Ardee said.

Eddie started to pace. He scratched the back of his neck.

"I was wondering," Eddie said. He methodically breathed in. "I was wondering, if, you know, wanted to get some coffee, later today, if not, no big deal." He stood still, his toes dug into the cold kitchenette vinyl flooring. His big toe almost blistered. He clenched his jaw.

"I don't know what to say," Ardee said. "Never thought you'd call, but, I. well-"

"I know, sorry," Eddie said. He smacked his hand on the counter top. He air punched at the refrigerator.

"I'm not a coffee drinker, I get that junk for Clevenger," Ardee said. She paused. "But, if you want, why don't you, come over, I'll fix you dinner."

Eddie could feel his heart thump; his scalp tingled.

"Dinner?" Eddie said.

"Yeah, how 'bout six or so," Ardee said. "The one thing that my mother passed on to me is my grandmother's best recipe."

"Yeah? I didn't know you cooked?" Eddie said.

"Well, I just need someone to cook for, right?" Ardee said. "Cooking is about sharing."

"Sure, sure, I'll, I'll be there," Eddie said. He felt like his body had been set on fire.

"I hope you like fried chicken?" Ardee asked.

Eddie exhaled. His vision blurred. He wobbled.

"I do," Eddie said.

"See you at six," Ardee said. "Just bring you."

# # #

At 4402 Anesidora Boulevard in Memphis, Charlene decided she would honor her commitment to her cousin Clevenger. It was a Sunday and she was certain what Clevenger would be doing. She imagined him wearing his vintage Confederate uniform as he sat up straight, hoisted atop his chestnut horse. She figured him bravely portraying a Master Sergeant at Perryville Battlefield about to lead a non-lethal, pseudo-charge into the other pasty white Union defenses that had driven to the battle in both foreign and domestic carbon emission vehicles.

"Hello Clevenger, it's Charlene," she said. She leaned her long legs across her family room leather couch.

"Oh, sorry, you got me by surprise," Clevenger said.

"It sounds like you're in the middle of one of your little battles? I'll be quick." Charlene said. She laughed.

"Okay, but I'm right in the middle of-" Clevenger said.

"I understand, young Edward was delightful, a nice young man. He conducted himself with style and grace," Charlene said. She chuckled. She put her big hands over her mouth. "I think the boy is just trying to find himself. Maybe give him a raise."

"Well okay, I see," Clevenger said. "Just a sec-"

Charlene could hear Clevenger trying to explain away the insult to the purity of the Civil War reenactment by bringing his cell phone to the battle scene.

"I'm back," Clevenger said.

"Oh, funny side-bar, Lionel gave him his socks, but otherwise, you have nothing to worry about," Charlene said. She covered her mouth, and quickly terminated the call.

Chapter Thirty Three

Captain Lovins drove his van past Nashville's soaring downtown office buildings, then past modest brick townhomes and homogenous shopping centers into an up-scale, spotlessly maintained, oak tree lined neighborhood. He vectored his van near Devine Grace Golf & Country Club, parking along a serene side street near the expansive back entry gate. He acknowledged some children riding their bikes. He charged toward the distressed white brick, Greek revival clubhouse trimmed with staunch dental molding.

Carrying an old leather golf bag with a set of clubs that he had bought earlier in the afternoon at Trevino & Watson Golf & Pawn Shop, Captain Lovins ignored the sign, Members Only. He marched through the solid mahogany double doors. Austere English and French period furniture had been set next to high-gloss white wainscoted paneling. English country toile fabric covered the walls. A hulking cherry stained grandfather clock chimed four o'clock in the afternoon. His military style boots dented the thick plush forest green carpet, flowing past common and intimate dining rooms. Past the club lounge, where a few members sat playing cards, he noticed a modest sign for the pro shop. He stepped downstairs.

Inside the pro shop, he found a young assistant professional, a lanky teenager with a thin bone structure and sunbaked skin. He had draped his arms over the shop's tempered glass counter framed in walnut reading a golf magazine. Behind him was a panoramic view of the golf course that had mostly emptied out for the day.

"Good afternoon," Captain Lovins said.

"Sir, can I help you?" the assistant pro asked. He stood up and quickly closed the magazine.

Captain Lovins fidgeted with the rusty club heads poking out from the golf bag as he strolled up to the counter. He pensively turned to examine the racks of golf clubs, sleeves of balls and spikeless golf shoes.

"I need your help," Captain Lovins said. He stared intently at the young man. "You have a young caddie I need to meet."

"Oh? Okay," the assistant pro said.

"Jose, Jr?" Captain Lovins said in a whispered tone. He leaned forward. "Hernandez."

"Yeah, I know him," the assistant pro said. He tapped at the club's sign in sheet. "Nice kid, head pro likes him."

"I'm not surprised from what I've been told," Captain Lovins said. He winked at the assistant pro. "Can you keep a secret?"

"Yeah, I guess," the assistant pro said. He shrugged. "Should I call the head pro, he just left."

"No, no I am hoping to keep this as quiet as possible," Captain Lovins said. He patted the young man on the arm. "You see, I'm the head of a special committee, our mission is to help under privileged children, love of our fellow man, so forth."

"Oh, that's cool," the assistant pro said. He nodded.

"Yeah, as you are well aware," Captain Lovins said. He nodded his head as glanced around the pro shop. "Like this place, not every child is born into a wealthy family."

"No kidding, most think they have magic DNA," the assistant pro said. The young assistant professional nodded in agreement, he stepped back; he stared to the right of Captain Lovins baldhead.

"Perhaps," Captain Lovins said. He sheepishly grinned.

"I think he's over at the driving range," the assistant pro said. "Did he win something?"

"A scholarship, sort of," Captain Lovins said. He patted his pants pocket to verify he had the package of gum. "But it's completely anonymous, we have a secret board that meets. He got picked because he seems to have some promise, someone noticed him, submitted him, he was up against thousands of others, but sometimes the board just goes on instinct, we picked him."

The assistant professional crossed his long arms. He shook his head and leaned against the counter.

"This is cool, he ain't got a pot to piss in," the assistant pro said. He grinned. He pointed up at the main building. "His dad works in the kitchen, mom too, I don't think she speaks hardly a word of English."

"I am hoping, with your help," Captain Lovins said. He leaned back over the glass counter. He nodded at the young man. "I'd like to spend some time talking to him, get to know him. Then I can report back to the board, can you help me make that happen?"

The assistant professional fidgeted with his pencil, coughed to clear his throat. After adjusting the pencils, he reviewed the blank tee time sheet.

"I guess," the assistant prof said.

"Can you ask him to caddie for me," Captain Lovins said. "Tell him I am thinking of becoming a member, he'll not be the wiser, I know I look mean, I wear the boots because of my back, got hurt from my military days, Halo jump, went wrong."

"I don't know," the assistant pro said. He grimaced. "I could get into hot water, the uppity members can be real prickly."

"Darn, I was afraid of that," Captain Lovins said. He started to back up. He scratched his square shaped chin. "I understand, oh well, I have to leave for business early, not sure I'll be back here anytime soon."

The assistant professional sighed. He wobbled.

"Okay, okay, but if anyone asks," the assistant pro said. "Ah, tell them you're a, inspecting the turf for chinch bugs."

"Oh, great idea," Captain Lovins said. He set the golf bag down. "If you're concerned, follow us around. We'll just be on the front nine, I doubt I'll even finish, and my back, it's not made for golf anymore." "Naw, no worries, he's a good kid, needs to get a break," the assistant pro said. He waved away the idea. "I'll go track him down, I'll send him to the first tee, head on out."

"You're too kind," Captain Lovins said. "I'll tell our board, I think one is a member here, but I can't tell you who, sorry, it's important our work goes unnoticed."

"Excuse me," the assistant pro said. "I'll get him." He scurried off to find Jose, Jr.

# # #

Jose, Sr. was nearby. He stood inside the country club's commercial grade kitchen, busily prepping celery, onions, and bell peppers. Jose, Jr.'s mother, Maria, was cleaning restrooms near the formal dining room.

"Come on, chop chop," the head chef said. He patted Jose, Sr., on his sweating shoulders as he supervised the busy kitchen staff. Nearby on a gas cooktop a large steaming pot was full of boiling potatoes. The loud sounds of pots banging against pots, and the clanging of dishes being sent through the hulking dishwasher and then stacked for the evening service staff.

"Yes, sir," Jose, Sr. said. He held a sharp knife; he wiped sweat from his forehead. He wore an all-white kitchen uniform.

"Good job, that's the way," the head chef said.

The young husband and wife, with their little boy Jose, Jr., had vamoosed from Mexico five years earlier. They had crawled across the US border, unnoticed by the human coyotes as they walked the dusty roads through Texas. They had a simple plan. They wanted to shield their child from abuse, drug lords, gangs and corruption. They prayed for a new prosperous life for their boy as they worked their way along the Blues trail near the banks of the Mississippi River then past Memphis and on toward Nashville where the heartbeat of country music picked at the soul of America.

Working at the country club, they thought the government would not notice them, simply hide in plain sight. But Professor Quan had noticed Jose, Jr.'s name in tiny black print from the Nashville Sun's sports section, at the bottom of page C4 from the results from a junior golf tournament. He was curious why the name was intermixed with numerous Anglophile names. He asked Captain Lovins to investigate his whereabouts and family history. He learned Jose, Jr. was born October 17, 2003 during the annual Orionid meteorite shower.

# # #

Next to the first tee box, Captain Lovins stood holding the old golf bag examining the golf clubs that looked like a bouquet iron of prehistoric weapons. It smelled of fresh cut grass, flowers, and it was situated beneath the massive clubhouse at the bottom of earthen stairs buttressed with railroad timbers. Down a steep ravine to Captain Lovins' right from behind the green painted groundskeeper shack, a boy appeared. He chased his skinny shadow past the branches of a willow tree, up the hill and he stood at attention in front of Captain Lovins.

"Hello, sir, I am Jose, Jr., I will caddie for you," he said. The scrawny boy had a white golf cap with the club's embossed symbol smashed over his straight jet-black hair. He had light brown skin. Captain Lovins thought he had happy hopeful seal brown eyes.

"Correct," Captain Lovins said.

Jose, Jr. without any direction from Captain Lovins dutifully grabbed the golf bag; he slung the leather tubular bag's strap over his bantamweight shoulders.

"What is your name, sir," Jose, Jr. asked.

"Sure you can carry that?" Captain Lovins asked.

"Oh, I may be small, but I am strong," Jose, Jr. said. He smiled up at Captain Lovins. He leaned forward to shift the weight of the bag across his lower back. "See? I am strong."

"Okay, I don't play much, what do I do next?" Captain Lovins asked. He gripped his hips. "Ah, and a, call me Edward."

"I am not allowed to call adults by their first name," Jose, Jr. said. He shrugged. He slightly grinned.

"Oh, then how about, Mr. Wilcox?" Captain Lovins said. He grinned down at Jose, Jr.

"Oh, sí," Jose, Jr. said. He trudged over to the wooden first tee markers. "You start by hitting the ball from behind those wooden markers. That a way, Mr. Wilcox." Jose, Jr. pointed his diminutive forefinger down the oak tree lined first fairway. A pastoral rolling landscape sloped gently from left to right with closely shaved green grass. He handed Captain Lovins a lacquered, persimmon wood-grained driver attached to a metal shaft with a worn rubber grip.

"Sir, you have no balls?" Jose, Jr. said as he dug inside the golf bags side zipper pockets. "I am sorry."

"What do you *mean*, I don't have any balls?" Captain Lovins asked. He stared down the fairway, he was certain had not a clue how to hit a golf ball, and the distance was intimidating.

"You have no balls to prey with," Jose, Jr. said. He shrugged with an innocent toothy smile.

"Oh, I thought they came with the bag," Captain Lovins said. He studied the course grounds dotted with a few hardy golfers. "So, where do I find balls to play with?"

"In the club house or you can use some of mine. I have them nearby in my golf bag," Jose, Jr. said. He shrugged; he stared up at Captain Lovins.

"Let's use some of your balls, I don't want to go back inside," Captain Lovins said. He tapped his wristwatch. "I'm on a schedule, need to keep moving."

"Wait here Mr. Wilcox," Jose, Jr. said. He carefully laid the golf bag on the ryegrass turf. The boy disappeared behind the nearby dented metal gardener shack. Quickly, he returned shifting forward as if a bole-legged cowboy weighted down with his pockets full of white orbs.

"Excellent, good work, good work," Captain Lovins said.

"You are welcome Mr. Wilcox," Jose, Jr. said. He placed one of the golf balls with a thick black stripe painted across the dimpled surface on a wooden tee. He dumped the rest of his driving range treasures inside one of the bag's zipper pockets.

"Thanks little man," Captain Lovins said as he death gripped the driver. He baseball swung, his boots stamped to the ground as the club head whiffed past the motionless golf ball. Strike one, Captain Lovins thought. He furrowed his eyebrows and clenched his jaw, not glancing over at the silent, Jose, Jr.

Jose, Jr. gracefully stared forward at the dark green four-inch high bluegrass rough that encircled the pale green fairway. After several attempts, the results were extreme curved shots that either duck hooked left, or banana sliced right. After two more dents added to the gardener shack, Captain Lovins huffed; he tapped the ground with the club head.

"I can find them for you," Jose, Jr. said. He waved for Captain Lovins to follow him over the modest slope and toward the fairway. Captain Lovins handed the driver back to Jose, Jr. as they sauntered halfway down the first fairway. After a few minutes, Jose, Jr. discovered one of the offending balls hidden in a deep thicket of rough, next to a husky oak tree trunk.

"Mr. Wilcox, over here," Jose, Jr. said. He waved at Captain Lovins like an airport signal caller standing on a hot tarmac.

Captain Lovins hacked at it; he then kicked it out into the fairway. He drilled his next shot with a three iron next to a smooth, powdery, synthetic sand trap.

"Ah, let's try another hole," Captain Lovins said as they walked toward the green. "Maybe I'll have better luck."

"Okay Mr. Wilcox," Jose Jr. said. He tugged at the bag on his lower back and he highway backpacker trudged toward the second hole teeing ground.

"Are you sure you can handle that?" Captain Lovins asked.

Jose, Jr. had sweated sunshine diamond-drips across his hairline. He smiled up at Captain Lovins.

"Oh, sí, sometimes I carry two bags," Jose Jr. said. "I do what they ask, I am strong. I make my father proud."

The second hole was a par 5; and it equaled the first hole in frustration for Captain Lovins. The turf pockmarked and scarred as Captain Lovins battled forward, traversing the fairway and rough with Jose, Jr. close behind towing the golf bag.

Captain Lovins could almost hear an old drill instructor scream inside his mind, "Left, Right, come on Lovins, show us what you've got, I think you're going to quit."

"This is a crazy game," Captain Lovins said.

"Oh, sí, it can be hard, I'm sorry," Jose, Jr., said.

"Why do people play it?" Captain Lovins asked.

"It's a fun game," Jose, Jr. said. He shrugged. "Be patient, the head professional tells me to be patient. He said listen to Mister Zen. But I do not know a Mister Zen."

"How so?" Captain Lovins asked. "Lesson's must be expensive?"

"He likes me, said I'm a good kid. He tells me to think in opposites, slower I swing, farther ball goes," Jose, Jr. said. He air gripped an invisible club. "Hands forward a bit, and let the god of gravity do the work, everything in harmony."

"God of gravity?" Captain Lovins said. He smirked.

"Sí, he tells me golf like faith," Jose, Jr. said. He pointed at down the fairway. "Silently pray in your mind, to trust." Jose, Jr. tightly shut his eyelids as if he was trying to remember how to translate Spanish into English.

"What?" Captain Lovins said.

"Pray away the evil fear, see the shot in my head," Jose, Jr. said. With his forefinger, he pointed and tapped at his temple. "And just let God grip the club for me, not so tight, but together as one, and just concentrate on a dimple on the ball, then to trust my swing."

"Just that simple?" Captain Lovins asked. He shrugged.

"Sí, all I do, I pray to be a great golfer, Mr. Wilcox," Jose, Jr. said. He gazed up at Captain Lovins. "I get on my knees and pray, every night, I know God listens."

At the third hole, Captain Lovins sat on a concrete bench with a marble marker memorializing a deceased member. Jose, Jr. stood nearby next to a wooden tee marker. A one hundred six yard par 3, it was positioned next to a free form pond centered by an ascending Phoenix Bird sculpture.

"What club do I use this time?" Captain Lovins asked. He huffed, he leaned forward, his elbows on his knees.

"I think you use the nine iron, I will put the ball on the tee for you," Jose, Jr. said. He scampered toward the tee box with a golf ball and tee. Captain Lovins grudgingly got up.

Covered in sweat, Captain Lovins swung at the first ball. It bounced off the sculpture, and landed in a premature, watery grave. He chopped the next shot into the pond. After he added several Urethane covered inhabitants to the growing aquatic cemetery, he handed the club back to Jose, Jr. and sat back down on the concrete bench. He wiped moisture from his face.

"Mr. Wilcox, I am sorry," Jose, Jr. said.

"It's okay, I have other talents," Captain Lovins said.

# # #

Inside the clubhouse kitchen, Jose, Sr. dropped his chef knife on the metal kitchen prep table. He stared down at the piles of chopped vegetables. He glanced around the busy commercial grade kitchen. He sensed the need to locate his son. After he wiped celery, onion, and bell pepper remnants off his stark white prep apron, he asked the executive chef if he could take a break.

"Did you get all the trinity prepped for me?" the head chef asked. He adjusted the tall chef's hat.

"Yes, yes sir. I am almost done," Jose, Sr. said. He nervously took off his apron. "I need to check on my son."

The head chef shrugged. He pointed his German made chef's knife at Jose, Sr. He pointed it for Jose, Sr. to flee.

"Go find junior," the head chef said. "but don't be gone long, got a lot of work to get done before tonight's service."

"Thank you, thank you," Jose, Sr. said as he scurried off toward the pro shop.

# # #

Out on the golf course, Captain Lovins had an idea how to advance his mission. He leaned back on the concrete bench.

"Hey, little man, why don't you show me some of that Mister Zen stuff you've learned?" Captain Lovins asked.

Jose, Jr. frowned. He stood motionless.

"I am not allowed. My father will get in trouble," Jose, Jr. said. He blankly stared down at his tennis shoes.

"No one is here, *I'll* protect you," Captain Lovins said. His fierce stare guaranteed Jose, Jr. instant membership credentials. "Look at me, think anybody will cause trouble?"

Jose, Jr. giggled. He grinned. He shrugged his shoulders and smiled over at Captain Lovins. He happily bounced over to the golf bag and carefully chose a golf club. As he confidently nodded, Captain Lovins noticed a highly competitive spark from Jose, Jr.'s brown eyes.

"I will try for you," Jose, Jr. said. He swiftly placed a weathered ball on a white tee. He walked behind the ball; he focused down the intended ball flight path across the pond toward the green. Jose, Jr. inhaled and exhaled. He blinked his eyelids several times. Then he closed his eyes. With practiced precision, Jose, Jr. moved astride the teed ball. His feet were about shoulder width apart, as he rhythmically danced at a blue's pianist's metronome pace. He rotated his hands microscopically forward, coiled his tiny body, his right hip slid back to allow his shoulders a full turn allowing his maturing back to face his intended target. After he paused for a microsecond at the top of his swing, with his hands just above his right ear, his face calm, confident, he returned to square the cast angled steel to compress the dimpled ball against the clubs grooves. It ejected the ball into the azure sky and the playful milky clouds. The orb flew the brief journey over the placid pond like an F4U Corsair landing safely inside the closely mowed kidney-shaped green. It taxied along the turf stopping just three feet from the cub marked with a white pole topped with a blue flag.

"Amazing," Captain Lovins said. He clapped his hands. "You're gifted, how did you learn to do all that?"

"Oh, the head professional showed me, he has me watch, oh, what his name?" Jose, Jr. said. He stared up and to the right into the sky. "Jake Saint something, and Lionel, I watch them on TV, he show me pictures of Mr. Jones swing, I am to do what they do. He told to see my shot, close my eyes to remember it like I take a picture, it works, see, I can see it."

"Well, it must work," Captain Lovins said.

"Ah ha, it work," Jose, Jr. said. He happily pointed at the green. "See, and I am to look at the grass, the grass is light, he told me as I walk toward the green, to remember if it is dark or light because it follow the sun light from God above."

"So?" Captain Lovins said.

"When I putt the ball, the sun will help me," Jose, Jr. said. He nodded. "It works, trust me. I am to pay attention to nature, the wind, time of day, he says listen to nature."

# # #

After the assistant professional told Jose, Sr. about the mysterious tough looking man asking about his son, he was now in a full out sprint. The assistant pro guessed his son might be near the third or fourth hole. He pushed his chubby body as fast as he could. He huffed, he strained. Past a row of laurel oaks, he chugged past his maintenance worker friends who were spraying chemicals on the grass to maintain the course's green hued theme park like appearance. Then he spotted his son and the big man, who appeared to be wearing military attire, as they strolled toward the fourth tee. He dove behind a bank of viburnum bushes, planted next to an electrical power station within earshot of the fourth hole tee box.

# # #

Captain Lovins noticed the Hispanic man dressed like Casper the Friendly Ghost in his stark white sous chef uniform. He stared down at Jose, Jr.

"So, a professional golfer?" Captain Lovins asked.

"Sí, Mr. Wilcox," Jose, Jr. said.

"Can you imagine it?" Captain Lovins asked.

"Si´, sí´," Jose, Jr. said. "I will work very hard. For when I get older, I have faith it will happen."

Captain Lovins took in a deep breath. He patted Jose, Jr. on his diminutive left shoulder.

"I wish you well. Jose, Jr. do you trust me?" He glanced over at the chubby man out of breath, certain he was the boy's father. He thought he should help calm the man.

"Si," Jose, Jr. said. He puzzlingly stared up at Captain Lovins. "I don't know."

"Because, I've got magical vitamin chewing gum, it will help you become a professional golfer. A friend of mine makes it. Do you want to try some?" Captain Lovins asked. He grabbed the dusty golf bag from Jose, Jr. before he responded. "Follow me, little man." Jose, Jr. skipped along behind as they arrived at the fourth hole tee box.

#

Jose, Sr. fidgeted behind the bushes, prepared to risk his life to defend his son. He searched through the leafy bush to find his son. He heard his son say. "My parents told me never to take from strangers." Sweat dripped down Jose, Sr.'s puffy face. He crawled along behind them in the grass, freshly planted flowers and dirt concealed by the bushes. He was happy his son listened to them.

#

"Absolutely, but this is *special* chewing gum," Captain Lovins said. He sarcastically twisted his head staring down at the Jose, Jr.

"Oh, you kid me," Jose, Jr. said. He giggled and grinned.

"Yeah, I'm sort of kidding you, here, chew on this for the rest of our walk, and let me know what you think," Captain Lovins said. He handed Jose, Jr. a gold foil wrapped piece of gum. His tiny brown hand accepted it. He placed it in his mouth. Captain Lovins popped in a placebo piece wrapped in silver foil.

"I like chewing gum," Jose, Jr. said. He bounced on his tiptoes across the tee box. He grabbed the golf bag back from Captain Lovins. "I will carry the bag."

"Yeah, dear friend of mine makes it, this is his test market product," Captain Lovins said. He shrugged. "It's only for special people, who the stars smiled down at."

As Professor Quan had theorized, Jose, Jr.'s teeth and jaw line crushed the gum material. His saliva would act as the catalysts to release the epigenetic mixture into his pink tissue. Then the payload would disperse into his blood stream and submerge into his body adding new gene instructions. His genome would forever be altered and affect his unborn children's children with specific protein instructions. A genetic code he devised to switch on the right protein instructions and turn off evil amino acids, and added the encouraging inner whispers to simply give and accept love and to sense pure evil.

Captain Lovins closely watched the little boy.

"Mister Wilcox, you look mean, but you a nice man, you not mean, are you?" Jose, Jr. asked. He kept chewing the gum.

"I guess so little man," Captain Lovins said. He winked down at Jose, Jr.

"I feel happy," Jose, Jr. said.

# # #

Jose, Sr. exhaled and wiped the sweat from his face, perplexed by his intuition and the strange man. Up off his knees, he brushed off the pine needles and oak leaves. He retreated to finish his prep work for Cajun/Creole night.

# # #

Captain Lovins observed Jose, Jr.'s father take a circuitous route back toward the clubhouse. Then he and Jose, Jr. spent the next hour walking the finely cut grounds at Divine Grace Golf & Country Club chatting about golf, life and Jose, Jr.'s future.

Chapter Thirty Four

Within a bygone section of Nashville, the golden sunset sparkled at its horizon, and a three-quarter moon began to emerge within a pale blue sky as Captain Lovins shepherded Jose, Jr. back toward the pro shop. Eddie parked his car along a weather-beaten brick street near Ardee's bungalow. From inside, Ardee had pulled back a shear lace curtain from behind a window separated into four sections by wooden muntins. She faintly waved down at Eddie. He waved back as he clutched the moist end of a bouquet of freshly purchased super market flowers. He walked up two concrete stairs onto the sturdy beadboard porch beneath exposed roof trusses as she pulled open the husky front door.

Standing on the entrance runner just inside Ardee's comfortable living room, Eddie kissed Ardee's warm cheek. She glided her fingers along his forearm as she admired the flowers.

"I guess those are for me?" Ardee asked. She wore a navy blue collard stretch dress with a beaded chain belt around her tiny waist.

"Yeah, sorry," Eddie said as he handed them to her.

"You look quite smart, Edward," Ardee said. She sniffed for the flowers fragrance, her thick blonde hair cascaded along her shoulders. "I love flowers, they share happiness, thank you."

The softly lit living room had comfortable furniture hidden under artful throws, and colorful decorative pillows. A scented candle glowed near the brick fireplace, and there were numerous strategically placed framed pictures of family and friends. He thought her lily and lavender perfume hid a secret love concoction, as he felt harmoniously warm within every living cell from his combed Christopher Clayton haircut down to his polished dress shoes.

"Nice place," Eddie said. He messed with the cuffs of his starched blue button down.

Ardee stepped forward and gave Eddie a warm kiss.

"I'm glad you're here," Ardee said. She smiled looking into his eyes. She backed up. "Follow me to the kitchen, help me cook, and put these in a vase."

"Sure," Eddie said. He happily followed her; his vision blurred strolling behind Ardee's slipstream.

"Edward, I thought we could have dinner out back," Ardee said. She nodded at a wide window with partially open shutters above the farmhouse sink. It overlooked a modest patio. "The weather's nice, and what not-"

"Why do you call me Edward?" Eddie asked. He leaned against the tiled counter top as Ardee searched a cupboard. The humble kitchen felt toasty from a pan baking potatoes in the oven, it had the aroma of chicken, spices, and perfume.

"I hate Eddie, that sounds like you were born to work the counter at a bowling alley," Ardee said. With a paring knife, she sliced the greenish flower stems at an angle, and carefully plunged each one into a simple glass vase.

"Bowling alley?" Eddie said. He chuckled. "That's not a real sport, besides, I hate those shoes."

"I think you're handsome, you're not an Eddie," Ardee said. She poured water under the flower petals into the vase. "Let me show you out back."

Eddie followed Ardee past the solid back door. A rickety fence blocked the nearby homes, the wooden plank porch shaded by tangled oak tree limbs.

"It's peaceful back here," Eddie said. He stared at the tiny strip of grass sprouting near the porch steps. "I think you're the prettiest girl I've ever seen."

Ardee set the vase in the center of the cypress table. She paused. She turned toward Eddie, she gently hugged him, and she pressed her cheek against his chest.

"We need to think about dinner, and not desert," Ardee said. She held his hand as they walked back inside the kitchen. "You do like fried chicken? You're not just being nice."

"What? My mother used to make it, ah, makes it," Eddie said. He shrugged. And Eddie thought it was just fate, his mother had perhaps found someone to share her time with, someone she could cook for, someone she could care for, and Eddie suspected it was just his turn to allow someone to love him, and for him to love them in return. He thought his father would have approved.

"Seriously, this is not a healthy meal?" Ardee said. She clicked on her gas cooktop, the flame ignited and she poured vegetable oil into her ancient cast iron skillet. "This skillet was my grandmother's, whenever I use it, I think of her."

"Whenever I eat fried chicken, I think of my mother," Eddie said. He stood near Ardee as she egg washed wrinkle skinned chicken drums, and with her dry hand rolled them in a pan filled with spiced flour specked with black pepper. "Then I remember my father, funny how the brain works."

"The secret to good fried chicken, buttermilk, time, hot, hot oil, not too much breading," Ardee said. She tipped her forefinger in a glass of water; she let a translucent drop fall into the oil. "Not ready, he's been gone along time?"

"He died just after Christmas, heart attack, they thought it was a genetic thing," Eddie said. He stared down at the solid tongue-in-groove floorboards. "I was thirteen, I can still see him lying there at the hospital, like he was sleeping, I've not liked the holidays since."

"Well aren't we the pair," Ardee said. She let another water teardrop fall into the hot oil. It sizzled as it dissipated into a gaseous oblivion. "Now we're talkin', I think the holidays are made up because it gets dark early in the winter, turn on all the lights so we don't all sit around being depressed, god forbid we actually sit and talk to each other."

"I like talkin' to you," Eddie said. He pulled back her dangling blonde hair. "It's like you can read my mind."

"Well, feelings mutual Mr. Wilcox," Ardee said. She snapped metal tongs at his pug nose. "Do you like white wine?"

"Sure," Eddie said.

"Over in the refrigerator, top shelf," Ardee said. With the tongs, she pointed at the stainless steel bottom-mount.

After Eddie uncorked the bottle, they sipped the cold wine with hints of apple, pear and citrus from crystal chardonnay glasses.

"Wedding gift I never sent back," Ardee said as she admired the wine glass. "Cheers."

"Cheers," Eddie said. "Sorry, the boys a fool-"

Ardee set the glass down on the kitchen counter. With the metal tongs, she flipped the frying chicken until they transformed into a flaky golden brown crusts. She covered the splattering oil with a round mesh cover.

"Don't want to catch fire," Ardee said. She shrugged. "I guess you need to have a little trauma in your life, I guess that's where wisdom hides, but only after."

"Did I ever tell you I beat him up?" Eddie said. Before taking another drink, he hid his grin behind the wine glass that reflected the fluorescent light.

"Mr. Wilcox, you know how to seduce a woman," Ardee said. She raised her wine glass up, and took a sip.

"Bobby was picking on an old friend of mine," Eddie said. He combed his hand through his brown hair. "You might have heard of him, Christopher Clayton, hair stylist?"

"Of course, but I can't afford to visit him," Ardee said. She scowled as she inspected the chicken. "Why are there people like Bobby? Pickin' at people, hurtin'em, always pickin'-"

"I don't know," Eddie said. He leaned against the doorframe. "Only time I've been in a fight, I think it's why Chris is my friend, why Jim Bob's still my friend. We sort of bonded that day. I think Chris still has a scar under his chin."

"Well, its Mr. Humperdinck's loss," Ardee said. She snapped the metal tongs. "I'll not be making him fried chicken, I don't understand Jim Bob, and his shenanigans, I don't really know."

And after a quiet moment of reflection, she finished frying the chicken, and they moved their feast outside under the twinkle from stars that time had not forgotten. The moon glowed in unison with the modest candle that reflected off the flower bouquet that dripped with tiny drops of moisture.

"Here goes," Eddie said. He held a chicken drum with his fingertips as if it were corn-on-the-cob.

Ardee and Eddie each bit into their chicken drums, leaving behind tiny golden morsels that stuck to their smiling glossed lips from the oil and fat.

"As good as your mother's?" Ardee asked. She grinned as if she already knew the answer.

"Oh, I think better," Eddie said. He wiped off his hands, and picked up the wine glass. "Cheers, thanks for cookin'."

"Well, thanks for callin'," Ardee said. She sipped wine from the glass; she set the glass on the table. "Comfort food, you're lucky you're not in jail with your bird brained friend."

"Jim Bob's not crazy, he's just lost," Eddie said. He scooped out scalloped potatoes from a baking dish. "Madam, may I?"

"Yes, darling, he's not lost now," Ardee said. She held her plate forward as Eddie served her potatoes. "He's gotten himself into quite a fix."

Eddie set the serving spoon within the steaming baking dish. He paused. He stared over at the candle.

"What's wrong," Ardee asked.

"I accidentally found him an attorney," Eddie said. He remembered that his Monday would be rather unusual. "My mother has, how do I say this without creeping myself out?"

"I look forward to meeting her," Ardee said. With her silver fork, she sliced her potatoes, and took a bite. "Mmm, I am a good cook, Jim Bob's got nothin' on me."

"Boyfriend? Yeah, I guess, named Simon Lewis," Eddie said.

Ardee wiped her mouth with a napkin. She set back and sipped the wine. She grinned at Eddie.

"Companion, I think that might be a softer way to say that," Ardee said. She giggled. She wiggled on the chair. "Good for her, I don't think we're old enough to be companions."

"True, well, he said he'd help get Jim Bob out of jail," Eddie said. He sipped his wine. "I think he made time for me tomorrow, I need to call him. I've never been to a lawyer's office, should prove to be an odd sensation."

"I would think," Ardee said.

"Yeah, he's even a tax attorney, how weird is that?" Eddie asked. He twisted the chicken drum in his fingertips as if he was basting it in the cool air.

"Life's just random," Ardee said. She shrugged; she drank wine. "And think, you grew up with my idiot ex."

"Can I tell you a secret?" Eddie asked. He smirked.

Ardee purposefully over-reacted; she carefully examined her patio. She sat slightly forward.

"Fun, I love me some secrets," Ardee said in a whispered tone. She raised her plucked eyebrow; then she winked.

"Regan Fryingpan, she's getting her haircut at Chris's," Eddie said. Then he thought about the creepy wish list. And of the bald headed dude. And the duffle bag hiding in his trunk. He mumbled. "Genome collection?"

"Yeah, what?" Ardee said. Her hands patted on the table. "Don't leave a girl hangin'."

"Oh, right, sorry," Eddie said. He leaned forward. "I'm going to act like I'm an assist to Chris. He thought I might get a kick out of being real close to someone famous."

Ardee sat back with her hand over her mouth.

"Edward the paparazzi spy, I shall not speak this evil," Ardee said. She laughed. "Are you serious?"

"Yeah, Monday night," Eddie said. He chuckled. "Maybe I'll get you a lock of her hair."

"We could sell it, make some loot," Ardee said.

"Yeah, but we'd pay our taxes," Eddie said. He took a gulp of wine. He clenched his teeth. "Right?"

"Yikes, that's a good point, don't mess with the IRS," Ardee said. She sat back and crossed her thin arms. "No, I'll let you keep it, I like living in my snow globe."

"Thanks, I think," Eddie said. He wiped off his mouth with a napkin. He gulped.

"I have a feeling about you, my Edward," Ardee said. She finger twirled her curled blonde hair. "I think you're destined for greatness."

"I don't know 'bout that," Eddie said. He shrugged.

"As I've gotten older, I've learned to listen to my instincts," Ardee said. She smiled. "Go be special, Edward."

"I loved your fried chicken," Eddie said.

"I hope you like desert?" Ardee said. She smiled over at Eddie; she sipped the wine, she licked the glass rim that reflected a kaleidoscope of soft colors across her smoldering eyes.

"Sure, you make something?" Eddie asked.

"Oh, just love," Ardee said. She leaned forward. She sighed. "Just me, all of me-"

Eddie rapidly blinked his eyelids. He pushed his right hand across the table to clutch Ardee's soft hand.

"I'd love desert," Eddie said. He sucked in the cool air.

"Homemade fried chicken," Ardee said. She kissed Eddie's hand. "It's the food of love."

Chapter Thirty Five

As Monday morning emerged, Eddie adjusted his eyesight to an unfamiliar space. The first tipoff he was not at his apartment, the aroma from perfume and not the moldy clothes he had stuffed in his hamper. And the other indication, the tangled blonde hair tickling under his chin connected to Ardee's warm naked body. He snuggled closer to her under the soft, clean bed sheets.

"Mornin' Edward," Ardee said. She sighed. She clutched his hand, and pulled him closer.

But far from the young lovers, Dr. Yin drove his four door sedan toward a tiny eastern Kentucky town, called Clayhole. He was unaware Ms. Prosperina's parasite came along for the ride as it slowly devoured his pineal gland.

Dr. Yin had an address plugged into his GPS for a diamond drill bit manufacturer, Brilliant Rock Bits. For several hours, he drove his car along the dusty two lane roads that corkscrewed through the hilly terrain. He dodged hulking dump trucks spewing dirt, and coal, as they hammered the rutted blacktop into submission. He searched for the facility that he was certain was a shadow business for Professor Quan and Captain Lovins. The privately held company's internet site was a cornucopia of information about every aspect for the drill bit industry and business. All their diamond drill bits were custom-made using state-of-the-art technology for numerous commercial projects. They created drill bits for coal mining, oil and gas rigs, and in particular for carving through the earth like a massive blind mole to create a pathway for super colliders. But the website was desert dry with ownership information or about the company's origins.

Dr. Yin flicked his GPS with his middle finger as it sporadically operated within the mountains. Then he realized he was lost, after he drove past the same shotgun style house guarded by a snarling German shepherd. And the same two-pump gas station across the street from a barnyard dotted with white feathered and black feathered roosters.

The sun was at its relative midmorning position, as he returned to Clayhole to ask for directions, buy an old-fashioned map, and perhaps find a restaurant for a late breakfast. He parked the formerly shiny car in an angled space on Main Street, across from him the two story stone courthouse as local business people stepped up the broad staircase. Down the one-way street, at the opposite corner from the post office was an active diner. He locked his car door with his remote, fed the meter; he walked toward the tempered glass front door, stenciled across with, White Flash. He buttoned his blue blazer, a group of old men sat next door on a long worn wooden bench witling pine shards onto gravel. The Caucasians and an African American wore bib overalls, mud splattered boots, and they licked the rolling papers tip ends and smoked their own cigarettes. One acknowledged him as he chawed tobacco, he spat at the ground, another tipped his railroad cap, but they did not stop witling, smoking or shooting the breeze about the dying coal business.

Within the narrow five-table diner, grease crackled with the scent from frying onions and hash browns, as steam particles floated up the commercial grade vent. He found the only unoccupied black vinyl swivel stool at the elbow of the chrome tipped salt and pepper laminate countertop.

"It ain't court day?" the waiter asked. She had her gangly grey hair back, her skin like a piece of marbled aged beef.

"Naw, it ain't," a man said. He sat next to Dr. Yin. He sipped black coffee from a white mug, and smashed his cigarette inside a black ashtray.

"Pardon?" Dr. Yin asked. He sat up straight as he put on his round wire-framed eyeglasses to read the paper menu.

"You ain't from here," the man said. His voice sounded like a slow tire leak. He pushed a buttermilk biscuit into a swirl of brown gravy and yellow egg yolk.

"Ah, no, I am not," Dr. Yin said.

"I'm sorry honey, thought you was a law man," the waiter said. She held a black handle decanter. "Coffee?"

"Yes, thank you," Dr. Yin said. He slipped the paper menu back into the metal crescent moon shaped condiment caddy.

"What can I get ya?" the waiter asked. She held the half-full coffee decanter up to offer refills down the row of weathered faces.

"Yes, I'd like an egg white only omelet, no butter, no cheese, with plain wheat toast," Dr. Yin said. He sipped the coffee, then added sugar and cream. He checked his PDA. "Oh, do you have yogurt smoothies?"

"Say that again?" the waiter asked. "Smooth what-"

Dr. Yin glanced up from staring down at his cell phone that did not have any signal strength. He sensed that every eyeball in the diner was staring at him. The cook turned around, he wiped his moist face with a towel, and stared over at the waiter. She shrugged.

"Ah, two eggs, scrambled, wheat toast," Dr. Yin said. He took off his glasses and slid them inside his jacket pocket.

"Lawyer type?" the man said. He nudged at Dr. Yin with a kindly grin. "Revenuer?"

"Revenuer? Pardon," Dr. Yin said.

"I'll translate honey, tax man?" the waiter said. In front of Dr. Yin she set a paper napkin and a metal fork and knife on the slick counter top.

"Oh, no, I know a few," Dr. Yin said. He sipped his hot carmel colored coffee. "Scientist, for the government, so to speak, say, perhaps you all can help me."

The waiter poured him more coffee and Dr. Yin added half-and-half and a packet of sugar.

"How so?" the waiter asked. Her moist, puffy forearm rested on the countertop.

"A company called, Brilliant Rock Bits?" Dr. Yin asked. He stared at her and the man sitting next to him. "Any idea where? I can't seem to find it, my GPS seems to have lost its connection, just weird, mountains should not-"

"Oh?" the man said. He grunted. "Imagine that-"

"Pardon?" Dr. Yin asked.

"Never heard of it," the waiter said. He snapped around and set the coffee carafe back onto a warmer.

"If I was you," the man said. He heaved his chest up under his red flannel shirt. "I'd not go roaming out there, it can get dangerous, easy to get lost."

The waiter set a white plate with scrambled eggs and wheat toast in front of Dr. Yin. She peeled off the paper customer ticket and slapped it next to the coffee mug.

"He's not kiddin'" the waiter said. "Need anythin' else?"

"No, this will work," Dr. Yin said. He tore the wheat toast apart. "Not like this is a war zone, or the projects, last I checked we are still in the United States."

"Revenuer's barge into those woods, lookin' for money," the man said. He filled a thin rolling paper with dried burley tobacco flakes, licked one end and candy wrapper twisted it together with his working-man fingertips. He lit it, took a drag and puffed out the smoke. "They don't come out, nobody finds nothin'."

"I'm not a *revenuer*, you mean drugs?" Dr. Yin asked. He chewed the bread with the scrambled eggs. He coughed.

"Yeah, but you sure look like one, besides, I don't go out there these days," the man said. He hacked a cough. "It ain't like I'm chicken, I got shot in Vietnam, government gave me trinkets for my troubles, it's just not the same these days."

"Ever heard of someone named Lovins, or a Quan?" Dr. Yin asked. He pulled out a piece of paper. "Have an address, any idea where this is?"

"More coffee?" the waiter asked. She glanced down at the paper, and the address.

"No thanks," Dr. Yin said.

"I'd let it go, son, you sort a, reminds me a bein' in Vietnam," the man said. He glanced up and down the bar. He waved his hand at the paper with the address on it. "You'll never find that place, besides, you stick out like I did, I wasn't supposed to be there, but I was doin' my duty, right?"

"More coffee," the waiter asked. She accidentally pushed Dr. Yin's hot coffee cup off the counter, and into his lap. "Oh, darn it, sorry."

Dr. Yin sprang back from the counter with a hot moist ring in the wrong spot on his pressed grey slacks.

"Damn, that stings," Dr. Yin said. He grabbed his private parts; he snatched several napkins and pressed them against his leg and groin.

"Oh, honey, I am so, sorry," the waiter said.

"Got ya good," the man said. He chuckled. "Need some ice?"

After a minute, Dr. Yin shook his head with his eyelids shut.

"Sorry, dear, breakfasts on the house," the waiter said.

"No, I'm fine," Dr. Yin said. He shoved open the front door, and marched out of the diner and onto the sidewalk. He stared down the street at the post office; he smacked his forehead with his right hand.

"Idiot, of course," Dr. Yin said. He stomped toward the post office. The customer line trudged along at broken conveyor belt speed. Dr. Yin huffed as he scooted past them and up to the only counter open for business.

"Get in line," the postal worker said. She shooed him away like a common house fly.

"But I-"Dr. Yin said. He turned and trudged away.

"You got to get a number," an old woman said. She pointed a boney finger up at the red plastic dispenser.

"Directions?" Dr. Yin asked. He looked down at the old woman. Her face was like moist bread dough.

"They real particular like that, got to have it," the old woman said. She patted him on the forearm. "You not from here-"

"No," Dr. Yin said. He yanked out the paper tongue sticking out from the dispenser. "And I'm not a *revenuer*."

"You best to do what they want," the old woman said.

"Thank you, ah, madam," Dr. Yin said. He shifted to the back of the line behind a puffy man, his gut slurped over his blue jeans. Dr. Yin stared down at his lucky number thirteen.

"Number one? Number one?" the postal worker asked. She locked her gaze over at the digital display. "Number one?"

"Wake up," Dr. Yin said. They turned to glare at him as if he had torn a hole into their space-time continuum.

"You'll get your turn," the postal worker said. She shooed at him. She inspected the crowd. "It's okay, number one?"

"Oh, I guess that me," a little girl said. She skipped over to the counter. "Can I buy stamps?"

The postal worker gazed down at the little girl. She smiled.

"Yes, honey child," the postal worker said.

The little girl threw paper currency and coins on the counter. She put her hands up as if she was under arrest.

"That much," the little girl said. "Grandma needs that much."

Dr. Yin's shoulders slumped. He sucked in stale oxygen through his puckered lips as stared down at the dirty tile floor. He waited the requisite twenty-five minutes; as each local had his or her moment to confer with the civil service queen mother. He read the FBI's most wanted list stapled to a cork-board; he shook his head at the profiles, aware the IRS had a much more dangerous unpublished list.

"Thirteen?" the postal worker asked. "Thirteen?"

"Me, me, my turn," Dr. Yin said. He strode up to the counter.

"Slow down, give you a stroke," the postal worker said. She leaned forward across the wooden service counter.

"I just need directions," Dr. Yin said. He yanked out the piece of paper with the address. He slid it over to the postal worker. "I need to find this address."

The postal worked slowly slid her eyeglasses attached to a beaded chain over her skinny neck up her long nose. She picked up the piece of paper and carefully read the address.

"Honey, I've lived in these parts, all my days," the postal worker said. She shrugged. "I have not a clue where this be-"

"What?" Dr. Yin said. "That's ridiculous."

"Simmer," the postal worker said. She handed back the piece of paper. She took off her eyeglasses. "For all I know, that could be a hundred different places, we don't deliver the mail out there, we not crazy."

Dr. Yin leaned back on his heels. He crossed his arms. "You all don't deliver?" Dr. Yin asked.

"Not out there, no sir," the postal worker said.

"Then how to they get their mail?" Dr. Yin asked.

The postal worker shook her head.

"You ain't real bright?" the postal worker said.

"I'll have you know I'm a PH.D.," Dr. Yin said. "I have more degrees than wall space."

"I am so, so impressed," the postal worker said. She pointed her forefinger to Dr. Yin's left like a crawling inchworm. "But you ain't got no common sense, now do ya, ever heard of a PO Box? Like that wall full of them, right there."

Dr. Yin turned and stared at the different sized metal boxes.

"True, but this address has to exist," Dr. Yin said. "This is a tax paying company, business is conducted, employees."

"I suppose, but anything with a rural route, means old. And I'm not allowed to tell anybody, anything," the postal worker said. "We have a code of conduct, I'm a civil servant."

"Surely, somebody knows," Dr. Yin said.

"Sorry," the postal worker said. She waved him away. "Number fourteen? Number fourteen?"

Dr. Yin left the post office and walked outside into the sulfur-invested air. He huffed; he trudged back to his car. He sat inside thinking through his options as the locals walked past him. He thought he could be back in Nashville before dinnertime, and besides he had important work to do, and he was not Ms. Prosperina's bag boy. But as he drove along the steep mountain highway under warm afternoon sunlight, he saw an intensely bright light of flash in his mind's eye, then the chrome front grill of a huge dump truck that smashed him and his car as it shoved it over a steep embankment, and for Dr. Yin, permanent darkness.

# # #

Back in Nashville, after Mr. Oppenheimer had broken back into Bertrand's home, and retrieved the thumb drive, Ms. Prosperina was enjoying her new taste for Kentucky bourbon; she was equally pleased to read Bertrand's file notes from his investigation into her background.

"Good boy," Ms. Prosperina said at the computer screen.

"Thank you, madam," Mr. Oppenheimer said. He stood nearby.

"I will need to find a replacement for Dr. Yin," Ms. Prosperina said. She licked her lips.

"Yes, madam," Mr. Oppenheimer said. He stared out of the of the hotel suite's bank of windows into the afternoon haze.

"Dr. Yin's lost his yang," Ms. Prosperina said. She sipped the liquid ambrosia. "This is quite lovely, and Mr. Screwtop, quite thorough, we'll pay them a cleanup visit."

Chapter Thirty Six

Before Ms. Prosperina influenced the parasite feasting on Dr. Yin's pineal gland to release its lethal bacterial payload, Eddie wiped away the bubbly dew from the rectangular bathroom mirror as Ardee's naked reflection emerged behind him from within the warm steam particle cloud. He peered up at the frosted lights; he thought his father might have said, "That's my boy!" He smiled as Ardee wrapped her arms around him.

"I had no idea my bathroom had a sauna feature," Ardee said. She kissed his neck. "You smell, you fell squeaky clean."

"Yeah, squeaky," Eddie said. He toweled off. "I used to hate Monday mornings, I better change my clothes."

"Naw, Clevenger won't notice," Ardee said. She slipped on a green terrycloth robe.

"You don't have to wear that," Eddie said.

"Oh? I've created a monster," Ardee said. She combed her wet hair, and then she squeezed it down to the tip ends to push out the moisture drops. "I think your shirt is on the kitchen floor, next to my dress, and my shoes, not sure what else."

"I guess it's okay," Eddie said. He shrugged. "Wait, I'll need to go back and get my suit, I have that lawyer, mothers-"

"Companion, her companion, Edward," Ardee said. She wiped her face with a hand towel. "Little part time job tonight?"

Eddie thought about the duffle bag hidden in his car's trunk. He glanced over at Ardee, she was shaking her hair dry with a soft cotton towel.

"Crap, I don't know what time, Simon said to call his office," Eddie said. He shrugged. "I'll go on to work, figure it out later, complicated day I guess."

"Can you do me a favor?" Ardee asked.

"Sure," Eddie said.

"Since things got, ah, rather wet in the shower," Ardee said. She combed her hair. "I don't usually wash my hair on Mondays, although you gave me a nice head massage like I was at a salon, among other things. Maybe you'll learn another technique tonight? I'm going to be late, can you be a saint and pickup Clevenger's coffee thing?"

"Sure, but you'll need to write it down?" Eddie asked.

"I can, he's rather picky," Ardee said. She smiled.

# # #

Eddie drove to work using an alternative route to a Starry Eyed Coffee Hut near a new homogenous strip mall that Ardee had directed him to. In the drive-thru line, he braked next to the hulking three paneled outside menu. A frowning black metal weather hood protected the microphone that crackled with static.

"How may we help you?" the barista asked. Her voice sounded like she was at the other end of a child's tin can string line.

"Ah, yeah," Eddie said. He held Clevenger's order written out on a piece of notebook paper that Ardee had kissed leaving behind her rosy red lip imprint. He grinned.

"Go ahead," the barista said.

"Sorry," Eddie said. He glanced at his rear view mirror and noticed the line that stretched behind him for two blocks with every make and model polluting the environment. And he sensed he was being watched after he looked up at the ubiquitous symbol for the restaurant chain with an all knowing eyeball staring down at him from within a golden five pointed star, there company slogan typed underneath, *in vivo coffea.*

"Hello?" the barista asked.

"Okay, sorry, first time," Eddie said. "I'd like a black-eyed, red eyed coffee with whipped cream, caramel-"

"I got it," the barista said. She chuckled. "Come up to the window, you must be a friend of Ardee's."

Eddie clutched the hot, tall coffee cup that had puked on his shirtsleeve as he skipped across the warm office parking lot; he scampered next to Ardee's desk, he set the coffee down.

"Just in time," Ardee said. She winked up at Eddie. "Let me get some tonic, that'll leave a stain."

"Thanks," Eddie said. He rapidly blinked his eyelids.

"What's wrong with your eyes?" Ardee asked.

"That barista friend, she gave me a free sample," Eddie said.

"She's like a drug pusher," Ardee said. She pointed at the coffee cup. "If you want a gut like Clevenger's-"

"No kidding, now I know why my father told me to drink it black," Eddie said. He shrugged. "Need some water, clear my mind because that stuff is potent, feel like I'm floating."

"I know, it's like Clevenger's addicted to this," Ardee said.

She winked at him. She pushed away Eddie's attempt at a public display of affection. "Not here." She wiggled away toward Clevenger's office door.

Eddie wobbled his way through the fabric walled cube world to the office kitchenette. He snagged a cold plastic bottle of water from the kitchenette's refrigerator.

Clevenger's bulbous moon shaped head appeared as he slurped down his coffee concoction.

"Well, well, glad to see you," Clevenger said.

"Yeah, nice to be back," Eddie said. He sucked in a deep breath. He twisted open the white plastic bottle top.

"I understand and you had quite a good time with the Turnbull's? Ardee said you got my coffee this morning, thank you, did good," Clevenger said. He stuck his gut out at Eddie. "Hey, you're not going to hold out on me are ya?"

"Sorry?" Eddie said. He wondered if Ardee had mentioned last night's fried chicken dinner.

"Lionel's socks or something or other, right?" Clevenger asked. He stroked the thick Civil War era mange hiding his mouth. He curiously stared at Eddie.

380

Eddie instantly clenched his fingers together which caused the water to shoot out geyser style from the bottle top.

"Sorry, well it's sort a true," Eddie said. He flicked the water drops off his hand and he grabbed a paper towel.

"Well that's cool," Clevenger said. He burped. "Sorry."

"Somebody made me a crazy offer, so I sold them," Eddie said. He coughed; He shrugged. "Who would believe me? You know."

Clevenger spindled with his pudgy fingers through his goatee. He nodded his head.

"Ah, too bad," Clevenger said. He slurped down more coffee.

"Sorry," Eddie said. He swigged down the last remaining drops of water from the plastic bottle.

"I guess I'd a done the same thing," Clevenger said. He rubbed his belly. "How much did you get?"

"Five hundred bucks," Eddie said. He stared down; he wondered if he might have just punched his ticket to hell.

"Good for you, Ha! Charlene thinks highly of you," Clevenger said. He waddled toward the opening. "Oh well, another exciting day sellin' insurance."

"Oh, Clevenger," Eddie said. He walked closer to Clevenger. "I need to meet a lawyer, my friend Jim Bob got into big trouble, my mothers', ah, companion offered to get him out."

"What'd he do?" Clevenger said. He sniffed. "Sellin' drugs or this coffee addiction? I'm kiddin', what's up?"

"Didn't pay his taxes," Eddie said. He gulped as he thought about his mother's deep freeze stuffed with US Treasury notes.

"Don't mess with them, no, no," Clevenger said. He whistled. "I get the shivers, you ever been audited?"

"No," Eddie said. He stared past Clevenger.

"If you ever make some money, or inherit some, they'll come a callin', I promise," Clevenger said. He shook his head. "It's like having a thick finger without a glove stuck up your yoo-hoo, like a permanent hemorrhoid that stings just to remind you like it's all high-and-mighty, and it is all knowing, all seeing." Clevenger scratched behind his ear.

"Ah, I never thought about it like that," Eddie said.

"But, yeah, insurance business ain't goin' anywhere," Clevenger said. He slogged forward. "Just let Ardee know."

"Thanks," Eddie said. He thought his ears were on fire as he thought about how easy he had gotten involved with Jim Bob's *friends.* "I'll let her know."

Eddie fought his way back through cube world corridor and collapsed onto his office chair. He dialed the number to Simon's office; a calm, professional voice greeted him. After being switched several times, Simon's assistant answered.

"Simon Lewis's office, this is Emily Dawn," she said.

"Yes, hello, I'm, ah Edward Wilcox," he said. He tapped the top of his office counter with a ballpoint pen.

"Mr. Wilcox, I've been expecting your call. Mr. Lewis has cleared his afternoon schedule, is one-thirty acceptable?" Emily Dawn asked. "He has a lunch meeting before."

"Absolutely," Eddie said. He stared over at his mother's picture he had tacked beneath the office cubes above storage.

"We will see you then, need directions?" Emily Dawn asked.

"Simon mentioned that Batman shaped building. Right?" Eddie asked. He shook his mouse to wake-up his computer.

"Yes, thirteenth floor, parking is under the building, we'll validate your ticket, check in at the front desk, and I'll come get you," Emily Dawn said. "Okay?"

"Yes, ma'am, I'll be there," Eddie said. He replaced the phone on its cradle. He pondered the rest of his day, and wondered how he swerved into being at Christopher Claytons at the same time Regan Fryingpan's scheduled to appear. He decided he wanted to quickly get the next transaction completed, get Jim Bob out of jail and *never, ever* get involved with these people again. He double-clicked his computer mouse to open WePay. He thought about how he should describe the hair. He stared up at the starless office ceiling tiles. He uncrossed his arms. He leaned forward and typed on the keyboard.

'Blond follicles and strands from a special person, perfect to add to anyone's genome collection.'

The black arrow dangled over the submit box. Eddie paused, and he glided his fingers through his partially dry hair. He took in a deep breath, he gulped and he clicked the mouse with his middle finger, and jerked back from his computer as if he had burned his hand by touching a hot cast iron stove.

"No going back now," Eddie whispered. He wondered how the rest of day would play out as he thought he was flying blind without any experience dealing with lawyers.

Chapter Thirty Seven

After Eddie had spent the rest of his morning nervously reviewing insurance applications, at high noon, he advised Ardee he was leaving for the day. She had blown a kiss at him, she had whispered she loved him, and she had swatted him on the behind.

"Companion, remember he's your mother's *companion*," Ardee had said. "Don't get me any hair, that was a joke, call me?"

"I'll call you," Eddie said. He had kissed her.

"Thank you," Ardee said. "Maybe come by, if you want." And as Eddie disappeared behind the office suite's smoked glass front doors, she had not a hint that she would not be able to sleep tonight. That she would anxiously stay awake, pacing back forth deep into the early morning wondering what had happened to Eddie. But not far from the office building, Ms. Prosperina sat inside her hotel suite tolerating lunch.

"No one cancels on me," Ms. Prosperina said. She pushed around her Caesar salad with a silver fork. "Who is this Simon Lewis? Tell me, the arrogant fool needs a lesson."

"Yes, Madam," Mr. Oppenheimer said. He flipped open his computer screen, it was set on a glass top coffee table.

"Tell me, I want details, nothing like a good personal detail to fire a warning shot," Ms. Prosperina said. She clenched her jaw; she glared over at Mr. Oppenheimer. "I am concerned Mr. Screwtop had a big mouth, thankfully, he can't talk now."

"We have his thumb drive," Mr. Oppenheimer said.

"Sneaky Mr. Screwtop, likely made a copy," Ms. Prosperina said. She hissed. "I need to make them concerned for their safety, encourage them to keep quiet, or pick at their greed."

Mr. Oppenheimer typed on the keyboard. He paused.

"He is well trained for his work," Mr. Oppenheimer said. He continued to study his computer screen. "MBA, JD from Ivy League schools, he has a bachelor's degree in divinity."

"Well, that's interesting," Ms. Prosperina said. She sipped her iced tea. She sneered. "I hate this carbon based vessel I'm trapped in, this food is disgusting. I wonder if it's in poor form for bourbon before noon? I'm not sure I care."

"I don't know," Mr. Oppenheimer said. He stared up at her.

"I should visit a distillery, go to Kentucky, buy a horse, a wonderfully wicked place, with bourbon, tobacco, horses, ah, I bet a delightful place," Ms. Prosperina said. She waved at Mr. Oppenheimer. "Go on-"

"Yes, Madam," Mr. Oppenheimer said. He adjusted his computer screen. "Well known for his taxation expertise, commercial litigation, quite formidable reputation, nothing to indicate he has had any criminal issues, no convictions, no obvious vice."

"Hmm, I would expect that, but what of his life, where is his flaw," Ms. Prosperina asked. She adjusted her petite body to an upright position. "He's all human, so he has a critical flaw."

"Early fifties, tall, he was a good athlete in his day, but studied on academic scholarships," Mr. Oppenheimer said. He shifted his forefinger along the computer pad. "Ah, his father was a Protestant minister, his mother a nurse. They are both deceased, he has no siblings I can find."

"Pity, that would have been fun," Ms. Prosperina said.

"He is a widower, wife died from a fatal stroke," Mr. Oppenheimer said. He clicked to another electronic web page.

"Well, good, he has felt pain," Ms. Prosperina said.

"Has grown children, grandchildren," Mr. Oppenheimer said. He grinned. He unbuttoned his jacket. "Ah, his social media page, yes, quite useful, many pictures, one moment madam."

Ms. Prosperina leaned back in the eagle clawed chair.

"Such fools, so easy to squeeze out their life like filtering toothpaste for a complete examination," Ms. Prosperina said. She chuckled. "Humanity, I feel this weakness in this body, but I have mastered it, I control it, love cannot harm me."

"Wait, he has a new picture," Mr. Oppenheimer said. He typed the keyboard. "From his daughter's social pages, a woman, let me search using her facial profile, one moment."

"Good boy," Ms. Prosperina said. She lit a cigarette.

"She is a widow, they go to the same church," Mr. Oppenheimer said. He typed. "They appear to be more than friends, a picture, they hold hands, new pictures with his children, smiling."

"Well, our saint cares for someone special," Ms. Prosperina said. She puffed out the smoke into dissipating grey rings floating toward the ceiling. "Tell me, yes, I want to know about her that is a useful flaw that he cannot easily hide."

"Name, Sophia Wilcox, husband was an Adam Wilcox, deceased," Mr. Oppenheimer said. He typed. "Old wedding photos, on her social page, ah, she has a child, a boy, one moment, let me lock onto his facial features." He typed. He shifted his forefinger across the computer pad.

Ms. Prosperina stood up, smoking; she strolled over to the suite's wet bar. She poured bourbon, neat, into a crystal highball. She studied the drink's auburn colored hue that she held up to the fluorescent lights.

"Now I understand why Mr. Screwtop called this his *mother's milk*," Ms. Prosperina said. She sipped, she savored the intense flavors; she licked her thin lips. "Just lovely, yes, I need to investigate this, just for me."

"Edward," Mr. Oppenheimer said. He chuckled.

"What's so funny?" Ms. Prosperina asked. She sucked in the cigarette smoke. She slowly released it from her pointy nose and mouth like a mythical flying serpent dragon.

"Edward *Tiberius* Wilcox, early twenties," Mr. Oppenheimer said. He shrugged. "Unremarkable, basic community college education, not much to note about him, works in insurance, goes by the name, Eddie."

"Oh, Edward is a much stronger name, Tiberius? How odd," Ms. Prosperina said. She shrugged and waved away the name. "Sophia, yes that is the flaw, I shall exploit her. He loves someone, she is an old widow, he will want to protect her. Yes, I have his Achilles heel as it might be said in this culture to ensure his silence and encourage his greed."

"Yes, Madam," Mr. Oppenheimer said.

"Go get the transportation," Ms. Prosperina said. She extinguished the cigarette; she slugged back the remaining bourbon. "I have an appointment to keep."

# # #

"Why are you calling?" Captain Lovins said. He clicked off his hotel room's television. "I took care of Jose, Jr., nice little guy, he'll be fun to follow."

"Find him, Edward, he is in grave danger," Professor Quan said. He panted against the cell phone microphone like an out of breath dog in heat.

"Calm down, details, give me details," Captain Lovins asked. He stood up, and he quickly zipped his backpack shut. "Focus-"

"Nashville, she is heading downtown, mad at a lawyer," Professor Quan said. "A Simon something, she knows Edward exists, there is a connection, with his mother."

"Weird, Edward left me a hint this morning," Captain Lovins said. He inspected the room to ensure he left nothing behind. "I reviewed his file, he has a childhood friend, owns an expensive barber shop. He went there. I think he stumbled onto one of the shopping list targets, Fryingpan woman, actress I think."

"No, no, she is too close, if she looks at him, she'll know, he is not ready," Professor Quan said. He moaned. "She will be unmerciful, she'll destroy him just to show off for me."

"I've got his car tagged," Captain Lovins said. He slung the backpack over his shoulder. "I can easily track him down, don't sweat this, it's a big town, odds are with us."

"He is flawed," Professor Quan said. "I sense something, this is not random, just find him before she does."

"Calm, I can do this," Captain Lovins said. He stood at attention inside the dark hotel room. "Calm, focus-"

"Yes, of course," Professor Quan said. "I don't care about the hair, I need to fix Edward first thing, need to find him."

"I'll find him," Captain Lovins said. He opened the metal door. He stopped in the carpeted hallway. "Then what?"

"I'm coming, I know what to do," Professor Quan said. "Set up a meeting, use any excuse, this has to happen now."

"I'll bait him," Captain Lovins said. He pulled at the backpack strap. "I know what to do, meet me at the doughnut shop, you know the one?"

"Yes, I do," Professor Quan said.

"There's an all-night General Beauregard's Fried Chicken nearby, I like the name," Captain Lovins said. He pushed past the side exit door and trotted outside toward his van. It was a cool morning splashed with brilliant sunlight. "It'll be empty, except for a few random drunks. You can sneak into town, and be out of here before she notices, and we can deal with Edward."

"Very well, I'm coming," Professor Quan said. "You'll know who I am when you see me."

# # #

Eddie tugged at his pure white starched dress shirt collar, he wondered if he had cinched his dad's favorite red club tie to tight around his neck. He stood on the marble floor inside the warm Batman shaped building's three story atrium; the human traffic was passing by him like random decaying nuclei being simultaneously attracted and repelled by each other. He verified the correct office suite from an inspection of the building's occupant legend for the law firm, Lewis, Milton, Wormwood & Screwtop.

"Thirteenth floor, I didn't think?" Eddie said. He shrugged. He searched for the correct elevator within the crowd of men and woman lost in business conversations. As he got inside the elevator packed like a doomed Kansas City cattle car, he thought the building gave him an odd sensation because as he had driven closer in the afternoon sunlight, he thought centered between the twin spires there was a massive eyeball staring down at him.

After the endless elevator ride up, and waiting for the other building occupants casually to get on or off, he cautiously walked up to the office suite's dark cherry wood reception desk. An attractive bleach blonde, her head partially concealed, stared up at Eddie.

"Hello, Mr. Wilcox?" she asked.

"Yes, I'm, ah, Mr. Wilcox," Eddie said. He wondered how she knew his name. He glanced around at the quiet reception area.

"Can we offer you coffee, water perhaps?" she asked.

"No, no, I'm fine-" Eddie said. He wiped perspiration from his flushed forehead. He tugged at his shirt collar.

"Please feel free to wait over in that alcove. I'll call Mr. Lewis's assistant," she said. She smiled.

"Thank you," Eddie said. He stumbled over to a soft, light brown, leather couch within a chair grouping, centered by a Shaker style storage coffee table. Fresh cut lilies were in a nearby Asian vase. Staring up at the crown molding and cottony textured starless ceiling tiles, he tried to think through Jim Bob's situation. He wondered how he would pay the legal costs in a tactful way, without being obvious by paying in blocks of frozen US currency. And he kept reflecting back to last night's fried chicken dinner, and Ardee. His heart muscle now spackled with her love that raced inside him, pumping oxygen into his blood stream to cycle the good news he felt deep within every cell that he was loved, and that he loved her in return.

"Mr. Wilcox?" Emily Dawn asked. She extended her open right hand to Eddie. She was tall, thin, with dark flowing hair and the spark of intellectual curiosity inside her dark irises.

"Yes," Eddie said. He took in a deep breath as he stood up.

"Please follow me," Emily Dawn said.

Eddie dizzily followed Emily Dawn down a narrow office corridor. Unaware, he strolled past Bertrand Screwtop's office, and then busy support staff shuffling virtual paper inside modest interior cubes.

"I guess I qualify as a member of cube world," Eddie said.

"What was that Mr. Wilcox?" Emily Dawn asked. She stopped.

"Oh, nothing, I work in cubes like these," Eddie said. He shrugged, and he messed with his shirt collar.

"Don't wear a tie much?" Emily Dawn asked. She gave Eddie a wide toothed smile.

"No, insurance office is rather casual," Eddie said.

"Mr. Lewis warned me you might be nervous," Emily Dawn said. She patted Eddie on the left shoulder. "It's okay, loosen your collar, you're in the best hands in the country. Seriously, I'm a lawyer as well, but I'd not want to have Mr. Lewis on the other side of the table, trust me. I'm learning all I can from him. And the IRS lawyers hate to see him show up, so, take a deep breath, he'll get this worked out. I've been researching all morning for your friend, Jim Bob, okay?"

"Thank you," Eddie said. He sensed his pulse slow down.

Emily Dawn waved her long fingers for Eddie to follow; she stopped at the corner office door with the name plate, Mr. Simon Lewis, Managing Partner. She leaned inside the doorway.

"Mr. Lewis, Mr. Wilcox is here," Emily Dawn said. She backed out of the doorway. Eddie walked forward into the office.

"Eddie," Simon said. "Come on in."

Simon's office had a panoramic view of downtown Nashville and western Tennessee. Beneath he could see how the Cumberland River snaking its path for several miles into the sunny haze; and toward western Kentucky and he thought the majestic Land Between the Lakes where he used to go hiking and fishing with his father. Those days were but a few happy memories from his childhood, a childhood cut short the day his father died. Eddie thought it like having a quiet constant every time he looked at something that triggered a memory of his father. He glanced back over at Simon, at least his mother was smiling again.

Simon sat behind a mahogany stained partners desk, banked by similar looking period sideboards.

"IRS will be rather surprised by Jim Bob's lawyer," Eddie said, as he stepped forward into the office.

"Quite right," Emily Dawn said. She shrugged. "Told ya-"

"I'm so pleased you have the confidence in me, and our firm to represent your friend, Jim Bob," Simon said. He stood up. He wore a white custom-fitted French cuff shirt, with pearl cuff links. "I hope you don't mind, I asked Emily Dawn to do an initial investigation as to the government's case."

Emily Dawn nudged Eddie further inside and guided him toward the intimate seating area. Eddie sat upright in a high back chair. Simon slinked in next to him on a soft couch.

"Mr. Lewis, I'm sorry, I don't want to waste your time," Eddie said. He realized his mother cavorted with a DNA gold medal lottery winner. "I feel stupid, I'm sorry."

Simon grinned over at Eddie. Eddie thought he had kind eyes.

"Now, you need not be concerned with all this rather ornate stuff, it's all for show. Our big business clients like to see this type presentation. I can assure you it is not my preference, besides, it's rather expensive," Simon said. He waved his hands as if to shoo away a housefly. He stared at Eddie. "I went to school so I could help people. You see, my father was a minister, really a philosopher at heart, all he ever wanted was for me to be a good man. So, I try, and I try to be a good lawyer. I'm nothing special."

"Yes sir," Eddie said. He could barely breathe. And he was certain his ears burned a lovely dark red shade.

"From what Emily Dawn has gathered, your buddy got himself involved with selling, how shall I say this?" Simon asked. He blushed looking up at Emily Dawn. He hesitated.

"It's okay," Emily Dawn said. She stood near Eddie as she covered her mouth with her hand.

"Very personal sports memorabilia?" Simon said. He chuckled. He shrugged. He leaned forward, with his elbows on his knees.

"Yeah," Eddie said. He sheepishly grinned. "He's unique."

"I'll say, anyway, problem, not remitting his owed taxes on the gain, not sure what the bases is, but," Simon said. He opened a file folder full of legal documents that Emily Dawn had handed down to him. "My suspicion is this type of underground commerce happens every day, and is not a matter of too much concern, not sure why they think he owes taxes on an internet transaction, something very odd going on here."

Eddie's palms were moist, so he shifted his arms forward along the chairs cushions to help keep them dry.

"I was unaware, he's always had a scheme to get rich, make a litter extra," Eddie said. He glanced up at Emily Dawn. She nodded. "You know-"

"Oh my lands," Simon said. His dark blue eyes peered over his spectacles. "The complaint alleges he earned over two hundred thousand dollars. I think you and I will agree that's not just a little extra income."

"Wow, I knew he was getting over his head that night, but-" Eddie said. He coughed. "Scary, it was weird, like I sensed the IRS was going to arrest him. Just didn't think, that way-"

"I'm certain that was not a pleasant experience. But I think we can get Jim Bob," Simon said. He paused. He took off his glasses and bit the tip end. He gazed at Eddie for assistance. "He does go by Jim Bob?"

"Yes, he has always gone by that name," Eddie said. "My middle names Tiberius, mom thinks it's Biblical, just sayin'."

Simon nodded and bit the end of his reading glasses frame.

"Interesting, your mother has a strong abiding faith," Simon said. He nodded. "Very well, I think we can get *Jim Bob* bailed out of Dorian-Hyde."

"Ah, that's great," Eddie said. He thought his internal temperature had dropped ten degrees.

Simon tapped his ink pen against the file folder and he furrowed his thick eyebrows. He glanced up at Emily Dawn.

"I don't mind telling you, that is a serious place to spend your time," Simon said. He set the pen down; he interlocked his long fingers. "Regardless, the case is under

Judge Plato's purview, and my experience he is typically quite reasonable."

"That's good, I guess," Eddie said.

"We can cover that later, but that is all the good news," Simon said. He flipped over the legal pages. Simon intently scanned through several pages of the legal file.

"Okay, bad news?" Eddie said. His felt his skin flush hot pink again. He tugged at his shirt collar.

"Again, don't jump to conclusions yet, it will be a matter of what I negotiate, and discuss with the prosecutor," Simon said. He shifted his long legs to get comfortable.

"Prosecutor?" Eddie said. He was jolted back by the word, *prosecutor.* He imagined a medieval executioner, hidden by a dark cloak clasped a curved scythe, with a tearful Jim Bob seated in a defendants chair as a jury hissed and pointed at him. "He's in big trouble?" His stomach churned acid, aware he had one hundred fifty thousand noninterest bearing United States Treasury Notes frozen together in the back of Mr. Lewis's, *companion's,* two-car garage next to the frozen sweet peas, mint chocolate chip ice cream and bags of hot wings.

"Eddie, the word *trouble* is a relative term, all right? He is not accused of murder, this type of case might get him a stiff fine, and maybe time served if we are lucky," Simon said. He stared out the windows. "Stay calm, I'll figure this out." He curiously stared over at Eddie.

"Yes sir," Eddie said. He thought Simon wondered if he knew more about Jim Bob's business. He gulped.

"Problem is- Emily Dawn had a chat with one of their lawyers, off the record, okay?" Simon asked Eddie. He stared at him.

"I, I understand," Eddie said.

Simon glanced up at Emily Dawn; she winked at Eddie and backed out of the office clicking the door tightly closed.

"Okay, the IRS lawyer thinks he might be involved with a hidden organization, mob like, dealing in body parts, DNA, whole mess of nasty stuff," Simon said. He shook his head. "They've been after them for decades. Unfortunately for Jim Bob, he's their only solid lead, which means they might try to put the screws to him." Simon closed the file folder.

"Jim Bob's not a criminal," Eddie said.

"Like a moth to the flame, he got burned, they might get a bit aggressive, they are ticked at these people," Simon said. He pursed his lips. "And they would not tell Emily precisely why, which is odd, very odd, this whole matter smells to me."

"Why?" Eddie asked. He could barely breathe. He had a thick mucous gulp. He thought he might pass out onto the Oriental rug.

"They usually charge them with something, at least make it appear legal," Simon said. He stared down at the carpet. "Let's just say, some secrets, even if you only have knowledge, didn't even get involved or doing anything, can be quite dangerous."

"I understand," Eddie said. He blinked his eyelids rapidly.

"Are you all right?" Simon asked. He took off his spectacles. "Emily Dawn? Ah, Emily?"

"I'll be alright, I think." Eddie said. He squirmed in the chair as his mind swirled as if the menacing bald man thrashed at him like a Midwestern tornado seeking the money.

Simon carefully watched Eddie. He tapped at the file folder.

"All right, I think you've had enough listening to me. Don't worry about your friend. I promise you, I'll get him the best possible option available under the law," Simon said. He winked at Eddie and he reached forward patted him on the knee.

"Okay, sounds good," Eddie said. But he heard people loudly arguing outside of Simon's office door. The sound of an angry scuffle, as Simon suspiciously glanced over at his office door. He glanced back at Eddie.

"Oh, and another thing, don't worry about our fee. I'm required to do a certain number of hours each year in what our professional custom calls, *pro bono* work," Simon said. He pointed with his forefinger down at the file. "Besides, to be completely honest, I'm intrigued with this case from the stand-point of internet commerce and privacy, okay?"

"Oh," Eddie said.

"Yes, new area of the law that continues to emerge," Simon said. He got up just as his office door flung open.

"I'm sorry," Emily Dawn said. She huffed. "This woman just barged in- she will not wait."

Ms. Prosperina marched into the expansive office as if she owned the planet.

"I was curious why you didn't respond," Simon said as Ms. Prosperina marched further into his office. He stared down at the diminutive woman. "And what seems to be the problem, madam?"

Eddie froze in the chair staring up at the petite woman wearing thick black sunglasses. And an expensive business suit.

"How dare you cancel my appointment," Ms. Prosperina said. Her hands folded behind. "I have important business, I cannot be delayed, I will not forget this-"

"Do you have a name?" Simon said. He held his hand out over at Eddie, as Eddie stood up. "Stay right there, Eddie, you're a client, and this person has interrupted our meeting."

"Ms. Prosperina," she said. She clenched her Germanic profile jaw line. "Your partner, Mr. Screwtop-"

Simon put his hands with his palms out.

"Simmer down, I know who you are," Simon said. He walked over toward his desk; he snapped a padded envelope off his credenza. He scowled back over at Ms. Prosperina. "And Bertrand had mailed this to me, his instruction was to only open if he died suddenly, or became incapacitated, which he most assuredly is. I'm his executor, might have to be the one to take him off life support, the man was stressed out because of you."

"That is not my problem," Ms. Prosperina said.

"Oh, I'm not surprised by your response," Simon said. He waved at her with the envelope. "Given what I read this morning off this thumb drive, you clearly lack a conscience."

Ms. Prosperina menaced further into the office. She smirked over at Eddie. She studied him for a moment. She waltzed near the expanse of office windows.

"Well, you should be proud, Mr. Screwtop was quite thorough," Ms. Prosperina said. She shrugged. "I'm a little woman, in a man's world, I play tough, I cannot tolerate weakness."

"I'm not obligated to look the other way," Simon said. His face was flushed red, his eyes blazed with conviction. "You, and your activities are an abomination to man."

"Abomination? What a word, do you learn that at divinity school? And is this little Eddie?" Ms. Prosperina asked. She glanced over at Eddie, as she walked along to inspect Simon's credenza littered with family photos. She pointed at the framed photo of Simon and Sophia. "Your female friend, Sophia?"

Simon moved between Ms. Prosperina and his credenza. He nudged her away.

"Eddie, don't let this sub-human scare you," Simon said. He pointed for Ms. Prosperina to leave. "Emily, escort Mr. Screwtop's former client from this office, call downstairs if you need extra security."

"Of course," Emily Dawn said. She waved at Ms. Prosperina. A confused young male associate stood next to her. "If you will please leave-"

"Oh? How disappointing," Ms. Prosperina said. She snatched off her sunglasses. She stared up at Simon.

But Simon did not budge, he stared right back at her without moving his gaze.

"Yes, I know about your unfortunate eyesight," Simon said. He continued to point for Ms. Prosperina to leave without looking away. "Any money's we have received from you will be returned before the close of business. This firm will not be involved with your secretive activities, and that secretive fellow, Quan, just seems to me you all are up to evil. We will not be engaged in your argument with him and what they are doing, of course, all in secret, if you have to be secretive, you're not our client type, which is not our business ethic."

Ms. Prosperina intently stared over at Eddie.

"Why are you so afraid?" Ms. Prosperina asked Eddie. She slowly strolled over toward him. "I'm just an old woman, looking someone in the eyes shows respect."

Eddie stared into her red and black irises. But Ms. Prosperina stopped as he stared back into Eddie's eyes. She scowled. She hissed. Her eyebrows narrowed. Then she snapped her stare back over at Simon.

"Emily, enough, call security," Simon said. He moved in between Ms. Prosperina and Eddie.

"That will not be necessary," Ms. Prosperina said. She turned away and strolled toward the doorway. She put her sunglasses on. "I can see my father has met this young man before, but clearly, he failed in his attempt, he is weak."

Eddie thought he had seen the face of evil.

"Let me put you on notice," Simon said. He stood in front of the shaking Eddie who wobbly stared down at his polished shoes. "I know about your secret IRS unit, I know you're heavily involved with agribusiness, cloning, all sorts of godless businesses. I am sure you have your tracks covered, but you'll slip up, good day madam."

Ms. Prosperina simply grinned at Simon. She turned and left the office suite. Emily Dawn followed behind as the office staff ogled at the menacing woman.

"Lock the door," Simon said. He watched her leave, he stepped back inside the office, he walked over and put his long fingers on Eddie's shoulder.

"You all right?" Simon asked. He squeezed Eddie's shoulder.

"I think so," Eddie said. He gulped. He sucked in a deep breath. "Like she was looking into my soul-"

"She uses her genetic defect to scare people," Simon said. He patted Eddie on the shoulder. "Don't let her trick you. My business partner, he's, he was I guess, willing to deal with questionable clients. I always warned him, but you know, Bertrand was, well, I think he's gone soon. But he was my friend, I never judged him."

Eddie glanced up at Simon who was wistfully staring out the smoked glass windows.

"Sorry," Eddie said.

Simon grunted. "I think everybody has a troubled friend, a person we hope might change, but never do."

"Guess I have Jim Bob," Eddie said.

"Yeah, well, I suppose so," Simon said. His eyes ringed in moisture. "I try not to judge, but, be a good listener, maybe lead by example, just hope for the best in people."

"Yeah," Eddie said.

"Regardless, you okay?" Simon asked. He pulled out a white linen handkerchief; he blew his nose and then wiped his eyes.

Eddie thought he had an out of body experience. As if the old woman had snatched his body off the planet and traveled with him into deep space toward a black void.

"I'll shake it off," Eddie said. He thought had seen death.

"All right," Simon said. "Sorry, we deal with complicated problems, I'll get Jim Bob out of there, so don't fret, okay?"

"Thank you, I'm all right," Eddie said. He left the office, walked past a disheveled Emily Dawn, and got into the elevator. It cycled down to the buildings underground parking garage. Like a condemned man, he trudged toward his car. He stared down at his dress shoes as he dug for his car keys.

"You contact me and then disappear to an attorney's office?" Captain Lovins asked. He stood next to Eddie's gas-guzzler fidgeting with his spider knife.

"Get away from me," Eddie said. He stopped and put his hands up as if he were prepared to lock into mortal combat.

"You have something to discuss?" Captain Lovins asked. He closely studied Eddie. "You okay? Look like you saw a ghost."

"How did you find me? I didn't think you worked this way?" Eddie said. He stuttered, his feet Medusa like frozen to the parking garages concrete slab.

"Don't insult me by acting stupid," Captain Lovins said. He stared at Eddie. "I tagged this junker, it's not hard, check back right wheel well."

Eddie aimlessly stared forward, he wobbled, his mind swirled with like he was floating at the top of the just flushed toilet bowl, and his rubber raft had a slow leak.

"I did send the email," Eddie said. He paused and took in a deep breath. "I can get you some of Regan Fryingpan's hair."

Captain Lovins closely studied Eddie, he kept carefully watching anyone the elevator doors, and up and down at the rows of parked cars.

"I suspected, but listen, the woman you just met, with red and black eyes," Captain Lovins said. He glanced at a nearby-parked car, as two executives got out and walked toward the elevators. "She is not what she seems."

"How do you know that?" Eddie said. He backed away from Captain Lovins.

"I'll not harm you," Captain Lovins said. He menaced forward. "But this is not the place, but know this, you mother's companion was quite brave. He sounds like a good man."

"I, I think so," Eddie said. He closed his eyes.

A mini-van coasted past them, its tires squeaked, as it turned the parking level corner towards the upper level. The stale garage air now smelled of gasoline, and exhaust.

"Go ahead to your foo-foo friend's barbershop," Captain Lovins said. He checked his wristwatch. "I have to keep moving."

"Yeah, he's a little better than a foo-foo barber," Eddie said, "you telling me you're interested?"

"We are, but I think you should meet someone," Captain Lovins said. He gripped his waste. "You'll get the hair?"

"I'll get the hair," Eddie said. He glanced around the parking garage. "There are enough cameras around here that they'll be able to track you down." He held his breath and clenched his jaw.

"No, this is blank spot, the drones, the ones in the sky, you cannot see, they are a different matter," Captain Lovins said. He sighed. "That is what I do, my employer cannot be outside for long, he has to remain hidden, but I'll let him explain that, but know this, Jim Bob is in danger, you are in danger, we need to meet, soon."

"Keep him out of this," Eddie said.

"Why?" Captain Lovins asked. "He's in it, you can't just back out of this, you crossed the Rubicon boys, sorry."

"I'm not an idiot, but Jim Bob's slow, he talks too much," Eddie said. His stomach muscles ached.

Captain Lovins clipped the spider knife onto his belt.

"Know this, all those that you love are in great danger," Captain Lovins said. He checked his watch again. "Listen, get the hair, I'll be waiting, the less you know, the better at this point, not knowing keeps you alive, I'll be in touch."

"They know about you, and your secrets," Eddie said.

"Oh, I am so, so scared Bambi, I know," Captain Lovins said. He crossed his arms. "You'll be watched from now on, and sorry, you will need to protect your friend, Ardee?"

"Leave her alone," Eddie said. He clenched his hands.

"Calm down, she's pretty, Edward you're going to have to trust me," Captain Lovins said. He glanced around the garage for any sign of Mr. Oppenheimer.

"I don't know," Eddie said.

"Listen, focus, if I wanted to hurt you, wanted that money in this trunk, I could easily get it, right?" Captain Lovins said.

"I suppose," Eddie said. He could not think straight.

"Get the hair, but do me a favor, real important, until you get to that barber shop, keep your cell phone off. In fact, take out the sim card. That phone is a sophisticated tracking device, I'll be in touch," Captain Lovins said. He glanced at the concrete pillars, the line of parked cars, then abruptly twisted and left the parking garage.

Eddie breathlessly mashed his hands on the car trunk. He inhaled the musty air. And he pulled off his tie, unbuttoned his shirt collar. He got back inside the car; he turned off his cell phone and plucked out the sim card. He nervously navigated back to his apartment complex parking lot. He got back inside his apartment, took off his suit, and took a warm shower. He did not care anymore if someone stole his car and the duffle bag. Soon, he had another job to do.

Chapter Thirty Eight

As Professor Quan paced inside his laboratory preparing to alter his appearance for his journey to Nashville, the raven black SUV stormed away from downtown Nashville.

"Drive, just drive," Ms. Prosperina said. She hissed. She lit a cigarette. "I am not sure if this was good luck, or bad luck."

"Madam?" Mr. Oppenheimer asked. In the driver side rear view mirror, he noticed the specter of the Batman shaped building's eyeball set between the twin spires, it appeared to watch the SUV speed down Church street.

"The woman's boy, Eddie," Ms. Prosperina said. She took a deep drag from the cigarette; the tip end glowed red-hot, it crackled like a wintertime fireplace. "My father, he's one of my father's *children*, I could see it, but how random."

"Dispose of him? Then the mother?" Mr. Oppenheimer asked. He stared at her using the interior rearview mirror.

"My father already knows, I wonder what he'll do," Ms. Prosperina said. She sighed. "Oh, you know that would give me great pleasure, thank you for asking. Good boy, but that would not challenge your skills. The boy only has puppy love in his heart - that is all I saw. How quaint, just a humanoid that lacks any special skills, a wasted life."

"Yes, Madam," Mr. Oppenheimer said. He continued to drive the SUV south by southwest away from downtown.

"I don't think the saint like Mr. Lewis will be of much concern," Ms. Prosperina said. With the SUV windows up, she flicked an ash from her smoke pluming cigarette.

"Yes, Madam," Mr. Oppenheimer said. He continued to drive along past busy bars, and restaurants in the West End, and then he drove past a vast hospital complex.

"What is over there?" Ms. Prosperina said. She pressed the down lever for the passenger-side back window. "Investigate, that is a strange government building."

Mr. Oppenheimer turned the SUV off the city street, and into a rolling landscaped green grass park. He weaved the SUV and parked along the curved sidewalk. Ms. Prosperina got out; she strolled up the concrete stairs, and up to the cast concrete aggregate museum's massive bronze front doors.

"At first, I thought this a government building," Ms. Prosperina said. She examined the doors mythic ornamentation. "But I remember now."

"It is an exact duplicate for the Parthenon, madam," Mr. Oppenheimer said. He shook the locked bronze interlocked snake door handles.

A young African American security guard walked up near the odd couple. She coughed, with her fist in front of her mouth.

"I'm sorry, closed on Mondays," the security guard said. She smiled. She adjusted her park ranger hat. "But you're free to walk around park, I'm sorry."

Ms. Prosperina did not acknowledge her. She strolled away.

"I want to go inside," Ms. Prosperina said.

"I'm very sorry," the security guard said.

"I'll handle this madam," Mr. Oppenheimer said. He unclipped his cell phone. As Ms. Prosperina strolled away, and along the buildings peristyle, she went past soaring Doric columns; she gazed over at a manmade lake edged with a concrete and stone rim backed with clusters of green drooping weeping willows and a colorful bouquet of blooming dogwoods.

"We are closed," the security guard said. She acknowledged Mr. Oppenheimer as she walked away.

"We shall see," Mr. Oppenheimer said with the cell phone next to his hard face.

Ms. Prosperina continued to stroll down the seventeen-column colonnade and an hour later returned to the front doors to find Mr. Oppenheimer standing next to a puzzled appearing older man wearing a blue blazer and grey slacks.

"Hello, I'm John Locke," he said. He held up the large skeleton door key; his hand shook from age and disease. "I'm retired, live close by, one of the docents here, happy to help."

"Ms. Prosperina," she said. She stood next to him. "I want to go inside, see her."

"Of course, being a former philosophy, well, I taught, this place is a treat," John said. He excitedly smiled; He happily shrugged. He clicked open the lock and pushed open the door with Mr. Oppenheimer's help. "It's amazing these, each door is seven and half ton, seven feet wide, twenty-four foot in height, and a foot thick, but even an old man can open them."

"Quite good craftsmanship, ya," Ms. Prosperina said. She gazed up at the doors, she strolled inside the building; the only sounds were her fashionable dress shoes walking along the highly polished floor.

"Ya, quite precise, madam," Mr. Oppenheimer said.

John Locke hustled to keep up with Ms. Prosperina.

"Yes, made in Nashville," John said. He stuffed the keys into his jacket pocket. "The Parthenon is open to the public, it is supported without great charge. We are quite fortunate." He coughed. "We are operated by a not-for profit, taxing us would ruin this balance of public and private cooperation, we do appreciate donations, I'm sure you understand."

"I see," Ms. Prosperina said. She stared up at the ornate painted ceiling as they strolled along.

"We have a nice art gallery-"John said. He glanced behind him at the menacing Mr. Oppenheimer.

"I just want to see her," Ms. Prosperina said. She looked intently over at John. "I need some inspiration, problem to solve."

"Oh, yes, quite right, Athena is the goddess of wisdom," John said as they walked together. After a few moments, they stood before the colossal replica of Athena Parthenos. John Locke huffed through his sanguine lips from the quick pace.

"Quite lovely," Ms. Prosperina said. She gazed up with her hands behind her.

"Athena the virgin, daughter from Zeus and Metis, this is forty-two feet high, eight ponds of gold leaf, the winged female in her hand is six feet tall, Nike, represents victory. She stands on a relief for the birth of Pandora, under that giant serpent," John said. He waved his hand toward her feet. He sucked in a deep breath. "A great deal of work by scholars to get her and this building exactly right, like the original from about 438 BC, the building, it is a bit of an optical illusion, like the original, it has no straight lines, amazing mathematical minds, and we think ourselves modern, such rubbish."

Ms. Prosperina walked up close to the massive gold serpent like a hissing cobra that appeared almost ready to strike her.

"Who owns her?" Ms. Prosperina said. She closely inspected the serpent. "I quite like her, quite beautiful."

"On her breast, the head of Medusa, that serpent represents the king of Athens, as it was told, she raised him, so she protected him, thus the shield. Sorry, she is not for sale," John said. He grinned. He fiddled with the door key in his pocket. "I think we'd have a riot, her gold, in part is from contributions from children's piggy banks."

Ms. Prosperina looked back at John Locke; she shrugged.

"Pity, I have a wonderful spot for her," Ms. Prosperina said.

John Locke wobbled forward; he waved at the artwork.

"Athena was the goddess of wisdom, culture, the arts, among other things, weaving," John said. He paused as he unbuttoned his blazer. "I hope this information interests, entertains you."

"Parthenon, and a virgin, interesting," Ms. Prosperina said.

"Ah, you are well ahead of me I see," John said.

"Parthenogenesis, human conception without a male," Ms. Prosperina said. She sighed as she patted for her pack of cigarettes. "Can I smoke in here?"

John Locke nervously waved his arms.

"No ma'am, absolutely not," John said. He chuckled.

"Oh, bad habit I suppose," Ms. Prosperina said. She strolled behind John. She glanced over at Mr. Oppenheimer. "Funny, my father wanted my first name to be Kore, he discovered much you see. As a boy he loved the idea behind chimera's, mixing things, and I suppose weaving things together, like DNA."

"I didn't want to say anything," John said. He stared over at the two level column supports. "Don't want to be insulting, Prosperone, Pandora and the like, not happy stories."

"How kind," Ms. Prosperina said. She smirked. "Yes, Kore, the maiden, goddess of the springtime, queen of the underworld."

John Locke and Mr. Oppenheimer quietly stood nearby, as Ms. Prosperina continued to inspect the masterful work of art that had meaning beyond myth.

"Athena, Zeus feared Metis, it was prophesy that she would conceive children more powerful than him," Ms. Prosperina said. She strolled around the work of art admiring all its meaning. "Father feared the child, a warrior goddess, Athena, a powerful woman in a man's world. How interesting, don't you think?"

"That is quite accurate," John said. He smiled up at Mr. Oppenheimer, who did not appear to have a sense of irony.

"Thank you, and of course poor, Prosperina, raped, tricked, dragged to Hades but then mother defends her daughter,"

Ms. Prosperina said. She smiled. She adjusted her glasses. "I've never had a taste for pomegranates, now would I?"

John Locke laughed, and he clapped his wrinkled hands.

"Quite enjoyable, yes, causes one to wonder about the morality of man," John said. He shrugged. He stared at the shiny, highly polished floor.

"Yes, what would a father do to, or for his child? If challenged," Ms. Prosperina said. She walked past John.

"Interesting question, a duality if you will, a constant pushing and pulling within life, nature, I suppose," John said. He buttoned his jacket.

"Time to leave," Ms. Prosperina said. She stared at John Locke. "Athena, she had wisdom, military victory, a female warrior with great patience and cunning?"

"I would think so," John said. Confused, he shifted to leave the museum walking just behind Ms. Prosperina and Mr. Oppenheimer. And just as suddenly, he waved goodbye as the black SUV drove away from the museum.

# # #

Mr. Oppenheimer drove out of the urban park space as Ms. Prosperina flicked her lighter. She took several drags.

"Find this boy," Ms. Prosperina said. She started to chuckle. "I'll not repeat what I've said, now, I'll try to forget, turn the radio on and I need to find some good Kentucky bourbon, I need to block him."

Chapter Thirty Nine

"Time does not stop, but for Edward?" Professor Quan said. He sighed. "A gift, I need to bring a gift, it would be rude otherwise." His dog curled up, asleep next to him on his old strata lounger. As he stroked her soft hair, he considered he would need to take his pet to a local hound dog hotel, and then proceed to drive to Nashville. First, he needed to devise a gift, and then to alter his appearance. He got up from his lounger and walked within his old laboratory savoring his genetic analyzer, his well-used equipment, and he scooted over to flip through their lists with names and dates of all the many children they had shared his secrets with, and now they were living happy, productive lives. But Edward was the outlier, the only child that had not become someone bigger than himself. He strolled, and paced in deep thought, and he finally quietly stood in front of his cold storage DNA sample room. He tapped on the cold glass, as he realized what the gift would be for Edward, and if needed, a deadly gift he would share with Ms. Prosperina. He opened the storage door, and went inside the artic like cold room to investigate his genetic treasures.

An hour later, Professor Quan stood in front of the DNA sequenced United States map. He searched for the correct numeric associations for his Voice Box Protocol machine. Tonight, it was his favorite character to recreate. He locked each ink stamp into a square tray. After which, he flicked an electrical switch, and the tray began to glow a pale auburn hue. From beneath, a cone shaped protein and carbon filter form focused the beam of spectral color through a bed of heated blue diamonds. Each diamond set at a harmonic angled position, relative to the center point. The tray captured each triangular prism's potential energy and liquefied the epigenetic mixture coated across each square tray.

Nearby, the Skin Sensor machine reacted from the introduction from the massive electrical current pulsing through the carbon fibers. The teak wood frame vibrated back and forth as if blankets hung outside on a clothesline begging a strong breeze to dry them. After he stripped off his multi-colored robe, he was naked before the vibrating intersecting triangles. He held up his epigenetic concoction that he had trapped inside a glass-mixing bowl sealed with a paraffin substance. He swished it in front of his face. His eyes glowed, covered by contact lenses made from silicone hydro gel to shield his corneas.

What an amazing array of genetic information in my conical collection, he thought.

"Elvis, now to Edward," Professor Quan said. He kissed the glass bowl thinking this might be the last time he used his old fashion machine. He continued to swish the viscous substance inside the bowl. Then he set it down on the carpet runner.

He walked to the side of the machine, and flipped open the black key pad on the left side of the teak panel. He pressed in a sequence relating to the mixtures unique profile. Professor Quan quickly scooted back over to the bowl; he pealed back the sealant, and exposed the recombinant DNA concoction to the filtered air within the antiseptic room. Without hesitation, in a practiced motion, he flung the contents into the frame's pink spider web fabric encircled within a magnetic ring. The heated carbon web absorbed the viscous oily mixture. It spread across the delicate silky surface like a hot pink wild fire as Professor Quan stepped forward onto the carpet runner. The teak wood frame released from the mouse pad couplings. The guide wire went slack. The frame levitated six-inches above the rubberized laboratory floor. It seemed to beckon Professor Quan to creep closer, and closer and closer. He scooted across the amber carpet. After he reached its apex, with his hands outstretched, his fingers and toes separated, he slowly, deeply breathed in and out; he knew the device's true magic generated from the xenon arc lamps hidden beneath the translucent false floor. The piercing light arrayed to penetrate through the Hope Diamond that reflected blue beams dispersing into a new moon circle.

"It was so simple," Professor Quan said. He chuckled remembering the day they stole the shiny rock. "Kiss, keep it simple stupid."

Then a rainbow of colors, green, cyan, blue and yellow cycled the protein's fluorescent energy, the web started to transfer heat to affect the web's amino acids, the electrical power sufficient to charge through the collagen-glazed fibers using the Hope Diamond's spectral fluorescence. Within a nanosecond, the mythical device waved back and forth, it wisped closer, and closer, until the surface, infused with the electrical charged naked tri-nucleotides, contacted his skin. Then it encapsulated him within the sticky membrane. The frame bent into two parts at the intersection of the red and white triangles. Like a brightly lit pinkish carnival ride, it spun counter-clockwise, oscillated the zero gravity honeycombs like sheets, and accelerated up to the speed of light. To the outward view, it was as if Professor Quan was hidden inside a life sized hot pink cotton candy ball. It pulsed, effused from the inside out living bubbles with Professor Quan immersed within the liquid core. After exactly three nano seconds the SS machine stopped spinning. It instantly shifted back to the mouse pad. The guide wire went taught, and held the frame's weight. The xenon arc light extinguished. And the massive diamond no longer blazed beneath the opaque floor. The system began to cool, but it radiated with intense heat. The sheets folded back apart.

Professor Quan emerged; his body had metamorphosed into a pudgy, pasty Caucasian. The carbon, protein, and hydrogen-based mixture had penetrated his skin at his cellular level as microscopic microbial hooks affixed the new skin. He appeared like a geriatric nude man that you hoped never to see at a Florida nudist colony. Carefully, delicately he stepped down the opposite side of the carpet runner, he turned left and quickly picked up the hot numbered ink stamps as the temporary skin began to cool.

Professor Quan grabbed the cold metal top of each stamp, and carefully followed his predetermined diagram. He pressed each device across his jugular and carotid arteries for three seconds. After which, he stood still and motionless as his outer skin dried from the emersion protocol. After, he would slip on the southern gentlemen's outfit he had pre-selected.

"Aw, I feel refreshed," Professor Quan said down at Waldo. His curious pet backed up on her hind legs, perplexed by the odd stranger with processed sugary white hair, and a goatee. She barked at him, she growled and pranced out the room in search of her master.

Chapter Forty

"You'll be the cute part-timer," Chris said at Eddie. He had shaved his head and dyed his facial hair burnt orange to conceal the nasty scar under his chin.

"You mean horny toad?" Jill Marie said. They exploded into cryptic blue laughter; unable to be composed, an hour before their new client, Regan, had had her people schedule a styling appointment.

"Funny," Eddie said. He was wearing a salon shirt.

"What do you seek?" Pedro asked. He wore a Nehru jacket. A mortal blood red tilak dot pasted between his bushy jet-black eyebrows. His intense brown eyes appeared almost amethyst black. "Edward, I never question my third eye, you seek something, or something seeks you."

"I'm fine," Eddie said. His spine arctic chilled, as if scanned at the subatomic level by Pedro's intense eyes.

"Your heart hurts," Pedro said. He gently put his right palm on Eddie's chest. "I can see, see pain within your aura."

"Dude, simmer," Chris said. "Eddie, he can't help it, it's the preacher man in him."

"Preacher? I do not understand," Pedro said.

"Never mind, when do I get an assistant?" Jill Marie asked.

"When I make you a star," Chris said. He glanced over at Pedro. "Maybe I meant shaman?"

"Shaman?" Pedro said. He shook his head. "If so, I am not gifted in that way, I do not have that gift."

"My name in lights," Jill Marie said. She leaned on her left elbow against her pedestal workstation. "Maybe you meant, guru?"

"Simmer, I'm over my head," Chris said. He waved his hands in the air. "Shiva, Bevo the Bull, maybe play some sitar jazz, I don't know, it's all confusing to me."

Eddie grinned over at Jill Marie. He tried to maintain focus and not get lost in their ideal chitchat and Pedro's curiosity. And he continually thought of Ardee, he felt safe near her. Now, he could not imagine being apart from her. But deep within his soul, the concept of love scared Eddie. It was temporary happiness, then death, for all good things end. But does true love die? Even puppy love, does it stay hidden and dormant inside the chambers of our invisible hearts as if a gentle whisper hidden within our cells.

"All right, what do I do, so I don't get into trouble and get beaten by Mr. Pedro?" Eddie asked.

"Oh, good question," Chris said. "What do you think, Pedro?"

"Trouble?" Pedro said. "I am a pacifist. I will not strike Edward, I am a non-violent anarchist."

"Anarchist? I love it when you talk dirty," Chris said.

"I know, no sense of humor. He has got no clue," Jill Marie said. "Just have him sweep up her trimmings, that way he does something useful, and doesn't stand there like a peeping tom."

"Great idea," Chris said. He snapped his fingers.

"Not dirty," Pedro said, "I am the anarchy of the lotus flower." He put his hands together.

Eddie smirked at them, but his heartbeats thumped inside his brain as he considered his next move, and then the meeting at the General Beauregard's Fried Chicken.

"Just tell me what to do," Eddie said. He shrugged. "Story of my life, right?"

Pedro stared into Eddie's eyes and intently moved closer toward him. He seemed to be examining Eddie's body.

"Edward, I fear for you," Pedro said. He searched Eddie's eyes. "You must be careful, evil spirits, dark forces."

"Dude, he's already wound tight," Jill Marie said to Pedro.

"I'm okay," Eddie said to Pedro. He gulped.

"No, look at me," Pedro said.

"Pedro, you'll make Eddie's hairs fall out," Chris said.

Pedro slinked in front of Eddie. His dark brown face whisper close, his now black pitted eyes locked Eddie into a cosmic time warp with the fog of ghosts of what would be.

"The darkest power approaches, the darkest power in the universe," Pedro whispered. He shook his head rapidly. He held Eddie's face within his warm hands. "You are in danger. If you survive, in the days, yes, the moments, the years ahead, you will feel the weight of all." The salon dripped golden silence.

Chris and Jill Marie blankly stared at each other. They knew Pedro did not make rash statements. Every night he studied the stars, he listened to meditative stillness of the ancients. His predictions had never been wrong. Now, they could barely feel their hearts beating. The salon was quiet as an empty cathedral.

"I'm okay," Eddie said. He coughed. "I think."

"No, what I see, I do not want to see," Pedro said. He began to breathe heavy loads of oxygen. He fearfully butterfly glided his right hand palm onto the center of Eddie's pulsating chest.

"Pedro, you're creeping me dude," Chris said.

Pedro closed his eyes, his hand near Eddie's chest.

"She is not one of us. Edward, you must be careful. You will be in great danger, a naga - Cobra serpent, seeks you," Pedro said. He quickly backed away from Eddie. A terrified flame flickered in his eyes, he stood stiff, erect, stone like.

"What? What?" Jill Marie asked.

"Dude," Chris said.

Eddie's feet felt frozen to the concrete salon floor. As if he stood at the intersection between desolate darkness and brilliant light.

"Edward, I do not want to say evil, it is better not to draw their attention. For they will come in due time, in the years ahead, you are about to evolve, if you live beyond tonight," Pedro said. He pressed his palms together. His chest heaved as his heart danced to a rhythmic electrical orchestra. "I will pray you seek wisdom, that you will seek courage. That you have the audacity to take great care of my soul, all our souls."

Chris clapped his hands together nervously.

"All righty then," Chris said. He hesitantly laughed. He snapped his fingers. He wiggled his narrow hips. "Enough of that, let's all dance, dance, dance."

# # #

"He's inside," Captain Lovins whispered. He sat sipping purified water, as the dwindling sunlight distilled harvest orange and yellow beams that licked the elfin shopping center within the reflected color prism. He had added an insurance policy, concerned Regan might try to arrive at the back door. And he had installed a tiny surveillance camera in the back of the two-story non-descript brick building, it was implanted under the decorative corbelling three-feet below the flat roofline. The lens opened to its widest aperture.

Across the eastern side of the half-empty rectangular parking lot, a metallic pale blue Germanic car, coasted into the complex. It parked near the salon's windowless front door. The expensive sport model blended within the posh upscale suburban environment. A petite blond-haired woman, she wore a baseball cap, had exited the driver side. Alone, she did not have an entourage, or any obvious security guard. She examined the salon door, but she appeared uncertain, because the salon had no signage. She made a cell call, and backed away from the door.

After a few moments, she shrugged and slipped her cell phone into her purse. She pulled back the salon door.

# # #

The hazy outside world invaded the dimly lit interior. As a female form, backlit by the evening light entered. She was fifteen minutes early. Frozen in mid-animated play, as if exposed by a fourth grade substitute teacher, two playmates, Mister Religious and the new kid, all collectively gave the white tail deer in the headlights gaze.

"Hello?" Regan said. She suspiciously examined the faces.

"Sorry, you're a just a bit early. I'm Christopher Clayton," he said. He quickly waltzed over to greet her.

"Well, thank you for squeezing me in on short notice," Regan said. She was simply dressed. The only two distinctive items hung on her thin wrist, a watch encrusted with diamonds within parallel channel locks, and her quilted bag. If you did not know her, you might think she was an upper middle class Nashville homemaker, who had escaped to visit her stylist.

"We were just talking amongst ourselves about how exciting it is to have your trust in our artistic vision."

Eddie's scalp tingled, as if; he was in a reality show, and he was the hidden contestant. But he hoped he was not the Star Trek new guy stand-in type, wearing the hunters orange uniform, who would get zapped dead standing next to the interplanetary playboy, Captain Kirk.

"I'm stunned that you have a salon right here in Nashville," Regan said. She smiled. "I grew up here, you know, what not."

The salon was showered with background music of distant thunder and lighting and rain. And it smelled of roses.

"You're such the petite stunner," Chris said.

"Why thank you," Regan said. She glanced over at Eddie. "Well, I can see that I'm the only one getting any attention around here. What's next?"

Chris encouraged everyone to assume their normal positions.

"Excellent, let me introduce you to my peeps," Chris said sarcastically, "this is Pedro my assistant."

"Madam," Pedro said. He did not look her in the eyes.

"Nice to meet you, Pedro," Regan said. "Call me Regan, Madam makes me feel like an old hooker."

"Yes," Pedro said. He stepped back, put his hands in prayer position and bowed slightly forward. He hummed.

Chris grinned down at Pedro.

"Sorry, he's rather intense," Chris said. He glided his arm forward. "Over here is Jill Marie. She handles my schedule and all things business." Chris winked over at Jill Marie.

"Pleasure to meet you, welcome," Jill Marie said. She shook Regan's hand like she was a prepubescent girl.

"Yes, great thank you," Regan said. She stared at Eddie.

Chris appeared baffled. He was uncertain how to introduce his new employee, and his grade school chum. Eddie stepped forward.

"I'm new here, I just help keep the place clean," Eddie stuttered. His cheeks flushed Georgia peach color.

"Exactly-" Chris said. He pointed at Eddie. "Of course you do, have to … start at the bottom."

"Eddie?" Regan asked. She suspiciously studied his face.

Chris ignored the question and slid between Regan and Eddie.

"Wonderful, Pedro please guide Regan over to a changing room, and then the right side salon chair," Chris said. He bowed a bit forward. "Excuse me." Chris moved over to a sink with a golden faucet and ritually washed his hands.

Pedro escorted Regan to a changing room.

Eddie watched her closely; he thought she seemed comfortable in her own skin. Jill Marie flipped through a fashion magazine.

After Regan returned from the changing room, Pedro skillfully wrapped a protective smock over her and positioned her facing the expansive mirrors, ringed with soft lights.

"Are you comfortable?" Pedro asked. He stood like a French waiter next to her, a warm towel draped over his forearm.

"Yes, thank you," Regan said.

"Can we offer you a glass of white Bordeaux, cappuccino or perhaps some still water?" Pedro asked. He stood up straight.

"Oh, no thanks, I'm fine," Regan said.

Then Chris and Pedro focused on their work and ignored Eddie.

But Regan glanced at Eddie's reflection from the mirror. Her eyes, Eddie thought, he was out of place, perhaps a journalist or maybe scalawag paparazzi.

"Wonderful, I think it best we discuss your expectations and what your vision might be?" Chris said. He slid onto a thick cushioned leather pedestal chair. He rolled his long angular body below her. Now parallel, he looked up directly into her eyes, as if he would absorb her every wish.

"I guess I'm hoping to take about an inch off the length. I like it straight, I guess. Because, I never know, if I get a part that they may need to create a new style or what not," Regan said. She studied her reflection then looked back at Chris. "I want a different color, nothing crazy, just a little different. You know, I just want to change things up."

Chris opened up his arms and stood up, as if an evangelist about to give Regan the good news before the laying on hands ceremony and welcoming her as a new tithing church member.

"Do you trust me?" Chris asked.

Eddie shifted forward; he tried to observe Regan's expression. He thought the question was odd.

"Well, I guess so. I'm sitting in your chair aren't I?" Regan said. She twisted her head as she smiled up at Chris.

"I will not touch your hair if you do not feel that I'm trustworthy, and believe that I'll give you my best. My reputation means more to me than any amount of money. That I'm true to my vision, being an artist, it's my most sacred cause," Chris said. He put his hands on his narrow hips.

"Oh, I see," Regan said. She studied her image, and then looked back up at the eccentric hair stylist. She took in a deep inhalation. "I'm an artist, I respect that. I do."

"Thank you, now I want you to relax, and allow the tranquil sounds to reinvigorate your mind," Chris said. He waved his hand like a magician. "Breathe in the red rose scent, and let your consciousness float to a distant planet."

Regan waved her forefinger at Chris.

"Oh honey, you're good," Regan said. She smiled. "I can't wait to see what you do next."

Christopher Clayton, an original, Eddie thought. He stood concealed by the salon's taffeta fabric barrier. Pedro somberly rolled their visionary sink behind Regan. After, Chris and Pedro skillfully repositioned her over the vessel. Pedro bathed her hair into a luxurious lather while simultaneously massaging her scalp. He took great care to be precise with just enough finger pressure on her scalp.

"Wow, you really know how to make a girl feel special," Regan said. She blinked her eyes. "I'm about to fall asleep."

Chris smiled down at her from within the bubble of his artistic self.

"Pedro enjoys making you feel special because, after all, you are unique. It was my life's vision to create a comfortable happy place within your mind. When you think of Christopher Clayton Originals, I want you to look forward to your the next visit," Chris said. He nodded at her.

Eddie shook his head. He grinned. His emotions tangled by the realization his grade school friend, who happened to perceive the world standing in different shoes. An old friend with whom he shared youthful personal stories, when they each had white tipped volcanic pimples at the tip end of their noses. When they laughed at Jim Bob after he got caught setting off smoke bombs in the school restroom. The countless times, they had tried to envision their grown-up lives on the school bus ride home; The friend who had come to his father's funeral;

who did not need to say anything; the friend who had quietly stood nearby with Jim Bob at the gravesite.

"A gold medalist," Eddie whispered. He sighed.

In reality, Eddie thought, Chris had created his own winning lottery ticket. And in a nanosecond, Chris sensed Eddie thinking about him. He glanced over at Eddie immersed within the fog of his art. A wordless gaze from one friend to another, Chris had grasped the admiration from his conservative friend's eyes. Eyes that never judged him, but wished the best that life offered.

Chris quickly turned away from Eddie to maintain his focus. His imperceptible vision located each individual hair strand. He created an elegant shape that flattered Regan's jaw line and accentuated her gorgeous face. Each scissor cut released the helical packed hair fibers that corkscrewed to the salon floor. Some were translucent, others mustard yellow and still others pale brown. Her foamy bare effervescence dispersed within each golden brown strand, now spread around the chair as if yellow tulip poplar leaves torn from their life giving branches, as it caught by a cold autumn breeze as they butterfly glided to the forest salon floor.

"Time to highlight," Chris said. He took a deep breath of the rose peddle scented air. As he created a color mixture and layered silvery foils within Regan's hair strands. After Chris examined his work, he said. "I'm done for now, please relax."

Regan closed her eyes and reclined in the comfort of the over-cushioned salon chair as if flying first class. In fact, she was so relaxed, from Chris' perfectly timed adulation; she slipped into a deep baby sleep.

"I think she's snoring?" Eddie said. Draped within a warm cotton blanket, her lips waved open from her rhythmic breath puffs. Her head covered in tin foil shards, as if a chaos theorist channeling leprechauns in the New Mexico Mountains.

"Oh, I know, happens all the time. Why, just last week Tobias Keifer chopped down several oak trees, I just love his natural blond curls, he's cool helping the troops, and all," Chris said. He brought his long, thin fingers to his lips, a starry twinkle from within his pale blue eyes. "I'm so bad."

"I think I better earn my pay," Eddie said. He sensed his window of opportunity, and waltzed through unsuspected past his friend. He swept up Regan's hair, and then marched to the curtained back room as if he was about to throw out the garbage. His scene was about to be over. With a practiced efficient move, he removed from within his back pocket a freezer bag; he stuffed the silky blond strands safely inside. Then Pedro appeared.

"Edward, this hair will open a dangerous door. What you think you seek is not your prize," Pedro said. He patted on Eddie's chest. "The nada snake seeks you-"

"I'll be all right," Eddie said. He gulped.

"I will pray for you," Pedro said. His eyes almost twinkled with tears. His lips quivered. "You are in great danger, a dark power I cannot see, or I will go blind, I am afraid."

"Thanks," Eddie said. "I guess, I guess I have to do this."

It was seven-thirty, time to leave, lest his unexplained freezer bag discovered by Chris. Eddie averted Pedro's solemn gaze. He slipped on a blue barn jacket, and dropped his cell phone inside his breast pocket.

"It's been a long day, been fun. Perhaps while she's conked-out, best I get back home," Eddie said. He acted as if infected by the yawns.

Pedro, Chris and Jill Marie all yawned in unison, each caught up with Eddie's contagious disease.

"Oh, okay, I'm glad you came by, it was a night to remember," Chris said quietly. He patted Eddie on his left shoulder.

"Later, sexy beast," Jill Marie whispered.

"I think it's about time to wake her up. I want her hair perfect," Chris said. He quickly rubbed his hand together.

"Edward, do not forgot what I said," Pedro said. He stared intently at Eddie. "What you seek, you do not have. Total darkness approaches you, I will pray for you all night. I will burn incense for you all night."

"Thank you, Pedro," Eddie said. He stared into Pedro's blank, coolly certain expression. He slid out the back door as the cool springtime air wisped across his flushed cheeks. The instant change in temperature perked him back into the conscious world.

# # #

"Well, he has emerged," Captain Lovins said. He paused as he waited for Eddie to get back in his car and turn on his cell phone. He sipped water and twisted to pop his stiff neck.

# # #

Eddie glanced at the buildings behind the salon, certain that they watched him. He crawled into his modest car. He slipped his sim card back in, and turned on his cell phone. It vibrated.

"Hello," Eddie said. He stared forward through the windshield across the shopping center parking lot.

"Edward, I know," Captain Lovins said.

"All right," Eddie said. He closed his eyes. He squeezed his right hand on the steering wheel.

"Be at the General Beauregard's Fried Chicken on Hubble Parkway, it's open twenty-four hours a day," Captain Lovins said. "Exactly one o'clock this morning. Leave your cell phone at home, have nothing electronic or cellular on you."

"I'll be there," Eddie said.

"You know what I look like. I will be inside. You follow, and bring the item for exchange," Captain Lovins said. "I will have the codes you need for the Swiss Bank account. Then my employer will present himself, Godspeed."

Chapter Forty One

While Mr. Oppenheimer sat inside the black SUV near Eddie's apartment complex, Eddie's cell phone alarm vibrated at the stroke of a digital midnight. From an over production of adrenaline and an empty stomach, his body shivered. On his hands and knees, Eddie sucked in a deep breath. With his forehead, he Spanish bulled open his closet door. He scanned his grey, shadowy bedroom. He saw only the faint outline of his bed and bookshelf. He waggled his head above his bed's rumpled flannel sheets. He wiggled back down and crawled out on all fours to search the apartment's main room through his half-open bedroom door. All appeared calm. He crept back to his closet's relative safety as he wondered how he had gotten into this nasty mess.

"Time to do this-" Eddie mumbled. He gradually tried to stand up, but his knees ached from being immobile for several hours. His thigh muscles twitched and strained, from the constant pressure from pushing against the closet door. He gulped for oxygen within the musty closet. As he leaned his right arm against a cardboard storage box for stability, written in black magic marker along the side panel, Dad's Stuff. But the corrugated top caved-in. His hand slid off, his right shoulder knocked open the sterile storage container. With the lid half-way off, it balanced and stuck to his sweaty elbow. The closet door was now partially open, as a parking lot lamp near Eddie's bedroom window illuminated the closet interior. Milky light reflected off shards of glass that flickered and sparkled like white diamonds. The corner of a picture frame peeked over the box edge. The frame held a poem stamped on parchment paper. Its glass cracked down the middle and it was falling apart at the corners from loosened tack nails.

Eddie thought for a moment. He had long since forgotten his father had given it to him. The occasion was after a grade school playground incident. Within his mind's eye, he could almost remember every detail as if the picture frame had transported him across time, to when he was twelve years old.

A fight had erupted one afternoon with the resident bully, Bobby Humperdinck, who had picked on his favorite target, Christopher Clayton.

"You're a faggot," Bobby screamed in Chris' ears.

"Leave me alone," Chris said. He slinked away from Bobby. His arms crossed. He fidgeted with his silver belt buckle, holding up his pressed blue jeans.

Eddie was playing with Jim Bob on a nearby swing set tempting fate, as they watched Chris peek around at the nearby schoolyard for a safe group of children. But there were none. He was alone. He was isolated, because he was different.

"What's wrong, sissy? Bet you are afraid of me?" Bobby said. He hissed. He scampered in front of Chris. He bumped him with his immature chest. He stuck his snarled face up at Chris.

"Come on now Bobby, no need to be a zipper-head," Jim Bob said. He yelled leaning against the swing set, out of breath, sweating, as he watched Eddie glide back and forth into the powder blue sky as if he was watching a tennis match. "Go Eddie, I think you might fly."

"Stay out of this, ya redneck," Bobby said. Then he twisted, he smacked Chris' pimply face and shoved him to the ground. "Big sissy, my daddy says you're a homo in training."

Chris fell back, his knees buckled. As he turned his head to see where he was falling, he tried to shield his face with his left hand, but he knocked his chin against the bottom edge of a metal slide. A sharp jagged sliver of metal slashed his naked skin, barely missing his carotid artery. Then a nasty gash opened a newly tapped oil well that gushed dark blood intended for his brain. Chris screamed. He cried. His shirt splattered along the collar. His face caked in blood, mixed with salty tears, green grass. Nervously, he tried to stop the bleeding with his trembling fingers. His terrified gaze darted back and forth, begging someone to help, for mercy.

But the now silent classmates were as if paper cutouts scattered across the green grass and blacktopped playground. They gawked. They looked at each other. They whispered to each other, but no one moved their feet. Except Eddie, he stopped freely gliding on the swing. He instinctively leaped off the swing mid arc and ran toward Chris.

"What're you go'en to do dip-wad?" Bobby said. His midget boxer fists up.

Eddie clenched his jaw. He stared down at Chris. Chris looked up at Eddie. Then, with a single motion, flyweight Eddie Wilcox drew back his left hand fist, spun forward and punched Bobby. As Bobby's nose began to bleed along his left side nostril, Eddie stopped, balanced his feet, shoulder width apart as his dad had shown him, and then nailed Bobby with a right hook to the eye.

"Leave him alone," Eddie said. His voice rumbled with rage.

"Oh, my eye, I can't see nothing," Bobby said as he cried.

"Get up and I'll blind your other eye," Eddie said.

But just as quickly Jim Bob bounced over to break up the fight. He held Eddie back from leaping onto Bobby.

"All right, back up now," Jim Bob said. He grappled Eddie back off Bobby. "Bobby I told you not to do that."

Eddie remembered his favorite grade school teacher Miss Deiser, sprang over to help Chris up, her favorite pink polyester pants suit was stained with Chris's blood.

"All of you, inside, as in now-" Miss Deiser said. She clutched Chris, with her fingers she put pressure on the wound. She hugged him close. "It will be okay dear, try to stay calm, just try to breathe."

"It hurts," Chris said. He moaned. He gulped for air.

Principal Harnisch suspended Eddie for three days. And Bobby got a week for being the instigator.

Eddie sat back reflecting over the distant, hazy memory. At home that night, his father had patted him on his diminutive left shoulder.

"It'll be okay," Adam had said. He frowned, and held Eddie tightly with both arms. "Your mother and I don't support violence, but you did the right thing to defend Chris." Adam then handed Eddie a package wrapped with a golden bow.

"Yes dear," Sophia said.

"I've kept this all my life wondering when I'd give it to you," Adam said. He clutched the gift in his hands. "As you get older, I'll not be there to defend you. You will have to figure out life on you own terms, perhaps this will give you inspiration, a little boost to face the world."

Eddie opened the package. He studied the frame, and read the words from an old poem.

"This is important dear," Sophia said. She stood close to her husband. Her right arm hugged his waist.

"This poem is special to me. Now I want you to have it. Perhaps someday in the not so distant future, you might find the words make sense," Adam said. He winked at Eddie. "Believe in yourself, make me proud by being an honorable man, and always know that I and your mother, love you unconditionally."

Eddie remembered his father brushed his shaggy bangs away from his eyes. And he kissed him on his forehead. He hugged him.

Inside his closet, Eddie slid back the cardboard box lid. He pulled out the cheap wooden frame. He switched on the closet's incandescent light. On his knees, Eddie scanned the poem written during the Victorian Age. His father seemed to like it, but Eddie was only twelve-years old when he gave it to him. He did not understand why his father wanted him to have it. Eddie read the simple, powerful words.

"Be a man," Eddie said. He sighed. He could visualize a perfect time capsule of his father Adam's face. The family was together at the dinner table devouring the last morsels of Sophia's special fried chicken dinner. He could almost hear Adam's boisterous laugh, as he teased his mother. He called her love. Eddie shrugged remembering his father always would say, "Hey love. Hey love this, Hey love that, I Love you." Adam had said the word *love* every time he talked to Sophia; he had always called her, his love. His father loved his mother.

Slowly, Eddie stood up inside his bedroom closet. His eyes dripped a river of happy tears. He held the talisman he had searched for, the thought that eluded him. The words he would never hear again. He knew his father loved him, too.

Eddie gently hugged the framed poem. He carefully placed it on his bookshelf. He glided his fingers along the frame's crumbled edges. It would be his paper compass to guide him through the cosmos and seek the Helix Nebula with the intense fatherly starlight that reflected him across time from where his father's spirit constantly had watched over him.

Eddie's heart filled with love, hope and courage, certain he would never feel lost again. His expression changed into the intense concentration of manhood. He flicked away the useless tears as he marched out into the unknown.

And as Eddie drove toward the General Beauregard's Fried Chicken restaurant, Mr. Oppenheimer called Ms. Prosperina.

"Madam," Mr. Oppenheimer said, as he drove behind Eddie's car, and he carefully monitored the tracking device.

"What have you for me," Ms. Prosperina said.

"The boy has left his apartment," Mr. Oppenheimer said. "I am following, if he simply goes to his girlfriend, I will return. If not, I will come collect you."

"Good, tell me nothing more," Ms. Prosperina said. "I need to have a clear mind."

Chapter Forty Two

Captain Lovins found the Dowsing Donut shop. After he parked his van, he walked toward the side glass doors and spied inside, confident he knew which person was Professor Quan.

"This how you expected me to appear?" Professor Quan asked. "Didn't mean for my hair to go crazy, kind of Einstein looking southern gentleman, but I decided it'll work."

Captain Lovins sat down across from Professor Quan. He nodded his head. He tapped his fingers along the hard plastic table. The restaurant was warm from the busy activity and the assembly line rolling out deep fried donuts.

"I think you out-did yourself this time," Captain Lovins said. He chuckled. "You sound a bit twangy, a bit gravely."

"Thank you," Professor Quan said. He sipped his coffee from an insulated cup.

"You'll never catch me in that machine," Captain Lovins said.

"Oh? Afraid of a little exterior modification," Professor Quan said. He adjusted his black Kentucky bow tie.

Captain Lovins focused on studying the other faces inside the donut shop. His weapon fully loaded, he interlocked his fingers across the tabletop, he was concerned Mr. Oppenheimer might appear.

"I'll take my chances," Captain Lovins said. The donut shop's neon sign flashed outside, as it beckoned those searching for a mid-night snack. Even at the late night hour, the shop half-full. People of all colors, race, religions, searched not just for the sugary food, but were trying to replace the hole in their own donut. "This is real dangerous."

"I know," Professor Quan said. He adjusted his legs and unbuttoned his white suit jacket. "She wants to try and scare me, or, she might just kill me if I don't give her the rocks."

"Think she's near, well, Edward's motivated to get his idiot friend out of jail, make some extra cash, and move on with his life," Captain Lovins said. He paused. "And he's got a girlfriend, she's pretty, so, if we keep him alive we can at least do some good tonight."

Professor Quan sipped his coffee. He stared up at the starless ceiling tiles. He smiled.

"I see, guess he is coming back to life, without us," Professor Quan said. "Amazing potential, but I'll fix him."

"Let's stay on point, Ms. Prosperina," Captain Lovins said. He tapped his fingers over near Professor Quan. Professor Quan stared over at Captain Lovins. He took off his black framed eyeglasses. He shrugged.

"Let's deal with Edward first," Professor Quan said.

"You arrive after me, let's say ten minutes and park in the back next to the dumpster. I will go inside and meet with

Edward. I'll give him the Swiss Bank account codes, and determine if it's safe for you to enter, if I think she lurks," Captain Lovins said. He diagramed his plan drawing with his forefinger across the tabletop.

"Fine with me, but don't worry about her," Professor Quan said. He stared past Captain Lovins at a young boy standing next to his father. "He should be home."

Captain Lovins turned to find him. He nodded in agreement.

"Yeah, my transmitter indicates he is headed there now," Captain Lovins said. Even though his old friend looked like someone else, he thought he had a resolute glint within his eyes, a look that comes from the certainty of truth, but there was something else there that he had not noticed before. "What?"

"Very well," Professor Quan said. He glided his pudgy fingers through the steam billowing from the hot coffee. He wiggled his white pant legs across the plastic bench and leaned his cane against the table. "This has to end, you're the only other person knows about the diamonds."

"But they know he exists. We have a window to reach out to him," Captain Lovins said. He glanced around the restaurant. "I don't like this, this is dangerous."

Professor Quan thought it was time to tell his old friend he had decided how to eradicate Ms. Prosperina.

"I'm tired of this, I'm tired," Professor Quan said. He stared at Captain Lovins. He pulled out a canister that resembled an asthma inhaler. "Once I give him this, she'll not mess with him. But I suspect she'll show up. The old girl is trying to be cunning, be Athena, block me from reading her mind. She's drunk from bourbon, and she smokes like she has iron lungs, witch."

"She'll kill you," Captain Lovins said.

"I'm counting on it," Professor Quan said. He shrugged. "Just let me deal with Edward, if she shows, after, take him to a safe place, a place he can hide for a few days."

Captain Lovins thought about all the time they had spent together, Professor Quan was his best friend. Now, he was about to say goodbye, but he knew it was the right thing to do, it was not a sacrifice, it was a conscious decision to protect unseen generations that would feel the freedom to love.

"You sure," Captain Lovins said. He frowned. He clenched his jaw line.

"Yes, just remember to pick up Waldo," Professor Quan said.

"I will," Captain Lovins said. He stared out the windows into the parking lot.

"You know, it's not just Biblical, the Pleiades cluster, Orion chasing the hot blue seven sisters," Professor Quan said. He pointed up toward the starry night sky. "Yahweh, Pyramids, the four forces of physics." He stared down at the restaurant's dirty tile floor. "But if you have love within you, there is a harmony within your cells that will emerge if induced by some electromagnetic force, a force yet to fully appear."

"Godspeed," Captain whispered. He clenched his jaw.

Professor Quan tapped on the table with his cane.

"If, when she appears, do not look back. He'll need some time, his mind will be on a serious bender, like he just got shot into space," Professor Quan said. He smiled. "But I'll be free, it'll be all right, if you're afraid of death, you've never lived, right?"

"Yeah," Captain Lovins said. He coughed. "I know-"

Professor Quan held up the steaming coffee cup. He examined the wisps of steam frothing over the sides.

"It's not the coffee, it's her manipulation," Professor Quan said. He set the cup down on the tabletop. "An innocent choice should not be used to enslave humanity."

# # #

Back on the hard concrete along Hubble Parkway, Eddie drove his jalopy into the spooky darkness, unaware Mr. Oppenheimer was tracking him. As he drove past his office complex, he decided to listen to his cell phone's voice mail. To his surprise, he had several messages waiting and numerous text messages from Ardee.

"Eddie, this is Simon. I think we are ahead of the game with Jim Bob, when you find a free moment, please contact Emily Dawn and she can fill you in. Take care." Click.

His voice mail rolled to the next message.

"Hey man, Jim Bob. That lawyer guy you got me, why he is a miracle worker. I am getting outta here-" Click.

Eddie thought his recent existence had turned into a series of odd moments that he could not reconcile. His voice mail rolled to the next message.

"I'm calling, say hi. How was Christopher's? Was it excitin'?" Ardee asked. Click.

Eddie clenched his teeth listening to Ardee's playful voice. His voice mail rolled to the next message.

"Eddie, it's Ardee again, wanted to say hi." Click.

His voice mail rolled to the next message.

"Eddie, its Ardee. Sorry, I do not want to seem like a pest, or a stalker, just wanted to hear your voice. Hope I did not creep, you out today. Did I do something wrong?" Click.

His voice mail rolled to the next message.

"Eddie, its Ardee again, sorry, I'm going to bed now, but you can call me back even if it's late. I miss you." Click.

His voice mail rolled to another message.

"It's real late, I know, but I hope you are okay? I hope I didn't do something to upset you?" she paused, "I am worried about you- I love you." Click.

"Dear god," Eddie said as the General Beauregard's Fried Chicken signage began to emerge. Eddie drove over a modest hump along the road. The General's smiling image beckoned. The square building looked like every fast food restaurant in Middle America. It had a sloped red metal roof and a precast concrete exterior, interspersed by windows and doors. It glowed from the inside out and illuminated the pitch-black environment as if it had trapped the sun. Above, a blue moon hung in visible orbit.

Eddie drove into the parking lot and glanced inside the restaurant to see if he detected Captain Lovins. Eddie scanned front to back. He discovered him on the right side of the reverse L shaped dining area. He sat alone.

# # #

"Madam," Mr. Oppenheimer said. He gripped the steering wheel with his leather driving gloves. "I would like to show you a classic American enterprise."

"Good boy," Ms. Prosperina said. "I'll be right down, waiting."

"Yes, madam," Mr. Oppenheimer said.

Chapter Forty Three

Professor Quan reclined inside his 1957 Roadmaster, with the convertible top up; he had parked near the dumpster behind the General Beauregard's Fried Chicken. He spotted Eddie in the parking lot walking toward the side glass door, he grinned.

# # #

"Stay cool," Eddie whispered as he loped past the glass double doors. The uninterested pointy paper hatted, polyester uniformed staff ignored him. The mostly empty restaurant had a distinct burnt grease and cigarette smoke fragrance. The airy Shanghai like pollution caused the neon restroom sign to blaze electric hot pink, revealing crayon mars along the winter white painted trim with a wallpaper pattern of a faith, hope and love country scene. Eddie tediously stepped toward Captain Lovins, who devoured the last carcass remnants of the General's famous six piece fried chicken dinner.

"Want some chicken? I love both light and dark meat. I enjoy the slight textural differences," Captain Lovins said. Attired in military garb, he wiggled his fingers covered with shiny grease. He methodically licked his fingertips one-by-one, with an icy stare up at Edward. "I prefer the classic recipe, not an extra crispy man."

"No thanks," Eddie said. His heart thumped.

"Too bad, you know we never have figured out that secret recipe," Captain Lovins said. He smirked up at Eddie. "I understand your attractive mother and girlfriend have *great* fried chicken recipes? I assume you brought Regan's hair?"

Eddie's face flushed scarlet, pulverized by the thought Captain Lovins knew about his mother, and Ardee.

"Yeah," Eddie said. His eyebrows furrowed. He gulped. "I know the IRS has been tracking you all for decades."

Captain Lovins leaned back. He crossed his arms.

"Don't you think I'm aware of them? Give me a little credit, *Edward*. I guess that high-powered lawyer, Mr. Lewis tipped you off, a faithful man, not like his partner, Mr. Screwtop. Dating your mother?" Captain Lovins said. He shook his head. "Now that's random, or just weird."

"What?" Eddie said.

"I'm well-trained to avert detection and, unlike you, I do my homework, " Captain Lovins said. He wiped off his hands with a moist hand-sanitizing wipe. "It's my job to know who I'm dealing with, you're not tough to track, cell phones, web browsing, it's all out there for anyone to find, you're a very unique number."

Eddie shifted on his brown shoes; he glanced behind him at the colorful rows of empty plastic tables and chairs.

"Doesn't seem like honest work to me," Eddie said. His stomach muscles stiffened. "This will the last time we meet."

"Sure, "Captain Lovins said. He chuckled. He swirled on the plastic seat to face Eddie. "You must be the luckiest fart in the world, go buy a lottery ticket, might make Charlene proud?"

Eddie thought he was frozen in time, his entire existence picked apart, he wondered what else they knew, his habits, his cell phone conversations, what else did they know.

"I made sure you, you knew I'm playing straight," Eddie said. He thought the restaurants bright fluorescent lights, coupled with the exterior darkness cloaked the evil eyes watching them.

"I'm curious, why is it that you don't use that gifted brain?" Captain Lovins said. He pursed his lips.

Eddie held his breath as his heart searched for oxygen.

"I've the hair," Eddie said. He stuttered and stammered. He sounded like a thirteen-year-old boy ravaged by puberty.

"Fine," Captain Lovins said. "My employer is nearby."

"Fine," Eddie said. He wimpy boy coughed.

"If you even so much as act like you're going to harm him, I'll drop you. I'll do it with my favorite spider knife," Captain Lovins said. He twirled his knife through his fingers.

A sweat bead glided down between Eddie's shoulder blades certain the bald headed man was not kidding.

"Take this thumb drive, it contains the Swiss bank account, its idiot proof, you'll figure it out. I'm not concerned with the item's authenticity," Captain Lovins said. He sucked in a deep breath as he glanced past Eddie. "You came alone?"

"Yeah," Eddie said. He thought the deal was about over.

"Lose the cell phone next time, I know it's blipping our location, if you've been tailed, IRS has an army you know," Captain Lovin said. He grinned up at Eddie. "Love that girl?"

"I don't know," Eddie said. "I guess-"

"Going to get Jim Boob out of prison?" Captain Lovins said. He enjoyed twisting Eddie's psyche screw ever so tight. He clipped his knife onto his belt.

"Yeah," Eddie said. He refused to scamper, even though his sphincter muscle had super glued his butt checks together into an exit only strategy.

"My employer wants to meet you," Captain Lovins said. He sent a text to Professor Quan. "Just be cool."

After a few minutes, inside the fast food emporium Professor Quan stood. He, Eddie and Captain Lovins stood in a triangular position. Captain Lovins situated between the ergonomic designed plastic bench and heatproof dining table. Eddie and Professor Quan stood in the dirty center aisle.

"Pleased to meet you young man," Professor Quan said.

"Hello," Eddie said. He stepped forward to shake the older man's hand. The grip seemed powerful, although his skin spongy. And Eddie was conflicted in an attempt to try to figure out who the man had a striking resemblance. The man's eyes his most remarkable feature, a dark brown backlit with an intense pure white light. He had dense processed sugar white hair, a fashionable well-maintained goatee and mustache, with thick, black horn rimmed eyeglasses.

# # #

Outside along the concrete street corner the black SUV parked. Ms. Prosperina inspected the restaurant. She gazed along the bank of windows until she noticed the old man standing near the back of the restaurant.

"That's him," Ms. Prosperina said. She tried to keep her mind blank. She sipped some bourbon. "I can barely think straight."

"Yes, madam," Mr. Oppenheimer said. "Focus on your childhood, the times you were left alone, to play with your chemistry set."

"I was quite bright, but alone," Ms. Prosperina said. She glanced down the street at the emptying bars, groups of drunken patrons stumbled toward the GBFC. "I see I have my opening."

"Yes, madam," Mr. Oppenheimer said.

# # #

"What now, never met a southern gentleman?" Professor Quan asked. He wore a purity white, three-button suit with a gold chain connected to a railroad pocket watch.

"I feel like I've seen you before," Eddie said. He scratched behind his right ear, he glance up and to his right at the starless ceiling tiles.

"Come now, we have never met, ah, not in person," Professor Quan said. He grinned. He waved toward a table. "Shall we have a seat? I believe you have some valuable merchandise you wish to exchange." They sat astride each other. Captain Lovins stepped back; he sat near the rear exit. He stared out the windows, and intently watched the doors.

"Well now, do you wish to offer me the item?" Professor Quan asked. He dangly pointed his pudgy finger over at Eddie.

"Yes, yes I do," Eddie said. He handed the freezer bag stuffed with Regan's hair strands over to Professor Quan. "What're you going to do with this stuff?"

"Well, let me think," Professor Quan said. He glanced over at Captain Lovins. He crossed his arms. "We try to help free humanity, to seek love."

Eddie crinkled his face. He thought the response was full of gushy, do-gooder crap found a thousand times over in his mother's shelf full of romance novels.

"Why the crazy list, I'm sure you can get this stuff by just calling these people," Eddie said. He glanced over at Captain Lovins. "I think, well, this is weird."

Professor Quan examined the hair strands. He stuffed the bag inside his coat breast pocket.

"Life's fingerprints are everywhere, but, I have to remain hidden, I did something stupid, so I need folks like you, to help me," Professor Quan said. He wiggled his bushy eyebrows. "Besides, this is no big deal, ever wonder if your own doctor might have sold off your DNA? They do it all the time, not a big deal, they own your genetic code, all nice and legal."

Eddie cocked his head up and rubbed his temple. He squinted with his eyes, and stared at Professor Quan.

"Maybe, I guess, I never thought about it, but what are you doing? And what's up with the list," Eddie asked. He shrugged.

"Oh, creating unique gifts for people and what-not," Professor Quan said. He grinned back over at Captain Lovins as he happily fishtailed his hands across the shiny tabletop.

Eddie sneaked a peek over at Captain Lovins, who menacingly stared back at him, and then looked behind him inspecting the restaurant. Eddie thought he was the toughest looking man he had ever seen, but he also seemed quite paranoid.

"You're making clones? Synthetic humans, I guess you clone Lionel or Regan, and all the other people on your list," Eddie said. He gulped. He exhaled. "Saw it on TV."

"Excuse me?" Professor Quan said. He glared at Edward. He glanced back over at Captain Lovins. Captain Lovins shrugged. He checked the security of his 9 mm weapon he had stuffed inside his back belt loop.

"I don't know," Captain Lovins said. He leaned forward. "He's a bit loopy tonight. Edward, you been drinking sugared up coffee? That stuff will put you in a narcoleptic haze."

Professor Quan bounced his cane off the tile floor.

"But that is very, very creative, I'll give you that," Professor Quan said. He chuckled. He clutched the cane. "Sorry, not quite, cloning is a waste of time. Humans are more than a collection of body parts, there is a harmony within our cells."

"Why are you being defensive?" Eddie asked.

"I'm not, you're lost, clones? Why is the world so obsessed with making us all homogenized every town looks the same, as if it's obese group think. Voyeur in like the Roman mob into the lives of paid fools," Professor Quan said. He huffed. He twirled the cane. "Live in a virtual reality created by our masters, besides clones are boring, I did much worse."

"Next, live executions, pay per view," Captain Lovins said. He nodded. "Then sell the carcass off for parts like an old '57 Chevy, right? That's where you're heading."

Eddie looked at them. He turned to look behind him.

"I don't understand," Eddie said. He glanced back at Captain Lovins. He looked back at the old man.

"Dump the voyeurism, be the next Elvis," Professor Quan said. He stared down at the dirty floor. He paused and slowly exhaled. "What a waste, clone? I did much worse. I helped create a real Frankenstein's monster, but I blame no one, but me."

"What?" Eddie said.

"Never mind," Professor Quan said. He gazed through the expansive glass windows back through time, at an Orwellian memory hole to a simpler existence, to a time before he seemingly opened a Pandora's Box. "I'm an old fool."

"How? Wait, you all paid me a lot of money," Eddie said. He gulped as he crinkled his face. "And it's like these people just appeared in front of me, did you cause that? Set me up?"

Professor Quan contemplated random nature, and if he had in fact sent out some cosmic wave that dropped Edward down a wormhole into another human dimension. If life was completely random, then how did we all get here? Are all our thoughts and actions already written within our genetic code?

"In a way, I suppose, stealing?" Professor Quan said. He shrugged. "You speed down the freeway, isn't that illegal too?"

Then from behind them, three drunken females suddenly wobbled through the back glass door, past the bathroom opening and whisked past Captain Lovins.

"Hey missy love, I didn't know it was Halloween?" the blonde girl said. She pointed at Professor Quan. She stumbled onto Eddie's lap. She puked burbled beer gas at Eddie.

"Wow, that dude's weird looking," the brunet woman said. She jumped forward, and high fived her friend. "It's a rockin' General Beauregard, back from the grave."

"I'd like to party with you, he's intense," the red head woman said. She did not show her face as she wobbled toward the front counter.

"Hey cutie, your grandpa looks like he's really out there, does he do Civil War reenactments? We should road trip, go bomb Fort Sumter again?" the blonde girl said to Eddie. Her domestic beer breath caused Eddie to turn this head; he shoved her up and nudged her off him.

"That's so cool," the brunet girl said as the girls cackled and bobbed past the restaurant corner, toward the stainless steal front counter.

But Professor Quan had watched them closely. He looked back over at Captain Lovins. A look that his life clock was about to stop ticking, and the future belonged to Edward.

"Come now, they gave you those specimens freely, he gave you his socks. She allowed her hair to be cut, and discarded the remnants to the trash heap," Professor Quan said. He nervously looked past Eddie. "Much of the hair is dead, but it only takes a small particle, tiny life still exists."

"Yeah, I guess," Eddie said.

Professor Quan snapped forward, he intently stared at Edward.

"Consider this, all you did was pick up discarded genetic material," Professor Quan said. He pulled out the small spray canister. "It's quite valuable for my experiments."

"Experiments?" Eddie asked. He leaned forward and tried to search deep within Professor Quan's eyes. "I'm not even sure you're real? You seem real, but something about you is just not right. And your experiments seem creepy."

"*Really*, I don't seem right? Creepy?" Professor Quan said. He shrugged and tapped his forefinger across his faux lips. "Well my experiments do have a purpose, primarily, to multiply life forward. You see, I did many bad things, and I theorize that if enough love is spread, that a harmony will inflate into the universe, and crowd out evil, dark matter, so to speak."

"You don't have-" Captain Lovins said.

"Why not," Professor Quan said. He waved him away.

"Then one day, something inside me changed, I woke up," Professor Quan said. He leaned back, sighed, and crossed his legs. "But you just want to be free from us, right?"

"Didn't think this through did you Huckleberry?" Captain Lovins said. He clutched his spider knife. He focused his stare toward the front of the restaurant.

"It's not that simple," Eddie said.

"Oh, I see," Professor Quan, said. He tapped the cane on the tile floor. "Poor little Edward, all alone. But now I can see you, no more hiding – Edward, life will change tonight."

"Jerk-off," Eddie said. His scruffy neck hair screamed after he heard Captain Lovins unclip his spider knife.

"It's okay, calm down, for now," Professor Quan said as he raised his cane. He turned to glower at Edward.

"Allow me to explain something to you Huck Finn. We are all in a silent war, a world war," Professor Quan said.

"Give me a break, I read the news," Eddie said. He fumbled with the thumb drive.

"You cannot hide, soon you will see why. I had to, but that was by my choosing," Professor Quan said. He leaned on his cane, as he stared forward. "But, in fact, no one has the luxury to hide anymore. All our lives are open books, most people get to be the bunny rabbit, a few, the falcon."

Professor Quan stopped talking. He intently stared forward. Eddie twisted to look behind him, but it was just a couple of drunken frat boys stumbling into the restaurant, post bar scene.

"Evil organizations that can easily steal our identity, they can even own your body, and you don't even know it," Professor Quan said. He squarely faced Eddie. "They make our food, filter the air we breathe, process the water we drink. They can alter mankind, and only they would know, rather Orwellian, a vast proletariat of bunny rabbits waiting to be feasted upon."

"Mister, I think you are out of your mind," Eddie said.

Professor Quan gripped the cane. He puckered his lips.

"I don't think so, listen, those thieves I mention, are not just obvious criminals. But governments that peer needlessly into innocent homes, like a nosy next-door neighbor," Professor Quan said. He huffed. He gulped. "They tell you how to raise your children. How to think, tell us God is dead. Soon, perhaps you will be ostracized because of your DNA sample." Professor Quan stared down at Edward's brown shoes. "But freedom, love, trumps evil, that's why evil hides like a snake in the grass."

"You're a nut-job," Eddie said. He sat up and leaned his shoulders back. "I knew I needed to do this for some odd reason. Take the hair, stay away. I'll take care of Jim Bob."

"Still think I'm crazy?" Professor Quan asked. He then patted Eddie on his left knee. "We'll stay away, don't you dare worry."

Eddie stared over at a leaning forward Captain Lovins. He appeared like a cat about to pounce on its prey.

"I'm confused, you're crazy, he's dangerous," Eddie said.

"You sure about this kid?" Captain Lovins asked. He glanced away. "I need to focus." He slowly breathed through his mouth.

"Oh, even more so now," Professor Quan said. He waved over at Captain Lovins. He glided his hand across the top of the cold, smooth plastic tabletop. "I like his hidden passion."

"Let's get this over with," Eddie said. He clenched his jaw. "I've got the money, said what I needed to say, I think-"

Captain Lovins glanced past Edward, his eyes moving left to right inspecting the restaurant behind him.

"I think you have a window," Captain Lovins said to Professor Quan. He purposefully moved behind Eddie as if to shield him.

"Give me a moment," Professor Quan said. He adjusted his eyeglasses up his nose. "Edward, mark my words, if you end up on the wrong side of the government, you might as well have never existed, do you understand?"

Eddie sat back and crossed his arms. He shook his head.

"You know, Jim Bob smashes gold tin foil over his head and channels the pyramids," Eddie said. He glanced behind him at the agitated Captain Lovins.

Captain Lovins flicked open his knife.

"Eddie? I like Edward better, just seems stronger to me. Your name should demand respect. Edward, demands respect, sounds strong and courageous," Professor Quan said. He patted Edward on his flushed check. "Wake up, all you are or ever will be is easily obtained. While you and your friends play video games, *the world burns outside, sorry, but I started the fire.*" Professor Quan sucked in a deep breath. He menacingly pointed at Eddie. "May I perform a magic trick for you? I want to prove something to you, to pay attention, to listen."

Eddie scooted away from Professor Quan. He shrugged his shoulders. He crinkled his lips.

"I guess-" Eddie mumbled.

"What if I walk over to that restroom opening, I will not hide. I don't like to hide. I'll stand under that pink neon sign. I will change my outward appearance, my skin, hair. I will lose some weight. Then, I will return to this hard plastic chair. Do you believe that will happen?" Professor Quan said.

Eddie contorted his face. He peeked behind him at the fidgeting Captain Lovins.

"Remember, time is short," Captain Lovins said.

"I don't think so, no, that's impossible," Eddie said. His voice calm resignation, certain the only way he would leave feet first, carted off on under a stark white sheet.

"Oh this will be interesting," Captain Lovins drolly said.

"Very well, I just want to prove to you how important it is to pay attention," Professor Quan said. He adjusted his black Kentucky bowtie. "Sure about what you see?" He balanced over his brown cane like a Broadway tap dancer. He slinked forward, his face uncomfortably close to Eddie's face. Then he waltzed away from Eddie, but he gazed back into Eddie's eyes. "This one-time-"

"I can see you," Eddie said. He thought the man smelled of pungent donuts and coffee.

Professor Quan steadily twisted and strolled toward the restrooms. He thought he needed to do this transformation one last time before she appeared.

"Watch *real* close, Edward," Professor Quan said as he snapped his fingers. In an instant, his suit jacket slumped around his shoulders. He barely caught his pants before dropping to his ankles. But what startled Eddie the most, the old man's hair, once a purity white, now amethyst black. Professor Quan twisted around, and strolled back toward Eddie.

Eddie's face deathly ashen, his vision blurred.

"Wha… wha…" Eddie whispered. His body wobbled.

"Well, you wanted to see what I really looked like. So, here I am," Professor Quan said. He patted Eddie's flushed cheek.

"What are you?" Eddie asked. He exhaled all the oxygen from his lungs. His lips gapped open. "Just don't hurt Ardee."

"How sweet," Professor Quan said. He sighed.

"I'm not going to hurt anybody," Professor Quan said. He dagger pointed at Edward. "Keep the money, you need it to get Jim Bob out of jail, right?"

"That's a nice kicker," Captain Lovins said. He chuckled.

Eddie held his breath, trying to figure out if he could escape. Then he realized Captain Lovins could easily track him down. He had left his cell phone in his carbon-fueled vehicle, a vehicle tagged with a tracking device.

"Edward, it's not about being," Professor Quan said. He snapped his fingers. "What you cynically call a sperm olympic champion, real champions work at their craft for years, for the love of it, it's all about love, passion."

"How do you know that?" Eddie asked.

"You are truly a naïve baby doe in the woods. The bald guy over there, rather thorough," Professor Quan said. He smiled over at Captain Lovins. He turned back to gaze down at Eddie. "You really think you can hide from the world?"

"What do you want?" Eddie said.

"Nothing – yet - you see Edward, every person is different. Your irises, your fingerprints, they are unique to you. Why, even identical twins become altered, their DNA is the same, but it is their life choices, it's about free will," Professor Quan said. He sat down. He pensively stared past Edward. "I cannot alter DNA, but I can alter how DNA is expressed, help someone seek love, happiness, I hope."

"I don't understand?" Eddie said. His chest pulsated from his overworked lungs. He gripped his knees.

"Courage and audacity, I like how that sounds," Professor Quan said. He proudly glanced over at Captain Lovins.

"I think you're on a roll," Captain Lovins said. He looked back over his shoulder. "Time is running out."

Professor Quan nodded his head.

"Edward, do you really think that it's a mistake or just dumb luck, as you think, that somehow people with magical talent emerge?" Professor Quan asked. He pulled out the spray canister.

"What?" Eddie asked. He clenched his jaw, glancing rapidly back and forth at Professor Quan and Captain Lovins.

"Pay attention, these people emerge all the time. I'll answer, it's NOT dumb luck," Professor Quan said. He snapped his fingers. "Just be a little self-reliant."

"You cannot be real," Eddie said. He sighed.

"Come now, I'm quite real," Professor Quan said. "Don't fear reality, time to stop hiding."

"Heads up," Captain Lovins said. As the two drunken women scurried back around the corner, they almost dropped their drum box full of the General's extra crispy, golden brown and delicious fried chicken. Captain Lovins stood up; he dangled his arms at his sides with a sinister stare. Both sobered up, confused that the fat grandpa with white hair had disappeared, and a much more intense appearing man wore his clothes. They scampered from the restaurant, not looking back, afraid they might turn into salt. And Captain Lovins noticed the red head was not with them. He glanced over at Professor Quan who nodded in agreement. He closed his eyes, and sucked in a deep breath.

"I do not play God, and I'm certainly not a god," Professor Quan said. He gave a quick glance over at Captain Lovins.

Eddie was certain it was a signal and he was about to be dragged off. "We work to guide the forgotten child. Maybe they are an orphan like us," Professor Quan said. He pointed at Captain Lovins. He leaned forward, his elbows on his knees. "There were moments in celestial time that we need to pay attention to, they guided the ancients, and I think they still communicate with us, we just need to listen, to watch."

"For what?" Eddie said. He clenched his teeth and started to cry. "This is nightmare, my life's been a big mistake."

"I don't think so, you are meant to be special," Professor Quan said. He fidgeted with the spray canister. "So, you're wondering why the list?"

"It's creepy," Eddie said. He stared at the spray canister; he thought it was likely some sort of poison.

"Here, take my hanky, no reason to cry," Professor Quan said.

Eddie wiped tears from his eyes. His eyebrows narrowed. Professor Quan stood up, he stared across the restaurant for a few seconds and then gazed down at the trembling Edward.

"You have a point, I'll give you that. If you look at it without context, you might get the wrong idea. But you might be

surprised by what shows up in DNA. It is not about being perfect, it's about courage. Just shine a blue laser light in the right
spot, pure light, pure love will appear, I promise."

"I think I'm going to throw-up," Eddie said. His heart
pounded against his chest. His body swarmed in sweat droplets.

"I made a new shopping list every year, not seeking perfection, but those that made mistakes but figured it out, that sort
of jazz," Professor Quan said. He heard a loud hiss. He heard
the snap of a serpent's dagger teeth. He glanced over at Captain
Lovins. "Know what happened the night you were born?"

"What?" Eddie said. He sprang up in front of Professor
Quan.

"Guess I woke you up?" Professor Quan said.

"Hang in there, it'll all be over soon," Captain Lovins said.
He put his hand on Edward's shoulder; he encouraged him to
sit down. Eddie gripped the bottom of his chair.

"Hear me out, the night you were born, in fact, the very
nano-second. As a massive Supernova lit up deep in space, it
was the exact moment of the winter solstice, it was heavenly
magic," Professor Quan said. He closed his eyes and took in
a slow, measured breath. "From death, there is rebirth in the
springtime, we will renew."

"This is crazy," Eddie moaned. "How do you know that?"

"Because I study the stars, just like the ancients, and I guess
I have been searching for you my whole life," Professor Quan
whispered. He tapped his smooth chin with his forefinger. "I
marked the date. You're meant to be special, I know it, I feel it,
I hope someday you will."

"Why? You're going to kill me," Eddie said. He shook his head, as if someone sucker punched him in the gut. Then he heard an even louder hiss, and then the screams.

Captain Lovins slipped forward, facing into the restaurant, his handgun hidden under his left thigh. But he clicked off the safety as several workers escaped toward the side door.

"That's not part of our game plan," Professor Quan said. He patted Edward's flushed cheek and chuckled. He stared forward. "We visited you many years ago, but we failed, I always listen to my inner voice, my instincts they never lie to me, tonight is not a mistake, it was simply meant to be."

Eddie's mind sank, drowning from a powerful spiral current he could not grasp. His essence bobbed up and down gulping for air. He sensed Captain Lovins lurked near him. He heard screams, he heard hisses, and he thought he was trapped inside a vivid nightmare. All he wanted to do was wake up.

"I have never seen you before," Eddie whispered. He covered his face with his moist hands, as he shook his head. "This is crazy, this is a nightmare."

"We act as caretakers, secrets from light particles found inside each of us," Professor Quan said. His brown eyes began to turn pitch black, back lit by a blue hot flame stoked from his passion. "I think that's where love hides."

"That's right," Captain Lovins said. He did not look back at Professor Quan. He pointed the weapon toward the corner of the restaurant's front counter. He slowly moved forward, he heard the hisses within the empty front counter.

"But, damn my immortal soul to burn in an eternal hellish flame if I chose not to act," Professor Quan said. He heard a louder hiss. He could hear the screams from the front counter staff running out the back of the restaurant. He watched the frat boys scamper past Captain Lovins and from the restaurant as if they had seen Medusa. "If you could only *see the world through my eyes*, to pear into the microbial past from the beginning of time, it's all right there."

"Nice," Captain Lovins said. He glared over at Professor Quan. He intently nodded at him. "Come on, she comes."

"Thank you dear friend," Professor Quan said. He bullwhip snapped his left hand fingers in front of Eddie's face.

"What?" Eddie asked. He rapidly blinked his eyelids. "What's going on?"

"The sand in my hourglass is almost empty, and I need to find someone special, someone predestined to protect humankind from my mistake," Professor Quan said. He handed Eddie the spray canister that resembled an asthmatic inhaler. "It's all in here, spray this into your lungs. It will save your life."

Professor Quan blankly stared over at Captain Lovins.

"She scares me too," Captain Lovins said. He shrugged. "She's over there, she hides behind that center counter."

"I don't know," Eddie said. He gripped the inhaler, examining it. Then he heard a loud hissing sound behind him. His skin started to chill as he heard skin slithering against tile.

"Edward, have you ever wondered why the stars come out at night, why monarch butterflies flock north, why sea turtles return to their breeding grounds, why the birds fly south for winter," Professor Quan said. He breathed out a long breath. "I think I know, and it's not just instincts, it's pure love. No one ever risks their life without love."

"I guess she waits for you," Captain Lovins said. He kept the weapon pointed forward. He could hear the serpent slithering, coiling behind the condiment counter. He could see the side outline of the cobra's hooded head, and saw its forked tongue.

Professor Quan snapped forward, he grasped Eddie's face within his hands.

"Enough! I staked our lives, Edward, we hide two black diamonds coated with her organic seeds, she'll enslave humanity, you'll see in a few seconds," Professor Quan said. He quickly yanked Eddie up shoving his hands under his armpits, and he dragged him into the back of the restaurant next to the bathroom opening. "Captain, protect him, I'll handle this."

"Am I going to die," Eddie whispered. His shoulders slumped.

"Non omnis moriar, not all of me will die," Professor Quan said. He scowled down at Eddie. "Just inhale, it's your choice, but what you will see, might help with your decision."

"Why me?" Eddie said. He whispered as he held the canister in his hand. He shook his head. "Am I dreaming?"

"No, fate I suppose," Captain Lovins said. He gripped Eddie's shoulders; he shoved him down and behind him. His weapon pointed up as Professor Quan strolled forward, toward the loud hisses.

Captain Lovins coughed to get Professor Quan's attention.

"I've got your back," Captain Lovins said.

"I know, nothing stops evil, nothing stops a bully, like someone with the courage to defend the weak, right? Isn't that in your code?" Professor Quan said. He clutched his brown cane. He stood up straight and walked past the restaurant corner.

"I don't understand," Eddie whispered.

"You'll be alright," Captain Lovins said. He kept his weapon up. "Just decide right now if you want to live or die, that canister will save your and many other lives, we are not trying to trick you, but you have to decide right now."

#

Professor Quan held his breath. Then he breathed in as deep as he could, and then slowly released the carbon dioxide. He mastered his emotions. He took his mind to a Zen place, his face calm, but resolute. He walked near the empty chrome counter littered with partially eaten chicken dinners; he could hear the drips from a leaking faucet, the sound of the cycling HVAC system. And then slithering of snake scales across the cold tiled flooring. He stood up straight. He coughed.

"Now, Kore, that's not like you to hide," Professor Quan said. From his left side, he watched Mr. Oppenheimer open the front glass door. His weapon drawn, he pointed it down at Captain Lovins. And the amber dot on Mr. Oppenheimer's forehead indicated Captain Lovins was pointing his weapon up at Mr. Oppenheimer.

"I am here madam," Mr. Oppenheimer said. The restaurant was completely empty; it was deathly quiet, save for a low hiss.

"Hello, father," Ms. Prosperina said as she slithered across the tile floor from behind an interior wall housing the fountain drink dispensers, napkins and condiments. She glided forward, her serpent head waved back and forth, as she revealed her colorful skin, her hooded Cobra head slinked back as if ready to strike Professor Quan. But her eyes, one black, one red, steady, they were certain, staring down at Professor Quan.

"Well, I sense you're a bit drunk," Professor Quan said. He moved to square his body with the giant serpent. "Are you showing off for me? You're quite amazing, what else can you morph into, another serpent, a bull, come now, I'm not scared."

"I find Kentucky bourbon," Ms. Prosperina said. She hissed, as her black forked tongue tested the air. "Fogs the mind, but you did not sense me, I have you now, father, you will give me, what is mine, or you will die."

"Yes, you're so much more powerful than me," Professor Quan said. He leaned his head to the side as he exposed his naked neck. "I guess you'll kill me, go ahead."

Ms. Prosperina's serpent head snapped its razor sharp fangs within a micron of Professor Quan's neck. She spat at him.

"I want you to suffer, first," Ms. Prosperina said. But she slithered past him and toward the restrooms. She stared down at Eddie and Captain Lovins. Eddie started to shake with fear, but Captain Lovins moved in front of him, blocking his vision. His weapon pointed over at Mr. Oppenheimer. Ms. Prosperina hissed and snapped at him. She turned and slithered back close to Professor Quan.

"Why this boy?" Ms. Prosperina asked. She stuck out her black forked tongue in front of his face. "I will kill all your children, I'll start with this one."

"Ya, he appears to be an asthmatic," Mr. Oppenheimer said. His weapon pointed down at Captain Lovins. "He seems to have lost his breath, keeps sucking on that inhaler, so weak."

"Come now, Kore," Professor Quan said. He walked between Ms. Prosperina's hooded cobra head and Captain Lovins and Edward. "You know better than that, he was born at the exact moment of the winter solstice, he is special to me."

Ms. Prosperina coiled and appeared prepared to strike.

"Of course, my father listens to God," Ms. Prosperina said. She hissed, she snapped her razor sharp fangs razor paper thin close to Professor Quan's placid face. "We both know, winter kills, this boy will die."

Professor Quan put his hands into prayer position in front of his face. He closed his eyes.

"Let it go, let this world go," Professor Quan said, "just live and seek happiness."

The serpent spat on Professor Quan, it coiled, and its long tail crushed a nearby plastic table and shoved it down the restaurants center aisle.

"Come now father, tell me I'm a mistake," Ms. Prosperina said. She snapped at him, she poked his forehead with her black tongue. "That I should have been aborted, you're the one that had the fascination with chimera."

"I was a stupid boy," Professor Quan said. He hummed a calming sound. "You knew what you were doing to Dr. Yin, he had not a clue, what you are, yes, you are my mistake."

"I enjoyed tormenting him," Ms. Prosperina said. She slithered, and coiled around Professor Quan as if he was the center pole for a caduceus. She stared down at Eddie. He stared at her, his face lost in shock. "I thought he might stumble into one of your formulas, but I knew you'd watch him, I knew you'd protect this child, who I will devour."

Professor Quan breathed out slowly, methodically. He stood still and resolute as Ms. Prosperina squeezed, and constricted him, her scaly skin glossed near his cheek.

"Captain, your bullets cannot hurt me," Ms. Prosperina said. She hissed at him.

"Yeah, but they'll slow you down," Captain Lovins said.

"Give me my meteorites, and I'll let the boy live," Ms. Prosperina said. Then she molted from the serpent form into a black hair wild boar. She shoved Professor Quan to the floor. She spat at Captain Lovins and Eddie. Eddie shook, but then the concoction from the inhaler finally caused him to wobble, his visions blurred and he lost consciousness, he slumped next to Captain Lovins.

"He is weak, the boy is weak," Mr. Oppenheimer said. He tightly gripped the gun handle. "Shall I kill them for you?"

Ms. Prosperina grunted, her red and black eyes stared down at Captain Lovins who did not take the weapon site dot off Mr. Oppenheimer's forehead.

"You'll never get them," Professor Quan said. He could smell the putrid scent from her tusks. He slid away from her hooves.

"I have my infrastructure in place," Ms. Prosperina said. She grunted. Her hooves snapped at the tile floor, cracking them into shards. "Now I want, what I want."

"Yes, I've read about your particle collider," Professor Quan said. He twisted up and shifted into a standing Buddhist pose, as she hoofed forward and spat.

"All I need is a particle, not even a grain of sand," Ms. Prosperina said. She molted into another serpent form, the head with sharp black goat horns. She slithered closer toward Eddie. Captain Lovins kept his weapon pointed at Mr. Oppenheimer as he kept between her and Eddie. Her black tongue poked at him.

"Never going to happen," Professor Quan said. "Kore, leave humanity be, leave that boy alone, you drunken witch."

"I'll find them, or the boy dies," Ms. Prosperina said. She leaned down; her black tongue darted near Eddie's face. "Of course, Dr. Yin could never find your original genetic starter, I wonder were that might be hiding? Perhaps I should be a mother, yes, a mother, use my own DNA."

"You'd make a terrible mother," Professor Quan said.

"Like you being such a thoughtful father?" Ms. Prosperina said. She hissed. "How rich- but you know there is nothing like the original material to replicate me and my people."

Professor Quan stood with his hands behind him.

"Go ahead," Professor Quan said. He waved her away. "Strike him dead, strike me dead, strike Captain Lovins dead."

The serpent spat at Professor Quan. It paused after it had coiled to strike. Then Ms. Prosperina molted back into her human form. She slipped on her black glasses. She intently examined Professor Quan.

"What did you do, father?" Ms. Prosperina asked. She faced Professor Quan. She stared up at him, studying him. Professor Quan shrugged.

"I thought you loved bacteria, viruses?" Professor Quan said. He waved his hand toward Eddie. "Go ahead, he's weak, right Mr. Oppenheimer? Or, just kill me instead, it's my fault, I'll never let you have those meteorites, you'll never get your hands on the organic material, I know you cannot parse your own DNA, you need the pure form, with all the code together."

Ms. Prosperina glared at Professor Quan. She walked behind him. She tapped her fingernails on the fast food laminate trash receptacle.

"What did you do? You old fool," Ms. Prosperina asked. She straightened her blouses cuffs.

"Shall I kill him, madam," Mr. Oppenheimer said.

"No, because then you'll be dead," Ms. Prosperina said. She stared down at Captain Lovins. "I presume you can shoot straight, for an old man."

Captain Lovins ignored the question. He shoved the comatose Eddie toward the side glass door; but he kept the gun pointed at Mr. Oppenheimer.

"If you harm the boy, his body will release a bacterial virus, a virus that will seek you, and only you, it will trigger your body to deteriorate, a bacteria, you do love bacteria?" Professor

Quan said. He walked behind her. "You'll be trapped in a dead body, then you'll die, and that body will begin to rot."

Ms. Prosperina shrugged. She backed away from Professor Quan; she strolled toward the front doors. She waved for Mr. Oppenheimer to follow.

"Well played father, but I came to you as a warning, give me what I want," Ms. Prosperina said. She turned to stare at Professor Quan. "I know where you are, they cannot be far from you, or, I will begin to send you not so kind messages on the evening news. Money does not mean much to me, but owning genetic information, I find that quite delightful."

"Kore, stop showing off, let me guess, you want to create a super race? Have humanity as your slaves, I know, it's in your DNA, that's my fault," Professor Quan said. He clenched his hands into fists. "But you know I distaste killing, death."

"I don't care, it has no effect on me," Ms. Prosperina said.

"Well, just so you know," Professor Quan said. He pointed down at Eddie. "He now has all my knowledge cycling inside his cells, as he sleeps he grows more and more powerful, someday, he will come looking for you, he'll eradicate you."

"Oh, that will be so much fun," Ms. Prosperina said. She morphed into a serpent head. She snapped at Professor Quan. She spat at him. "I'll be waiting."

"Stop showing off," Professor Quan said. "I knew you'd come looking for me, so, you found me, now go away. And if you persist in hurting people, then I will seek you."

"This is not over, I will find your children, I will begin to inflict pain, or simply give me the meteorites, choose," Ms. Prosperina said. She motioned for Mr. Oppenheimer to leave; he pushed back the glass door, his weapon still drawn. "But you've been warned, that is my last courtesy for you, father. I have a generation to care for, my people need to be reborn, you know my DNA is flawed, I need the genetic purity, but you know that, father, now don't you? But I know where you are, you cannot hide from me."

Professor Quan stepped forward.

"I'm not your father," Professor Quan said. He walked in between Captain Lovins and Mr. Oppenheimer's line of sight. "Put your gun away Mr. Oppenheimer. Kore, your real fathers are dead, and exactly where they should be, in hell. Leave humanity alone, I know hidden even in your cells, there is love, allow it to grow, don't fight it."

"Hardly, you've left me with any other choices," Ms. Prosperina said. She stopped at the doorway. She took off her glasses and glared at Professor Quan with her red and black irises. "Pain, it's coming, and you're welcome, *father.*"

Professor Quan watched her walk away as she disappeared within the darkness. He turned, and walked back over to Captain Lovins, and the comatose Eddie.

"Take him to a safe place," Professor Quan said.

"I will, but what did you do?" Captain Lovins asked.

"I didn't have a choice, either," Professor Quan said. He shook his head as he kneeled down next to Eddie. He carefully stroked Edward's hair. "As Edward grows stronger, I'll grow progressively weaker. It's just the nature of things, I couldn't take the chance, that canister had all my secrets, it had all that I am, as he learns, I will begin to die."

"Well, this sucks," Captain Lovins said. He pulled Edward toward him. "I thought she'd kill us, just for fun. But she really needs those black diamonds?"

"Yes, her genetic code is a jumbled mess," Professor Quan said. He grinned. "She knows it, the particle collider was her attempt to find a pure strand of her genetic code, she failed, but she'll be back, she'll not give up."

"No doubt," Captain said. He stuffed his weapon behind him into his pants. He clutched Eddie by his armpits; he raised him up and over his shoulder and carried him past the doorway and outside.

"I'll check your car for a transmitter, or if the knucklehead messed with it," Captain Lovins said. He pushed the side door open. "By the way, I don't have a parasite in me, do I?"

"Oh, no, I lied," Professor Quan said. He shrugged. "He does, and I do, it's my way of providing Edward protection."

"Even so, that's one nasty woman," Captain Lovins said. He gently placed Edward onto the passenger side seat. "Hell hath no fury, just saying, I had no idea she would be that nasty."

"Yeah, she's not a she, but I had to figure out how to slow IT down, I thought she might do something permanent, being a bit drunk, if she had I'd be dead, but so would she," Professor Quan said. He stared out into the darkness. He nodded. "But she'll be back, I know she keeps scheming."

# # #

Later that morning, as Professor Quan drove back into the darkness of Appalachia, Captain Lovins hoisted Eddie onto his shoulder. He trudged across the quiet, tree lined residential street; he climbed up the two stairs onto Ardee's front porch. He carefully leaned Eddie onto the wooden flooring, and balanced him against the door jam. He gently knocked on the tempered glass front door. Captain Lovins backed away from the door. He stood under the roof pitch, hidden in the darkness as Ardee cautiously opened the front door.

"Eddie," Ardee said. She began to cry, as she fell to her knees, she hugged him. Her blond hair was tangled, her housecoat was pulled tight. But she stopped, she sensed she was not alone, as she looked up she noticed Captain Lovins' shadow cast along the wooden porch. "Who, who are you? What have you done to him?"

Captain Lovins stepped forward. He bent down.

"He'll be out for a while," Captain Lovins said. He kept his hands and arms open, and he backed up to create more space between them. "Never tell him about me."

"Why, I don't understand, what did you do to him?" Ardee asked. She tightly hugged Eddie. "I'll call the police, I've been terrified all night, I knew something was wrong."

An owl hooted from the darkness, perched on an ancient oak tree. The moon was beginning to fade into morning.

"I dare not tell you, it would put your life in danger," Captain Lovins said. He glanced around the front porch and inspected the still neighborhood. "His car is at a General Beauregard's Fried Chicken, the keys are in his pocket. He has a lot of money in the trunk, he has a thumb drive in his pocket as well, more resources for his journey, be very careful, he will not remember much, for now."

"What? He's kind, he wouldn't hurt anyone," Ardee said.

"Just know this, there are powerful forces that mean to harm, to kill, to maim, they do not discriminate between races, sex, the rich or the poor," Captain Lovins said. He stared over at Ardee. "I am a simply a soldier, my code demands I protect the weak, that code is my bond. The reason I stepped forward many years ago. From this day forward, Edward will begin to change."

"How so?" Ardee said. She wiped the tears from her eyes.

"He will grow strong, his mind, it will become quite powerful," Captain Lovins said. He glanced away as he thought of the fact Professor Quan had guaranteed his own death. "He will be in great danger, those forces know he exists, but I will watch, I will protect him as long as I live. You will need to be aware, do you understand?"

"No, I do not," Ardee said. She protectively hugged Edward. "I'm calling the police, know that."

Captain Lovins stood up. He interlocked his fingers.

"Yes, you can do that, know this, many years ago, Edward was chosen," Captain Lovins said. He shrugged. "I don't know why, that's beyond me. But within his cells, he has a hidden power to protect humanity. Someday, he will instinctively know, but only he can decide, it's his choice."

"This is a nightmare," Ardee said.

"In a sense, but always remember, love is more powerful than hate," Captain Lovins said. He leaned forward. "Let me take him inside, then I'll immediately leave, no harm will come to him or you, that is not what I do."

Ardee wiped the tears from her eyes. She scanned the quiet, dark residential street.

"I suppose," Ardee said.

Captain Lovins marched forward, as Ardee opened the front door. He clutched Edward and carried him into the bedroom. Then he turned, and left the house. Ardee locked the door, she watched him march onto the sidewalk, and he disappeared past the far street corner behind a neighbor's house with a single security light on near the front door.

# # #

Edward awoke with a feather pillow under his head. A multi-colored blanket draped across his mortal shell. Gazing up, he realized he was in Ardee's bedroom. And it was as if he was watching a movie, as her smooth plaster ceiling blazed with an endless kaleidoscope of shiny stars and distant planets. The vast celestial radiance beckoned him to float from the soft bed and into the colorful DNA pattern of deep space and glide beyond infinity at the speed of light. He reached his hand toward the intense light; he blinked his eyes and adjusted to the hazy gloom. He wobbled up, as if standing within deep space, as if immersed within a gyrating Milky Way particle shower from the moon's reflected light from the sun. A foggy perception reverberated within his consciousness that he had been out that night, but he was not drunk from wine, nor did he remember being at any particular place, at any particular time, for any particular reason, he simply knew he existed.

Lost in a cosmic sea, Edward sensed the Iris Nebula watched him from afar, attracting him with powerful magnetic currents to seek unknown destinations. To swim within a tidal wave crashing against an endless sandy shore, as if his foamy bare essence was naked to a blue moon.

Later, dawn began to emerge above the visible horizon. Golden sun light beams began to overcome the dark night. Edward listened to the stillness; he sensed his lungs fill with oxygen, the thump of his heartbeat. Unique ideas, perceptions, and wonderful new inventions cycled through his mind. Careful not to disturb Ardee, he attempted to walk off his pure energy, curious why he was unable to turn off his electrified brain illuminating a constant waterfall of a generation's hopes and dreams.

Outside in the moist, grey morning, a mist cascaded off the warm street. Steadily, heavy raindrops bounced off the shingled roof. Then the heavens opened up a tempest storm, Edward closed his eyes, it sounded like chicken frying in his mother's cast iron skillet. He thought of his father. He looked down at Ardee. As a distant rumble shook the translucent window, as Edward stood behind the glass panel, he smiled. He was home.